The Great Air Fryer
Cookbook for Beginners 2023

2000 Days of Simple, Budget-Friendly & Easy-Breezy Air Fryer Recipes to Enjoy With Your Family and Friends incl. Tasty Desserts Special

Alice M. Ondricka

Table of Contents

Chapter 1 Breakfasts

Chapter 2 Family Favorites

Chapter 3 Fast and Easy Everyday Favorites

Chapter 4 Poultry

Chapter 5 Beef, Pork, and Lamb

Chapter 6 Fish and Seafood   49

Chapter 7 Snacks and Appetizers

Chapter 8 Vegetables and Sides

Chapter 9 Vegetarian Mains
77

Chapter 10 Desserts
82

Appendix 1: Air Fryer Cooking Chart
89

INTRODUCTION

Welcome to the delightful world of air frying, where the sizzle of crispy perfection meets the joy of guilt-free cooking. In this air fryer cookbook, we embark on a culinary adventure that will transform your kitchen into a hub of flavor, health, and culinary creativity.

Air frying has emerged as a revolutionary cooking method, capturing the hearts and taste buds of food enthusiasts worldwide. It offers a healthier alternative to traditional frying, allowing you to indulge in your favorite crispy treats without the excess oil. But air frying is so much more than just a way to reduce calories. It is a gateway to unlocking a whole new realm of culinary possibilities.

Within the pages of this cookbook, you'll discover a treasure trove of recipes designed specifically for air fryers. From delectable appetizers to mouthwatering main courses and even sweet sensations, each recipe has been crafted to maximize flavor and texture, ensuring every bite is a culinary delight. Get ready to experience the magic of air frying as it transforms simple ingredients into extraordinary dishes.

But this cookbook is more than just a collection of recipes. It is a guide that will empower you to become a master of air frying. I'll share with you the fundamental techniques, tips, and tricks that will elevate your air frying skills to new heights. From achieving the perfect crispy exterior to maintaining succulent tenderness inside, you'll learn the secrets to creating culinary masterpieces that will impress even the most discerning palates.

As we embark on this flavorful journey, rest assured that dietary preferences and restrictions have been taken into consideration. You'll find a diverse range of recipes that cater to various needs, including vegetarian, gluten-free, and dairy-free options. Everyone deserves to enjoy the delights of air frying, regardless of their dietary choices, and this cookbook strives to provide inclusive culinary experiences.

Prepare to be amazed as you witness the power of air frying to transform your favorite comfort foods into healthier versions without sacrificing taste. Crispy fries, golden onion rings, tender chicken, succulent seafood, and an array of delectable desserts are just a taste of what awaits you. This cookbook will inspire you to think beyond the traditional, to experiment with flavors and ingredients, and to create unique dishes that reflect your personal culinary style.

So, whether you're a novice in the kitchen or a seasoned home cook, I invite you to embark on this culinary adventure with me. Let's dive into the art of air frying, unlocking a world of flavor, health, and endless culinary possibilities. Get ready to revolutionize your cooking, surprise your taste buds, and impress your family and friends with each delectable dish you create.

Let's turn up the heat, savor the crunch, and embrace the joys of air frying. Welcome to a world of flavor, health, and culinary delight. Happy air frying!

Chapter 1 Breakfasts

Berry Muffins

Prep time: 15 minutes | Cook time: 12 to 17 minutes | Makes 8 muffins

1⅓ cups plus 1 tablespoon all-purpose flour, divided
¼ cup granulated sugar
2 tablespoons light brown sugar
2 teaspoons baking powder
2 eggs
⅔ cup whole milk
⅓ cup safflower oil
1 cup mixed fresh berries

1. In a medium bowl, stir together 1⅓ cups of flour, the granulated sugar, brown sugar, and baking powder until mixed well. 2. In a small bowl, whisk the eggs, milk, and oil until combined. Stir the egg mixture into the dry ingredients just until combined. 3. In another small bowl, toss the mixed berries with the remaining 1 tablespoon of flour until coated. Gently stir the berries into the batter. 4. Double up 16 foil muffin cups to make 8 cups. 5. Insert the crisper plate into the basket and the basket into the unit. Preheat the unit by selecting BAKE, setting the temperature to 315°F (157°C), and setting the time to 3 minutes. Select START/STOP to begin. 6. Once the unit is preheated, place 4 cups into the basket and fill each three-quarters full with the batter. 7. Select BAKE, set the temperature to 315°F (157°C), and set the time for 17 minutes. Select START/STOP to begin. 8. After about 12 minutes, check the muffins. If they spring back when lightly touched with your finger, they are done. If not, resume cooking. 9. When the cooking is done, transfer the muffins to a wire rack to cool. 10. Repeat steps 6, 7, and 8 with the remaining muffin cups and batter. 11. Let the muffins cool for 10 minutes before serving.

Broccoli-Mushroom Frittata

Prep time: 10 minutes | Cook time: 20 minutes | Serves 2

1 tablespoon olive oil
1½ cups broccoli florets, finely chopped
½ cup sliced brown mushrooms
¼ cup finely chopped onion
½ teaspoon salt
¼ teaspoon freshly ground black pepper
6 eggs
¼ cup Parmesan cheese

1. In a nonstick cake pan, combine the olive oil, broccoli, mushrooms, onion, salt, and pepper. Stir until the vegetables are thoroughly coated with oil. Place the cake pan in the air fryer basket and set the air fryer to 400°F (204°C). Air fry for 5 minutes until the vegetables soften. 2. Meanwhile, in a medium bowl, whisk the eggs and Parmesan until thoroughly combined. Pour the egg mixture into the pan and shake gently to distribute the vegetables. Air fry for another 15 minutes until the eggs are set. 3. Remove from the air fryer and let sit for 5 minutes to cool slightly. Use a silicone spatula to gently lift the frittata onto a plate before serving.

Strawberry Tarts

Prep time: 15 minutes | Cook time: 10 minutes | Serves 6

2 refrigerated piecrusts
½ cup strawberry preserves
1 teaspoon cornstarch
Cooking oil spray
½ cup low-fat vanilla yogurt
1 ounce (28 g) cream cheese, at
room temperature
3 tablespoons confectioners' sugar
Rainbow sprinkles, for decorating

1. Place the piecrusts on a flat surface. Using a knife or pizza cutter, cut each piecrust into 3 rectangles, for 6 total. Discard any unused dough from the piecrust edges. 2. In a small bowl, stir together the preserves and cornstarch. Mix well, ensuring there are no lumps of cornstarch remaining. 3. Scoop 1 tablespoon of the strawberry mixture onto the top half of each piece of piecrust. 4. Fold the bottom of each piece up to enclose the filling. Using the back of a fork, press along the edges of each tart to seal. 5. Insert the crisper plate into the basket and the basket into the unit. Preheat the unit by selecting BAKE, setting the temperature to 375°F (191°C), and setting the time to 3 minutes. Select START/STOP to begin. 6. Once the unit is preheated, spray the crisper plate with cooking oil. Working in batches, spray the breakfast tarts with cooking oil and place them into the basket in a single layer. Do not stack the tarts. 7. Select BAKE, set the temperature to 375°F (191°C), and set the time to 10 minutes. Select START/STOP to begin. 8. When the cooking is complete, the tarts should be light golden brown. Let the breakfast tarts cool fully before removing them from the basket. 9. Repeat steps 5, 6, 7, and 8 for the remaining breakfast tarts. 10. In a small bowl, stir together the yogurt, cream cheese, and confectioners' sugar. Spread the breakfast tarts with the frosting and top with sprinkles.

Gold Avocado

Prep time: 5 minutes | Cook time: 6 minutes | Serves 4

2 large avocados, sliced
¼ teaspoon paprika
Salt and ground black pepper, to taste
½ cup flour
2 eggs, beaten
1 cup bread crumbs

1. Preheat the air fryer to 400ºF (204ºC). 2. Sprinkle paprika, salt and pepper on the slices of avocado. 3. Lightly coat the avocados with flour. Dredge them in the eggs, before covering with bread crumbs. 4. Transfer to the air fryer and air fry for 6 minutes. 5. Serve warm.

Pita and Pepperoni Pizza

Prep time: 10 minutes | Cook time: 6 minutes | Serves 1

1 teaspoon olive oil
1 tablespoon pizza sauce
1 pita bread
6 pepperoni slices
¼ cup grated Mozzarella cheese
¼ teaspoon garlic powder
¼ teaspoon dried oregano

1. Preheat the air fryer to 350ºF (177ºC). Grease the air fryer basket with olive oil. 2. Spread the pizza sauce on top of the pita bread. Put the pepperoni slices over the sauce, followed by the Mozzarella cheese. 3. Season with garlic powder and oregano. 4. Put the pita pizza inside the air fryer and place a trivet on top. 5. Bake in the preheated air fryer for 6 minutes and serve.

Mexican Breakfast Pepper Rings

Prep time: 5 minutes | Cook time: 10 minutes | Serves 4

Olive oil
1 large red, yellow, or orange bell pepper, cut into four ¾-inch rings
4 eggs
Salt and freshly ground black pepper, to taste
2 teaspoons salsa

1. Preheat the air fryer to 350ºF (177ºC). Lightly spray a baking pan with olive oil. 2. Place 2 bell pepper rings on the pan. Crack one egg into each bell pepper ring. Season with salt and black pepper. 3. Spoon ½ teaspoon of salsa on top of each egg. 4. Place the pan in the air fryer basket. Air fry until the yolk is slightly runny, 5 to 6 minutes or until the yolk is fully cooked, 8 to 10 minutes. 5. Repeat with the remaining 2 pepper rings. Serve hot.

Cajun Breakfast Sausage

Prep time: 10 minutes | Cook time: 15 to 20 minutes | Serves 8

1½ pounds (680 g) 85% lean ground turkey
3 cloves garlic, finely chopped
¼ onion, grated
1 teaspoon Tabasco sauce
1 teaspoon Creole seasoning
1 teaspoon dried thyme
½ teaspoon paprika
½ teaspoon cayenne

1. Preheat the air fryer to 370ºF (188ºC). 2. In a large bowl, combine the turkey, garlic, onion, Tabasco, Creole seasoning, thyme, paprika, and cayenne. Mix with clean hands until thoroughly combined. Shape into 16 patties, about ½ inch thick. (Wet your hands slightly if you find the sausage too sticky to handle.) 3. Working in batches if necessary, arrange the patties in a single layer in the air fryer basket. Pausing halfway through the cooking time to flip the patties, air fry for 15 to 20 minutes until a thermometer inserted into the thickest portion registers 165ºF (74ºC).

Sausage and Cheese Balls

Prep time: 10 minutes | Cook time: 12 minutes | Makes 16 balls

1 pound (454 g) pork breakfast sausage
½ cup shredded Cheddar cheese
1 ounce (28 g) full-fat cream cheese, softened
1 large egg

1. Mix all ingredients in a large bowl. Form into sixteen (1-inch) balls. Place the balls into the air fryer basket. 2. Adjust the temperature to 400ºF (204ºC) and air fry for 12 minutes. 3. Shake the basket two or three times during cooking. Sausage balls will be browned on the outside and have an internal temperature of at least 145ºF (63ºC) when completely cooked. 4. Serve warm.

Bacon Hot Dogs

Prep time: 5 minutes | Cook time: 15 minutes | Serves 4

3 brazilian sausages, cut into 3 equal pieces
9 slices bacon
1 tablespoon Italian herbs
Salt and ground black pepper, to taste

1. Preheat the air fryer to 355ºF (179ºC). 2. Take each slice of bacon and wrap around each piece of sausage. Sprinkle with Italian herbs, salt and pepper. 3. Air fry the sausages in the preheated air fryer for 15 minutes. 4. Serve warm.

Cheddar-Ham-Corn Muffins

Prep time: 10 minutes | Cook time: 6 to 8 minutes per batch | Makes 8 muffins

¾ cup yellow cornmeal	½ cup shredded sharp Cheddar
¼ cup flour	cheese
1½ teaspoons baking powder	½ cup diced ham
¼ teaspoon salt	8 foil muffin cups, liners
1 egg, beaten	removed and sprayed with
2 tablespoons canola oil	cooking spray
½ cup milk	

1. Preheat the air fryer to 390°F (199°C). 2. In a medium bowl, stir together the cornmeal, flour, baking powder, and salt. 3. Add egg, oil, and milk to dry ingredients and mix well. 4. Stir in shredded cheese and diced ham. 5. Divide batter among the muffin cups. 6. Place 4 filled muffin cups in air fryer basket and bake for 5 minutes. 7. Reduce temperature to 330°F (166°C) and bake for 1 to 2 minutes or until toothpick inserted in center of muffin comes out clean. 8. Repeat steps 6 and 7 to cook remaining muffins.

Gyro Breakfast Patties with Tzatziki

Prep time: 10 minutes | Cook time: 20 minutes per batch | Makes 16 patties

Patties:	½ teaspoon fine sea salt
2 pounds (907 g) ground lamb	½ teaspoon garlic powder, or 1
or beef	clove garlic, minced
½ cup diced red onions	¼ teaspoon dried dill weed, or
¼ cup sliced black olives	1 teaspoon finely chopped fresh
2 tablespoons tomato sauce	dill
1 teaspoon dried oregano leaves	For Garnish/Serving:
1 teaspoon Greek seasoning	½ cup crumbled feta cheese
2 cloves garlic, minced	(about 2 ounces / 57 g)
1 teaspoon fine sea salt	Diced red onions
Tzatziki:	Sliced black olives
1 cup full-fat sour cream	Sliced cucumbers
1 small cucumber, chopped	

1. Preheat the air fryer to 350°F (177°C). 2. Place the ground lamb, onions, olives, tomato sauce, oregano, Greek seasoning, garlic, and salt in a large bowl. Mix well to combine the ingredients. 3. Using your hands, form the mixture into sixteen 3-inch patties. Place about 5 of the patties in the air fryer and air fry for 20 minutes, flipping halfway through. Remove the patties and place them on a serving platter. Repeat with the remaining patties. 4. While the patties cook, make the tzatziki: Place all the ingredients in a small bowl and stir well. Cover and store in the fridge until ready to serve. Garnish with ground black pepper before serving. 5. Serve the patties with a dollop of tzatziki, a sprinkle of crumbled feta cheese, diced red onions, sliced black olives, and sliced cucumbers. 6. Store leftovers in an airtight container in the refrigerator for up to 5 days or in the freezer for up to a month. Reheat the patties in a preheated 390°F (199°C) air fryer for a few minutes, until warmed through.

Mini Shrimp Frittata

Prep time: 15 minutes | Cook time: 20 minutes | Serves 4

1 teaspoon olive oil, plus more	shrimp, drained
for spraying	Salt and freshly ground black
½ small red bell pepper, finely	pepper, to taste
diced	4 eggs, beaten
1 teaspoon minced garlic	4 teaspoons ricotta cheese
1 (4-ounce / 113-g) can of tiny	

1. Spray four ramekins with olive oil. 2. In a medium skillet over medium-low heat, heat 1 teaspoon of olive oil. Add the bell pepper and garlic and sauté until the pepper is soft, about 5 minutes 3. Add the shrimp, season with salt and pepper, and cook until warm, 1 to 2 minutes. Remove from the heat. 4. Add the eggs and stir to combine. 5. Pour one quarter of the mixture into each ramekin. 6. Place 2 ramekins in the air fryer basket and bake at 350°F (177°C) for 6 minutes. 7. Remove the air fryer basket from the air fryer and stir the mixture in each ramekin. Top each frittata with 1 teaspoon of ricotta cheese. Return the air fryer basket to the air fryer and cook until eggs are set and the top is lightly browned, 4 to 5 minutes. 8. Repeat with the remaining two ramekins.

Quick and Easy Blueberry Muffins

Prep time: 10 minutes | Cook time: 12 minutes | Makes 8 muffins

1⅓ cups flour	1 egg
½ cup sugar	½ cup milk
2 teaspoons baking powder	⅔ cup blueberries, fresh or
¼ teaspoon salt	frozen and thawed
⅓ cup canola oil	

1. Preheat the air fryer to 330°F (166°C). 2. In a medium bowl, stir together flour, sugar, baking powder, and salt. 3. In a separate bowl, combine oil, egg, and milk and mix well. 4. Add egg mixture to dry ingredients and stir just until moistened. 5. Gently stir in the blueberries. 6. Spoon batter evenly into parchment paper-lined muffin cups. 7. Put 4 muffin cups in air fryer basket and bake for 12 minutes or until tops spring back when touched lightly. 8. Repeat previous step to bake remaining muffins. 9. Serve immediately.

Cheesy Scrambled Eggs

Prep time: 2 minutes | Cook time: 9 minutes | Serves 2

1 teaspoon unsalted butter

2 large eggs

2 tablespoons milk

2 tablespoons shredded Cheddar

cheese

Salt and freshly ground black pepper, to taste

1. Preheat the air fryer to 300°F (149°C). Place the butter in a baking pan and cook for 1 to 2 minutes, until melted. 2. In a small bowl, whisk together the eggs, milk, and cheese. Season with salt and black pepper. Transfer the mixture to the pan. 3. Cook for 3 minutes. Stir the eggs and push them toward the center of the pan. 4. Cook for another 2 minutes, then stir again. Cook for another 2 minutes, until the eggs are just cooked. Serve warm.

Breakfast Sammies

Prep time: 15 minutes | Cook time: 20 minutes | Serves 5

Biscuits:

6 large egg whites

2 cups blanched almond flour, plus more if needed

1½ teaspoons baking powder

½ teaspoon fine sea salt

¼ cup (½ stick) very cold unsalted butter (or lard for dairy-free), cut into ¼-inch pieces

Eggs:

5 large eggs

½ teaspoon fine sea salt

¼ teaspoon ground black pepper

5 (1-ounce / 28-g) slices Cheddar cheese (omit for dairy-free)

10 thin slices ham

1. Spray the air fryer basket with avocado oil. Preheat the air fryer to 350°F (177°C). Grease two pie pans or two baking pans that will fit inside your air fryer. 2. Make the biscuits: In a medium-sized bowl, whip the egg whites with a hand mixer until very stiff. Set aside. 3. In a separate medium-sized bowl, stir together the almond flour, baking powder, and salt until well combined. Cut in the butter. Gently fold the flour mixture into the egg whites with a rubber spatula. If the dough is too wet to form into mounds, add a few tablespoons of almond flour until the dough holds together well. 4. Using a large spoon, divide the dough into 5 equal portions and drop them about 1 inch apart on one of the greased pie pans. (If you're using a smaller air fryer, work in batches if necessary.) Place the pan in the air fryer and bake for 11 to 14 minutes, until the biscuits are golden brown. Remove from the air fryer and set aside to cool. 5. Make the eggs: Set the air fryer to 375°F (191°C). Crack the eggs into the remaining greased pie pan and sprinkle with the salt and pepper. Place the eggs in the air fryer to bake for 5 minutes, or until they are cooked to your liking. 6. Open the air fryer and top each egg yolk with a slice of cheese (if using).

Bake for another minute, or until the cheese is melted. 7. Once the biscuits are cool, slice them in half lengthwise. Place 1 cooked egg topped with cheese and 2 slices of ham in each biscuit. 8. Store leftover biscuits, eggs, and ham in separate airtight containers in the fridge for up to 3 days. Reheat the biscuits and eggs on a baking sheet in a preheated 350°F (177°C) air fryer for 5 minutes, or until warmed through.

Strawberry Toast

Prep time: 10 minutes | Cook time: 8 minutes | Makes 4 toasts

4 slices bread, ½-inch thick

Butter-flavored cooking spray

1 cup sliced strawberries

1 teaspoon sugar

1. Spray one side of each bread slice with butter-flavored cooking spray. Lay slices sprayed side down. 2. Divide the strawberries among the bread slices. 3. Sprinkle evenly with the sugar and place in the air fryer basket in a single layer. 4. Air fry at 390°F (199°C) for 8 minutes. The bottom should look brown and crisp and the top should look glazed.

Mushroom-and-Tomato Stuffed Hash Browns

Prep time: 10 minutes | Cook time: 20 minutes | Serves 4

Olive oil cooking spray

1 tablespoon plus 2 teaspoons olive oil, divided

4 ounces (113 g) baby bella mushrooms, diced

1 scallion, white parts and green parts, diced

1 garlic clove, minced

2 cups shredded potatoes

½ teaspoon salt

¼ teaspoon black pepper

1 Roma tomato, diced

½ cup shredded mozzarella

1. Preheat the air fryer to 380°F(193°C). Lightly coat the inside of a 6-inch cake pan with olive oil cooking spray. 2. In a small skillet, heat 2 teaspoons olive oil over medium heat. Add the mushrooms, scallion, and garlic, and cook for 4 to 5 minutes, or until they have softened and are beginning to show some color. Remove from heat. 3. Meanwhile, in a large bowl, combine the potatoes, salt, pepper, and the remaining tablespoon olive oil. Toss until all potatoes are well coated. 4. Pour half of the potatoes into the bottom of the cake pan. Top with the mushroom mixture, tomato, and mozzarella. Spread the remaining potatoes over the top. 5. Bake in the air fryer for 12 to 15 minutes, or until the top is golden brown. 6. Remove from the air fryer and allow to cool for 5 minutes before slicing and serving.

Baked Egg and Mushroom Cups

Prep time: 5 minutes | Cook time: 15 minutes |
Serves 6

Olive oil cooking spray
6 large eggs
1 garlic clove, minced
½ teaspoon salt
½ teaspoon black pepper
Pinch red pepper flakes

8 ounces (227 g) baby bella mushrooms, sliced
1 cup fresh baby spinach
2 scallions, white parts and green parts, diced

1. Preheat the air fryer to 320°F (160°C). Lightly coat the inside of six silicone muffin cups or a six-cup muffin tin with olive oil cooking spray. 2. In a large bowl, beat the eggs, garlic, salt, pepper, and red pepper flakes for 1 to 2 minutes, or until well combined. 3. Fold in the mushrooms, spinach, and scallions. 4. Divide the mixture evenly among the muffin cups. 5. Place into the air fryer and bake for 12 to 15 minutes, or until the eggs are set. 6. Remove and allow to cool for 5 minutes before serving.

Hearty Cheddar Biscuits

Prep time: 10 minutes | Cook time: 22 minutes |
Makes 8 biscuits

2⅓ cups self-rising flour
2 tablespoons sugar
½ cup butter (1 stick), frozen for 15 minutes
½ cup grated Cheddar cheese,

plus more to melt on top
1⅓ cups buttermilk
1 cup all-purpose flour, for shaping
1 tablespoon butter, melted

1. Line a buttered 7-inch metal cake pan with parchment paper or a silicone liner. 2. Combine the flour and sugar in a large mixing bowl. Grate the butter into the flour. Add the grated cheese and stir to coat the cheese and butter with flour. Then add the buttermilk and stir just until you can no longer see streaks of flour. The dough should be quite wet. 3. Spread the all-purpose (not self-rising) flour out on a small cookie sheet. With a spoon, scoop 8 evenly sized balls of dough into the flour, making sure they don't touch each other. With floured hands, coat each dough ball with flour and toss them gently from hand to hand to shake off any excess flour. Put each floured dough ball into the prepared pan, right up next to the other. This will help the biscuits rise, rather than spreading out. 4. Preheat the air fryer to 380°F (193°C). 5. Transfer the cake pan to the basket of the air fryer. Let the ends of the aluminum foil sling hang across the cake pan before returning the basket to the air fryer. 6. Air fry for 20 minutes. Check the biscuits twice to make sure they are not getting too brown on top. If they are, re-arrange the aluminum foil strips to cover any brown parts. After 20 minutes, check the biscuits by inserting a toothpick into the center of the biscuits. It should come out clean. If it needs a little more time, continue to air fry for two extra minutes. Brush the tops of the biscuits with some melted butter and sprinkle a little more grated cheese on top if desired. Pop the basket back into the air fryer for another 2 minutes. 7. Remove the cake pan from the air fryer. Let the biscuits cool for just a minute or two and then turn them out onto a plate and pull apart. Serve immediately.

Egg White Cups

Prep time: 10 minutes | Cook time: 15 minutes |
Serves 4

2 cups 100% liquid egg whites
3 tablespoons salted butter, melted
¼ teaspoon salt
¼ teaspoon onion powder

½ medium Roma tomato, cored and diced
½ cup chopped fresh spinach leaves

1. In a large bowl, whisk egg whites with butter, salt, and onion powder. Stir in tomato and spinach, then pour evenly into four ramekins greased with cooking spray. 2. Place ramekins into air fryer basket. Adjust the temperature to 300°F (149°C) and bake for 15 minutes. Eggs will be fully cooked and firm in the center when done. Serve warm.

Sausage Stuffed Poblanos

Prep time: 15 minutes | Cook time: 15 minutes |
Serves 4

½ pound (227 g) spicy ground pork breakfast sausage
4 large eggs
4 ounces (113 g) full-fat cream cheese, softened
¼ cup canned diced tomatoes

and green chiles, drained
4 large poblano peppers
8 tablespoons shredded Pepper Jack cheese
½ cup full-fat sour cream

1. In a medium skillet over medium heat, crumble and brown the ground sausage until no pink remains. Remove sausage and drain the fat from the pan. Crack eggs into the pan, scramble, and cook until no longer runny. 2. Place cooked sausage in a large bowl and fold in cream cheese. Mix in diced tomatoes and chiles. Gently fold in eggs. 3. Cut a 4-inch to 5-inch slit in the top of each poblano, removing the seeds and white membrane with a small knife. Separate the filling into four servings and spoon carefully into each pepper. Top each with 2 tablespoons pepper jack cheese. 4. Place each pepper into the air fryer basket. 5. Adjust the temperature to 350°F (177°C) and set the timer for 15 minutes. 6. Peppers will be soft and cheese will be browned when ready. Serve immediately with sour cream on top.

Spinach and Swiss Frittata with Mushrooms

Prep time: 10 minutes | Cook time: 20 minutes | Serves 4

Olive oil cooking spray
8 large eggs
½ teaspoon salt
½ teaspoon black pepper
1 garlic clove, minced
2 cups fresh baby spinach

4 ounces (113 g) baby bella mushrooms, sliced
1 shallot, diced
½ cup shredded Swiss cheese, divided
Hot sauce, for serving (optional)

1. Preheat the air fryer to 360°F(182°C). Lightly coat the inside of a 6-inch round cake pan with olive oil cooking spray. 2. In a large bowl, beat the eggs, salt, pepper, and garlic for 1 to 2 minutes, or until well combined. 3. Fold in the spinach, mushrooms, shallot, and ¼ cup of the Swiss cheese. 4. Pour the egg mixture into the prepared cake pan, and sprinkle the remaining ¼ cup of Swiss over the top. 5. Place into the air fryer and bake for 18 to 20 minutes, or until the eggs are set in the center. 6. Remove from the air fryer and allow to cool for 5 minutes. Drizzle with hot sauce (if using) before serving.

Maple Granola

Prep time: 5 minutes | Cook time: 40 minutes | Makes 2 cups

1 cup rolled oats
3 tablespoons pure maple syrup
1 tablespoon sugar
1 tablespoon neutral-flavored oil, such as refined coconut,

sunflower, or safflower
¼ teaspoon sea salt
¼ teaspoon ground cinnamon
¼ teaspoon vanilla extract

1. Insert the crisper plate into the basket and the basket into the unit. Preheat the unit by selecting BAKE, setting the temperature to 250°F (121°C), and setting the time to 3 minutes. Select START/STOP to begin. 2. In a medium bowl, stir together the oats, maple syrup, sugar, oil, salt, cinnamon, and vanilla until thoroughly combined. Transfer the granola to a 6-by-2-inch round baking pan. 3. Once the unit is preheated, place the pan into the basket. 4. Select BAKE, set the temperature to 250°F (121°C) and set the time to 40 minutes. Select START/STOP to begin. 5. After 10 minutes, stir the granola well. Resume cooking, stirring the granola every 10 minutes, for a total of 40 minutes, or until the granola is lightly browned and mostly dry. 6. When the cooking is complete, place the granola on a plate to cool. It will become crisp as it cools. Store the completely cooled granola in an airtight container in a cool, dry place for 1 to 2 weeks.

Pumpkin Donut Holes

Prep time: 15 minutes | Cook time: 14 minutes | Makes 12 donut holes

1 cup whole-wheat pastry flour, plus more as needed
3 tablespoons packed brown sugar
½ teaspoon ground cinnamon
1 teaspoon low-sodium baking powder
⅓ cup canned no-salt-added

pumpkin purée (not pumpkin pie filling)
3 tablespoons 2% milk, plus more as needed
2 tablespoons unsalted butter, melted
1 egg white
Powdered sugar (optional)

1. In a medium bowl, mix the pastry flour, brown sugar, cinnamon, and baking powder. 2. In a small bowl, beat the pumpkin, milk, butter, and egg white until combined. Add the pumpkin mixture to the dry ingredients and mix until combined. You may need to add more flour or milk to form a soft dough. 3. Divide the dough into 12 pieces. With floured hands, form each piece into a ball. 4. Cut a piece of parchment paper or aluminum foil to fit inside the air fryer basket but about 1 inch smaller in diameter. Poke holes in the paper or foil and place it in the basket. 5. Put 6 donut holes into the basket, leaving some space around each. Air fry at 360°F (182°C) for 5 to 7 minutes, or until the donut holes reach an internal temperature of 200°F (93°C) and are firm and light golden brown. 6. Let cool for 5 minutes. Remove from the basket and roll in powdered sugar, if desired. Repeat with the remaining donut holes and serve.

Breakfast Hash

Prep time: 10 minutes | Cook time: 30 minutes | Serves 6

Oil, for spraying
3 medium russet potatoes, diced
½ yellow onion, diced
1 green bell pepper, seeded and diced

2 tablespoons olive oil
2 teaspoons granulated garlic
1 teaspoon salt
½ teaspoon freshly ground black pepper

1. Line the air fryer basket with parchment and spray lightly with oil. 2. In a large bowl, mix together the potatoes, onion, bell pepper, and olive oil. 3. Add the garlic, salt, and black pepper and stir until evenly coated. 4. Transfer the mixture to the prepared basket. 5. Air fry at 400°F (204°C) for 20 to 30 minutes, shaking or stirring every 10 minutes, until browned and crispy. If you spray the potatoes with a little oil each time you stir, they will get even crispier.

Not-So-English Muffins

Prep time: 5 minutes | Cook time: 10 minutes |
Serves 4

2 strips turkey bacon, cut in half crosswise
2 whole-grain English muffins, split
1 cup fresh baby spinach, long stems removed
¼ ripe pear, peeled and thinly sliced
4 slices Provolone cheese

1. Place bacon strips in air fryer basket and air fry at 390°F (199°C) for 2 minutes. Check and separate strips if necessary so they cook evenly. Cook for 3 to 4 more minutes, until crispy. Remove and drain on paper towels. 2. Place split muffin halves in air fryer basket and cook for 2 minutes, just until lightly browned. 3. Open air fryer and top each muffin with a quarter of the baby spinach, several pear slices, a strip of bacon, and a slice of cheese. 4. Air fry at 360°F (182°C) for 1 to 2 minutes, until cheese completely melts.

Vegetable Frittata

Prep time: 10 minutes | Cook time: 19 minutes |
Serves 1 to 2

½ red or green bell pepper, cut into ½-inch chunks
4 button mushrooms, sliced
½ cup diced zucchini
½ teaspoon chopped fresh oregano or thyme
1 teaspoon olive oil
3 eggs, beaten
½ cup grated Cheddar cheese
Salt and freshly ground black pepper, to taste
1 teaspoon butter
1 teaspoon chopped fresh parsley

1. Preheat the air fryer to 400°F (204°C). 2. Toss the peppers, mushrooms, zucchini and oregano with the olive oil and air fry for 6 minutes, shaking the basket once or twice during the cooking process to redistribute the ingredients. 3. While the vegetables are cooking, beat the eggs well in a bowl, stir in the Cheddar cheese and season with salt and freshly ground black pepper. Add the air-fried vegetables to this bowl when they have finished cooking. 4. Place a cake pan into the air fryer basket with the butter using an aluminum sling to lower the pan into the basket. Air fry for 1 minute at 380°F (193°C) to melt the butter. Remove the cake pan and rotate the pan to distribute the butter and grease the pan. Pour the egg mixture into the cake pan and return the pan to the air fryer, using the aluminum sling. 5. Air fry at 380°F (193°C) for 12 minutes, or until the frittata has puffed up and is lightly browned. Let the frittata sit in the air fryer for 5 minutes to cool to an edible temperature and set up. Remove the cake pan from the air fryer, sprinkle with parsley and serve immediately.

Easy Buttermilk Biscuits

Prep time: 5 minutes | Cook time: 18 minutes |
Makes 16 biscuits

2½ cups all-purpose flour
1 tablespoon baking powder
1 teaspoon kosher salt
1 teaspoon sugar
½ teaspoon baking soda
8 tablespoons (1 stick) unsalted butter, at room temperature
1 cup buttermilk, chilled

1. Stir together the flour, baking powder, salt, sugar, and baking powder in a large bowl. 2. Add the butter and stir to mix well. Pour in the buttermilk and stir with a rubber spatula just until incorporated. 3. Place the dough onto a lightly floured surface and roll the dough out to a disk, ½ inch thick. Cut out the biscuits with a 2-inch round cutter and re-roll any scraps until you have 16 biscuits. 4. Preheat the air fryer to 325°F (163°C). 5. Working in batches, arrange the biscuits in the air fryer basket in a single layer. Bake for about 18 minutes until the biscuits are golden brown. 6. Remove from the basket to a plate and repeat with the remaining biscuits. 7. Serve hot.

Apple Rolls

Prep time: 20 minutes | Cook time: 20 to 24 minutes |
| Makes 12 rolls

Apple Rolls:
2 cups all-purpose flour, plus more for dusting
2 tablespoons granulated sugar
1 teaspoon salt
3 tablespoons butter, at room temperature
¾ cup milk, whole or 2%
½ cup packed light brown sugar
1 teaspoon ground cinnamon
1 large Granny Smith apple, peeled and diced
1 to 2 tablespoons oil
Icing:
½ cup confectioners' sugar
½ teaspoon vanilla extract
2 to 3 tablespoons milk, whole or 2%

Make the Apple Rolls 1. In a large bowl, whisk the flour, granulated sugar, and salt until blended. Stir in the butter and milk briefly until a sticky dough forms. 2. In a small bowl, stir together the brown sugar, cinnamon, and apple. 3. Place a piece of parchment paper on a work surface and dust it with flour. Roll the dough on the prepared surface to ¼ inch thickness. 4. Spread the apple mixture over the dough. Roll up the dough jelly roll-style, pinching the ends to seal. Cut the dough into 12 rolls. 5. Preheat the air fryer to 320°F (160°C). 6. Line the air fryer basket with parchment paper and spritz it with oil. Place 6 rolls on the prepared parchment. 7. Bake for 5 minutes. Flip the rolls and bake for 5 to 7 minutes more until lightly browned. Repeat with the remaining rolls. Make the Icing 8. In a medium bowl, whisk the confectioners' sugar, vanilla, and milk until blended. 9. Drizzle over the warm rolls.

Green Eggs and Ham

Prep time: 5 minutes | Cook time: 10 minutes | Serves 2

1 large Hass avocado, halved and pitted
2 thin slices ham
2 large eggs
2 tablespoons chopped green onions, plus more for garnish

½ teaspoon fine sea salt
¼ teaspoon ground black pepper
¼ cup shredded Cheddar cheese (omit for dairy-free)

1. Preheat the air fryer to 400°F (204°C). 2. Place a slice of ham into the cavity of each avocado half. Crack an egg on top of the ham, then sprinkle on the green onions, salt, and pepper. 3. Place the avocado halves in the air fryer cut side up and air fry for 10 minutes, or until the egg is cooked to your desired doneness. Top with the cheese (if using) and air fry for 30 seconds more, or until the cheese is melted. Garnish with chopped green onions. 4. Best served fresh. Store extras in an airtight container in the fridge for up to 4 days. Reheat in a preheated 350°F (177°C) air fryer for a few minutes, until warmed through.

Spinach Omelet

Prep time: 5 minutes | Cook time: 12 minutes | Serves 2

4 large eggs
1½ cups chopped fresh spinach leaves
2 tablespoons peeled and chopped yellow onion

2 tablespoons salted butter, melted
½ cup shredded mild Cheddar cheese
¼ teaspoon salt

1. In an ungreased round nonstick baking dish, whisk eggs. Stir in spinach, onion, butter, Cheddar, and salt. 2. Place dish into air fryer basket. Adjust the temperature to 320°F (160°C) and bake for 12 minutes. Omelet will be done when browned on the top and firm in the middle. 3. Slice in half and serve warm on two medium plates.

Chimichanga Breakfast Burrito

Prep time: 10 minutes | Cook time: 10 minutes | Serves 2

2 large (10- to 12-inch) flour tortillas
½ cup canned refried beans (pinto or black work equally well)

4 large eggs, cooked scrambled
4 corn tortilla chips, crushed
½ cup grated Pepper Jack cheese
12 pickled jalapeño slices

1 tablespoon vegetable oil
Guacamole, salsa, and sour

cream, for serving (optional)

1. Place the tortillas on a work surface and divide the refried beans between them, spreading them in a rough rectangle in the center of the tortillas. Top the beans with the scrambled eggs, crushed chips, pepper jack, and jalapeños. Fold one side over the fillings, then fold in each short side and roll up the rest of the way like a burrito. 2. Brush the outside of the burritos with the oil, then transfer to the air fryer, seam-side down. Air fry at 350°F (177°C) until the tortillas are browned and crisp and the filling is warm throughout, about 10 minutes. 3. Transfer the chimichangas to plates and serve warm with guacamole, salsa, and sour cream, if you like.

Breakfast Pita

Prep time: 5 minutes | Cook time: 6 minutes | Serves 2

1 whole wheat pita
2 teaspoons olive oil
½ shallot, diced
¼ teaspoon garlic, minced
1 large egg

¼ teaspoon dried oregano
¼ teaspoon dried thyme
⅛ teaspoon salt
2 tablespoons shredded Parmesan cheese

1. Preheat the air fryer to 380°F(193°C). 2. Brush the top of the pita with olive oil, then spread the diced shallot and minced garlic over the pita. 3. Crack the egg into a small bowl or ramekin, and season it with oregano, thyme, and salt. 4. Place the pita into the air fryer basket, and gently pour the egg onto the top of the pita. Sprinkle with cheese over the top. 5. Bake for 6 minutes. 6. Allow to cool for 5 minutes before cutting into pieces for serving.

Two-Cheese Grits

Prep time: 10 minutes | Cook time: 10 to 12 minutes | Serves 4

⅔ cup instant grits
1 teaspoon salt
1 teaspoon freshly ground black pepper
¾ cup milk, whole or 2%
1 large egg, beaten

3 ounces (85 g) cream cheese, at room temperature
1 tablespoon butter, melted
1 cup shredded mild Cheddar cheese
1 to 2 tablespoons oil

1. In a large bowl, combine the grits, salt, and pepper. Stir in the milk, egg, cream cheese, and butter until blended. Stir in the Cheddar cheese. 2. Preheat the air fryer to 400°F (204°C). Spritz a baking pan with oil. 3. Pour the grits mixture into the prepared pan and place it in the air fryer basket. 4. Cook for 5 minutes. Stir the mixture and cook for 5 minutes more for soupy grits or 7 minutes more for firmer grits.

Breakfast Meatballs

Prep time: 10 minutes | Cook time: 15 minutes |

Makes 18 meatballs

1 pound (454 g) ground pork breakfast sausage
½ teaspoon salt
¼ teaspoon ground black pepper

½ cup shredded sharp Cheddar cheese
1 ounce (28 g) cream cheese, softened
1 large egg, whisked

1. Combine all ingredients in a large bowl. Form mixture into eighteen 1-inch meatballs. 2. Place meatballs into ungreased air fryer basket. Adjust the temperature to 400ºF (204ºC) and air fry for 15 minutes, shaking basket three times during cooking. Meatballs will be browned on the outside and have an internal temperature of at least 145ºF (63ºC) when completely cooked. Serve warm.

Jalapeño Popper Egg Cups

Prep time: 10 minutes | Cook time: 10 minutes |

Serves 2

4 large eggs
¼ cup chopped pickled jalapeños
2 ounces (57 g) full-fat cream

cheese
½ cup shredded sharp Cheddar cheese

1. In a medium bowl, beat the eggs, then pour into four silicone muffin cups. 2. In a large microwave-safe bowl, place jalapeños, cream cheese, and Cheddar. Microwave for 30 seconds and stir. Take a spoonful, approximately ¼ of the mixture, and place it in the center of one of the egg cups. Repeat with remaining mixture. 3. Place egg cups into the air fryer basket. 4. Adjust the temperature to 320ºF (160ºC) and bake for 10 minutes. 5. Serve warm.

Mozzarella Bacon Calzones

Prep time: 15 minutes | Cook time: 12 minutes |

Serves 4

2 large eggs
1 cup blanched finely ground almond flour
2 cups shredded Mozzarella cheese

2 ounces (57 g) cream cheese, softened and broken into small pieces
4 slices cooked sugar-free bacon, crumbled

1. Beat eggs in a small bowl. Pour into a medium nonstick skillet over medium heat and scramble. Set aside. 2. In a large microwave-safe bowl, mix flour and Mozzarella. Add cream cheese to the bowl. 3. Place bowl in microwave and cook 45 seconds on high to melt cheese, then stir with a fork until a soft dough ball forms. 4. Cut a piece of parchment to fit air fryer basket. Separate dough into two sections and press each out into an 8-inch round. 5. On half of each dough round, place half of the scrambled eggs and crumbled bacon. Fold the other side of the dough over and press to seal the edges. 6. Place calzones on ungreased parchment and into air fryer basket. Adjust the temperature to 350ºF (177ºC) and set the timer for 12 minutes, turning calzones halfway through cooking. Crust will be golden and firm when done. 7. Let calzones cool on a cooking rack 5 minutes before serving.

Egg and Bacon Muffins

Prep time: 5 minutes | Cook time: 15 minutes |

Serves 1

2 eggs
Salt and ground black pepper, to taste
1 tablespoon green pesto

3 ounces (85 g) shredded Cheddar cheese
5 ounces (142 g) cooked bacon
1 scallion, chopped

1. Preheat the air fryer to 350ºF (177ºC). Line a cupcake tin with parchment paper. 2. Beat the eggs with pepper, salt, and pesto in a bowl. Mix in the cheese. 3. Pour the eggs into the cupcake tin and top with the bacon and scallion. 4. Bake in the preheated air fryer for 15 minutes, or until the egg is set. 5. Serve immediately.

Portobello Eggs Benedict

Prep time: 10 minutes | Cook time: 10 to 14 minutes

| Serves 2

1 tablespoon olive oil
2 cloves garlic, minced
¼ teaspoon dried thyme
2 portobello mushrooms, stems removed and gills scraped out
2 Roma tomatoes, halved lengthwise
Salt and freshly ground black

pepper, to taste
2 large eggs
2 tablespoons grated Pecorino Romano cheese
1 tablespoon chopped fresh parsley, for garnish
1 teaspoon truffle oil (optional)

1. Preheat the air fryer to 400ºF (204ºC). 2. In a small bowl, combine the olive oil, garlic, and thyme. Brush the mixture over the mushrooms and tomatoes until thoroughly coated. Season to taste with salt and freshly ground black pepper. 3. Arrange the vegetables, cut side up, in the air fryer basket. Crack an egg into the center of each mushroom and sprinkle with cheese. Air fry for 10 to 14 minutes until the vegetables are tender and the whites are firm. When cool enough to handle, coarsely chop the tomatoes and place on top of the eggs. Scatter parsley on top and drizzle with truffle oil, if desired, just before serving.

Creamy Cinnamon Rolls

Prep time: 10 minutes | Cook time: 9 minutes | Serves 8

1 pound (454 g) frozen bread dough, thawed
¼ cup butter, melted
¾ cup brown sugar
1½ tablespoons ground cinnamon
Cream Cheese Glaze:

4 ounces (113 g) cream cheese, softened
2 tablespoons butter, softened
1¼ cups powdered sugar
½ teaspoon vanilla extract

1. Let the bread dough come to room temperature on the counter. On a lightly floured surface, roll the dough into a 13-inch by 11-inch rectangle. Position the rectangle so the 13-inch side is facing you. Brush the melted butter all over the dough, leaving a 1-inch border uncovered along the edge farthest away from you. 2. Combine the brown sugar and cinnamon in a small bowl. Sprinkle the mixture evenly over the buttered dough, keeping the 1-inch border uncovered. Roll the dough into a log, starting with the edge closest to you. Roll the dough tightly, rolling evenly, and push out any air pockets. When you get to the uncovered edge of the dough, press the dough onto the roll to seal it together. 3. Cut the log into 8 pieces, slicing slowly with a sawing motion so you don't flatten the dough. Turn the slices on their sides and cover with a clean kitchen towel. Let the rolls sit in the warmest part of the kitchen for 1½ to 2 hours to rise. 4. To make the glaze, place the cream cheese and butter in a microwave-safe bowl. Soften the mixture in the microwave for 30 seconds at a time until it is easy to stir. Gradually add the powdered sugar and stir to combine. Add the vanilla extract and whisk until smooth. Set aside. 5. When the rolls have risen, preheat the air fryer to 350ºF (177ºC). 6. Transfer 4 of the rolls to the air fryer basket. Air fry for 5 minutes. Turn the rolls over and air fry for another 4 minutes. Repeat with the remaining 4 rolls. 7. Let the rolls cool for two minutes before glazing. Spread large dollops of cream cheese glaze on top of the warm cinnamon rolls, allowing some glaze to drip down the side of the rolls. Serve warm.

Chapter 2 Family Favorites

Coconut Chicken Tenders

Prep time: 10 minutes | Cook time: 12 minutes |
Serves 4

Oil, for spraying	¾ cup panko bread crumbs
2 large eggs	1 teaspoon salt
¼ cup milk	½ teaspoon freshly ground
1 tablespoon hot sauce	black pepper
1½ cups sweetened flaked coconut	1 pound (454 g) chicken tenders

1. Line the air fryer basket with parchment and spray lightly with oil. 2. In a small bowl, whisk together the eggs, milk, and hot sauce. 3. In a shallow dish, mix together the coconut, bread crumbs, salt, and black pepper. 4. Coat the chicken in the egg mix, then dredge in the coconut mixture until evenly coated. 5. Place the chicken in the prepared basket and spray liberally with oil. 6. Air fry at 400°F (204°C) for 6 minutes, flip, spray with more oil, and cook for another 6 minutes, or until the internal temperature reaches 165°F (74°C).

Buffalo Cauliflower

Prep time: 15 minutes | Cook time: 5 minutes |
Serves 6

1 large head cauliflower, separated into small florets	⅔ cup nonfat Greek yogurt
1 tablespoon olive oil	½ teaspoons Tabasco sauce
½ teaspoon garlic powder	1 celery stalk, chopped
⅓ cup low-sodium hot wing sauce	1 tablespoon crumbled blue cheese

1. In a large bowl, toss the cauliflower florets with the olive oil. Sprinkle with the garlic powder and toss again to coat. Put half of the cauliflower in the air fryer basket. Air fry at 380°F (193°C) for 5 to 7 minutes, until the cauliflower is browned, shaking the basket once during cooking. 2. Transfer to a serving bowl and toss with half of the wing sauce. Repeat with the remaining cauliflower and wing sauce. 3. In a small bowl, stir together the yogurt, Tabasco sauce, celery, and blue cheese. Serve with the cauliflower for dipping.

Chinese-Inspired Spareribs

Prep time: 30 minutes | Cook time: 8 minutes |
Serves 4

Oil, for spraying	½ cup beef or chicken stock
12 ounces (340 g) boneless pork spareribs, cut into 3-inch-long pieces	¼ cup honey
	2 tablespoons minced garlic
1 cup soy sauce	1 teaspoon ground ginger
¾ cup sugar	2 drops red food coloring (optional)

1. Line the air fryer basket with parchment and spray lightly with oil. 2. Combine the ribs, soy sauce, sugar, beef stock, honey, garlic, ginger, and food coloring (if using) in a large zip-top plastic bag, seal, and shake well until completely coated. Refrigerate for at least 30 minutes. 3. Place the ribs in the prepared basket. 4. Air fry at 375°F (191°C) for 8 minutes, or until the internal temperature reaches 165°F (74°C).

Beef Jerky

Prep time: 30 minutes | Cook time: 2 hours | Serves 8

Oil, for spraying	brown sugar
1 pound (454 g) round steak, cut into thin, short slices	1 tablespoon minced garlic
¼ cup soy sauce	1 teaspoon ground ginger
3 tablespoons packed light	1 tablespoon water

1. Line the air fryer basket with parchment and spray lightly with oil. 2. Place the steak, soy sauce, brown sugar, garlic, ginger, and water in a zip-top plastic bag, seal, and shake well until evenly coated. Refrigerate for 30 minutes. 3. Place the steak in the prepared basket in a single layer. You may need to work in batches, depending on the size of your air fryer. 4. Air fry at 180°F (82°C) for at least 2 hours. Add more time if you like your jerky a bit tougher.

Pork Burgers with Red Cabbage Salad

Prep time: 20 minutes | Cook time: 7 to 9 minutes | Serves 4

½ cup Greek yogurt	pork
2 tablespoons low-sodium mustard, divided	½ teaspoon paprika
1 tablespoon lemon juice	1 cup mixed baby lettuce greens
¼ cup sliced red cabbage	2 small tomatoes, sliced
¼ cup grated carrots	8 small low-sodium whole-wheat sandwich buns, cut in
1 pound (454 g) lean ground	half

1. In a small bowl, combine the yogurt, 1 tablespoon mustard, lemon juice, cabbage, and carrots; mix and refrigerate. 2. In a medium bowl, combine the pork, remaining 1 tablespoon mustard, and paprika. Form into 8 small patties. 3. Put the sliders into the air fryer basket. Air fry at 400ºF (204ºC) for 7 to 9 minutes, or until the sliders register 165ºF (74ºC) as tested with a meat thermometer. 4. Assemble the burgers by placing some of the lettuce greens on a bun bottom. Top with a tomato slice, the burgers, and the cabbage mixture. Add the bun top and serve immediately.

Beignets

Prep time: 30 minutes | Cook time: 6 minutes | Makes 9 beignets

Oil, for greasing and spraying	1 cup milk
3 cups all-purpose flour, plus more for dusting	2 tablespoons packed light brown sugar
1½ teaspoons salt	1 tablespoon unsalted butter
1 (2¼-teaspoon) envelope active dry yeast	1 large egg
	1 cup confectioners' sugar

1. Oil a large bowl. 2. In a small bowl, mix together the flour, salt, and yeast. Set aside. 3. Pour the milk into a glass measuring cup and microwave in 1-minute intervals until it boils. 4. In a large bowl, mix together the brown sugar and butter. Pour in the hot milk and whisk until the sugar has dissolved. Let cool to room temperature. 5. Whisk the egg into the cooled milk mixture and fold in the flour mixture until a dough forms. 6. On a lightly floured work surface, knead the dough for 3 to 5 minutes. 7. Place the dough in the oiled bowl and cover with a clean kitchen towel. Let rise in a warm place for about 1 hour, or until doubled in size. 8. Roll the dough out on a lightly floured work surface until it's about ¼ inch thick. Cut the dough into 3-inch squares and place them on a lightly floured baking sheet. Cover loosely with a kitchen towel and let rise again until doubled in size, about 30 minutes. 9. Line the air fryer basket with parchment and spray lightly with oil. 10. Place the dough squares in the prepared basket and spray lightly with oil. You may need to work in batches, depending on the size of your air fryer. 11. Air fry at 390ºF (199ºC) for 3 minutes, flip, spray with oil, and cook for another 3 minutes, until crispy. 12. Dust with the confectioners' sugar before serving.

Meringue Cookies

Prep time: 15 minutes | Cook time: 1 hour 30 minutes | Makes 20 cookies

Oil, for spraying	1 cup sugar
4 large egg whites	Pinch cream of tartar

1. Preheat the air fryer to 140ºF (60ºC). Line the air fryer basket with parchment and spray lightly with oil. 2. In a small heatproof bowl, whisk together the egg whites and sugar. Fill a small saucepan halfway with water, place it over medium heat, and bring to a light simmer. Place the bowl with the egg whites on the saucepan, making sure the bottom of the bowl does not touch the water. Whisk the mixture until the sugar is dissolved. 3. Transfer the mixture to a large bowl and add the cream of tartar. Using an electric mixer, beat the mixture on high until it is glossy and stiff peaks form. Transfer the mixture to a piping bag or a zip-top plastic bag with a corner cut off. 4. Pipe rounds into the prepared basket. You may need to work in batches, depending on the size of your air fryer. 5. Cook for 1 hour 30 minutes. 6. Turn off the air fryer and let the meringues cool completely inside. The residual heat will continue to dry them out.

Churro Bites

Prep time: 5 minutes | Cook time: 6 minutes | Makes 36 bites

Oil, for spraying	1 tablespoon ground cinnamon
1 (17¼-ounce / 489-g) package frozen puffed pastry, thawed	½ cup confectioners' sugar
1 cup granulated sugar	1 tablespoon milk

1. Preheat the air fryer to 400ºF (204ºC). Line the air fryer basket with parchment and spray lightly with oil. 2. Unfold the puff pastry onto a clean work surface. Using a sharp knife, cut the dough into 36 bite-size pieces. 3. Place the dough pieces in one layer in the prepared basket, taking care not to let the pieces touch or overlap. 4. Cook for 3 minutes, flip, and cook for another 3 minutes, or until puffed and golden. 5. In a small bowl, mix together the granulated sugar and cinnamon. 6. In another small bowl, whisk together the confectioners' sugar and milk. 7. Dredge the bites in the cinnamon-sugar mixture until evenly coated. 8. Serve with the icing on the side for dipping.

Phyllo Vegetable Triangles

Prep time: 15 minutes | Cook time: 6 to 11 minutes | Serves 6

3 tablespoons minced onion
2 garlic cloves, minced
2 tablespoons grated carrot
1 teaspoon olive oil
3 tablespoons frozen baby peas, thawed
2 tablespoons nonfat cream cheese, at room temperature
6 sheets frozen phyllo dough, thawed
Olive oil spray, for coating the dough

1. In a baking pan, combine the onion, garlic, carrot, and olive oil. Air fry at 390°F (199°C) for 2 to 4 minutes, or until the vegetables are crisp-tender. Transfer to a bowl. 2. Stir in the peas and cream cheese to the vegetable mixture. Let cool while you prepare the dough. 3. Lay one sheet of phyllo on a work surface and lightly spray with olive oil spray. Top with another sheet of phyllo. Repeat with the remaining 4 phyllo sheets; you'll have 3 stacks with 2 layers each. Cut each stack lengthwise into 4 strips (12 strips total). 4. Place a scant 2 teaspoons of the filling near the bottom of each strip. Bring one corner up over the filling to make a triangle; continue folding the triangles over, as you would fold a flag. Seal the edge with a bit of water. Repeat with the remaining strips and filling. 5. Air fry the triangles, in 2 batches, for 4 to 7 minutes, or until golden brown. Serve.

Meatball Subs

Prep time: 15 minutes | Cook time: 19 minutes | Serves 6

Oil, for spraying
1 pound (454 g) 85% lean ground beef
½ cup Italian bread crumbs
1 tablespoon dried minced onion
1 tablespoon minced garlic
1 large egg
1 teaspoon salt
1 teaspoon freshly ground black pepper
6 hoagie rolls
1 (18-ounce / 510-g) jar marinara sauce
1½ cups shredded Mozzarella cheese

1. Line the air fryer basket with parchment and spray lightly with oil. 2. In a large bowl, mix together the ground beef, bread crumbs, onion, garlic, egg, salt, and black pepper. Roll the mixture into 18 meatballs. 3. Place the meatballs in the prepared basket. 4. Air fry at 390°F (199°C) for 15 minutes. 5. Place 3 meatballs in each hoagie roll. Top with marinara and Mozzarella cheese. 6. Place the loaded rolls in the air fryer and cook for 3 to 4 minutes, or until the cheese is melted. You may need to work in batches, depending on the size of your air fryer. Serve immediately.

Old Bay Tilapia

Prep time: 15 minutes | Cook time: 6 minutes | Serves 4

Oil, for spraying
1 cup panko bread crumbs
2 tablespoons Old Bay seasoning
2 teaspoons granulated garlic
1 teaspoon onion powder
½ teaspoon salt
¼ teaspoon freshly ground black pepper
1 large egg
4 tilapia fillets

1. Preheat the air fryer to 400°F (204°C). Line the air fryer basket with parchment and spray lightly with oil. 2. In a shallow bowl, mix together the bread crumbs, Old Bay, garlic, onion powder, salt, and black pepper. 3. In a small bowl, whisk the egg. 4. Coat the tilapia in the egg, then dredge in the bread crumb mixture until completely coated. 5. Place the tilapia in the prepared basket. You may need to work in batches, depending on the size of your air fryer. Spray lightly with oil. 6. Cook for 4 to 6 minutes, depending on the thickness of the fillets, until the internal temperature reaches 145°F (63°C). Serve immediately.

Pecan Rolls

Prep time: 20 minutes | Cook time: 20 to 24 minutes | Makes 12 rolls

2 cups all-purpose flour, plus more for dusting
2 tablespoons granulated sugar, plus ¼ cup, divided
1 teaspoon salt
3 tablespoons butter, at room temperature
¾ cup milk, whole or 2%
¼ cup packed light brown sugar
½ cup chopped pecans, toasted
1 to 2 tablespoons oil
¼ cup confectioners' sugar (optional)

1. In a large bowl, whisk the flour, 2 tablespoons granulated sugar, and salt until blended. Stir in the butter and milk briefly until a sticky dough forms. 2. In a small bowl, stir together the brown sugar and remaining ¼ cup of granulated sugar. 3. Place a piece of parchment paper on a work surface and dust it with flour. Roll the dough on the prepared surface to ¼ inch thickness. 4. Spread the sugar mixture over the dough. Sprinkle the pecans on top. Roll up the dough jelly roll-style, pinching the ends to seal. Cut the dough into 12 rolls. 5. Preheat the air fryer to 320°F (160°C). 6. Line the air fryer basket with parchment paper and spritz the parchment with oil. Place 6 rolls on the prepared parchment. 7. Bake for 5 minutes. Flip the rolls and bake for 5 to 7 minutes more until lightly browned. Repeat with the remaining rolls. 8. Sprinkle with confectioners' sugar (if using).

Cheesy Roasted Sweet Potatoes

Prep time: 7 minutes | Cook time: 18 to 23 minutes |

Serves 4

2 large sweet potatoes, peeled and sliced	vinegar
1 teaspoon olive oil	1 teaspoon dried thyme
1 tablespoon white balsamic	¼ cup grated Parmesan cheese

1. In a large bowl, drizzle the sweet potato slices with the olive oil and toss. 2. Sprinkle with the balsamic vinegar and thyme and toss again. 3. Sprinkle the potatoes with the Parmesan cheese and toss to coat. 4. Roast the slices, in batches, in the air fryer basket at 400ºF (204ºC) for 18 to 23 minutes, tossing the sweet potato slices in the basket once during cooking, until tender. 5. Repeat with the remaining sweet potato slices. Serve immediately.

Mixed Berry Crumble

Prep time: 10 minutes | Cook time: 11 to 16 minutes

| Serves 4

½ cup chopped fresh strawberries	1 tablespoon honey
½ cup fresh blueberries	⅔ cup whole-wheat pastry flour
⅓ cup frozen raspberries	3 tablespoons packed brown sugar
1 tablespoon freshly squeezed lemon juice	2 tablespoons unsalted butter, melted

1. In a baking pan, combine the strawberries, blueberries, and raspberries. Drizzle with the lemon juice and honey. 2. In a small bowl, mix the pastry flour and brown sugar. 3. Stir in the butter and mix until crumbly. Sprinkle this mixture over the fruit. 4. Bake at 380ºF (193ºC) for 11 to 16 minutes, or until the fruit is tender and bubbly and the topping is golden brown. Serve warm.

Berry Cheesecake

Prep time: 5 minutes | Cook time: 10 minutes |

Serves 4

Oil, for spraying	1 large egg
8 ounces (227 g) cream cheese	½ teaspoon vanilla extract
6 tablespoons sugar	¼ teaspoon lemon juice
1 tablespoon sour cream	½ cup fresh mixed berries

1. Preheat the air fryer to 350ºF (177ºC). Line the air fryer basket with parchment and spray lightly with oil. 2. In a blender, combine the cream cheese, sugar, sour cream, egg, vanilla, and lemon juice and blend until smooth. Pour the mixture into a 4-inch springform pan. 3. Place the pan in the prepared basket. 4. Cook for 8 to 10 minutes, or until only the very center jiggles slightly when the pan is moved. 5. Refrigerate the cheesecake in the pan for at least 2 hours. 6. Release the sides from the springform pan, top the cheesecake with the mixed berries, and serve.

Avocado and Egg Burrito

Prep time: 10 minutes | Cook time: 3 to 5 minutes |

Serves 4

2 hard-boiled egg whites, chopped	plus additional for serving (optional)
1 hard-boiled egg, chopped	1 (1.2-ounce / 34-g) slice low-sodium, low-fat American cheese, torn into pieces
1 avocado, peeled, pitted, and chopped	
1 red bell pepper, chopped	4 low-sodium whole-wheat flour tortillas
3 tablespoons low-sodium salsa,	

1. In a medium bowl, thoroughly mix the egg whites, egg, avocado, red bell pepper, salsa, and cheese. 2. Place the tortillas on a work surface and evenly divide the filling among them. Fold in the edges and roll up. Secure the burritos with toothpicks if necessary. 3. Put the burritos in the air fryer basket. Air fry at 390ºF (199ºC) for 3 to 5 minutes, or until the burritos are light golden brown and crisp. Serve with more salsa (if using).

Fried Green Tomatoes

Prep time: 15 minutes | Cook time: 6 to 8 minutes |

Serves 4

4 medium green tomatoes	½ cup panko bread crumbs
⅓ cup all-purpose flour	2 teaspoons olive oil
2 egg whites	1 teaspoon paprika
¼ cup almond milk	1 clove garlic, minced
1 cup ground almonds	

1. Rinse the tomatoes and pat dry. Cut the tomatoes into ½-inch slices, discarding the thinner ends. 2. Put the flour on a plate. In a shallow bowl, beat the egg whites with the almond milk until frothy. And on another plate, combine the almonds, bread crumbs, olive oil, paprika, and garlic and mix well. 3. Dip the tomato slices into the flour, then into the egg white mixture, then into the almond mixture to coat. 4. Place four of the coated tomato slices in the air fryer basket. Air fry at 400ºF (204ºC) for 6 to 8 minutes or until the tomato coating is crisp and golden brown. Repeat with remaining tomato slices and serve immediately.

Elephant Ears

Prep time: 5 minutes | Cook time: 5 minutes | Serves 8

Oil, for spraying
1 (8-ounce / 227-g) can buttermilk biscuits
3 tablespoons sugar

1 tablespoon ground cinnamon
3 tablespoons unsalted butter, melted
8 scoops vanilla ice cream (optional)

1. Line the air fryer basket with parchment and spray lightly with oil. 2. Separate the dough. Using a rolling pin, roll out the biscuits into 6- to 8-inch circles. 3. Place the dough circles in the prepared basket and spray liberally with oil. You may need to work in batches, depending on the size of your air fryer. 4. Air fry at 350°F (177°C) for 5 minutes, or until lightly browned. 5. In a small bowl, mix together the sugar and cinnamon. 6. Brush the elephant ears with the melted butter and sprinkle with the cinnamon-sugar mixture. 7. Top each serving with a scoop of ice cream (if using).

Steak Tips and Potatoes

Prep time: 10 minutes | Cook time: 20 minutes | Serves 4

Oil, for spraying
8 ounces (227 g) baby gold potatoes, cut in half
½ teaspoon salt
1 pound (454 g) steak, cut into ½-inch pieces

1 teaspoon Worcestershire sauce
1 teaspoon granulated garlic
½ teaspoon salt
½ teaspoon freshly ground black pepper

1. Line the air fryer basket with parchment and spray lightly with oil. 2. In a microwave-safe bowl, combine the potatoes and salt, then pour in about ½ inch of water. Microwave for 7 minutes, or until the potatoes are nearly tender. Drain. 3. In a large bowl, gently mix together the steak, potatoes, Worcestershire sauce, garlic, salt, and black pepper. Spread the mixture in an even layer in the prepared basket. 4. Air fry at 400°F (204°C) for 12 to 17 minutes, stirring after 5 to 6 minutes. The cooking time will depend on the thickness of the meat and preferred doneness.

Cajun Shrimp

Prep time: 15 minutes | Cook time: 9 minutes | Serves 4

Oil, for spraying
1 pound (454 g) jumbo raw shrimp, peeled and deveined
1 tablespoon Cajun seasoning
6 ounces (170 g) cooked kielbasa, cut into thick slices
½ medium zucchini, cut into ¼-inch-thick slices

½ medium yellow squash, cut into ¼-inch-thick slices
1 green bell pepper, seeded and cut into 1-inch pieces
2 tablespoons olive oil
½ teaspoon salt

1. Preheat the air fryer to 400°F (204°C). Line the air fryer basket with parchment and spray lightly with oil. 2. In a large bowl, toss together the shrimp and Cajun seasoning. Add the kielbasa, zucchini, squash, bell pepper, olive oil, and salt and mix well. 3. Transfer the mixture to the prepared basket, taking care not to overcrowd. You may need to work in batches, depending on the size of your air fryer. 4. Cook for 9 minutes, shaking and stirring every 3 minutes. Serve immediately.

Chapter 3 Fast and Easy Everyday Favorites

Corn Fritters

Prep time: 15 minutes | Cook time: 8 minutes | Serves 6

1 cup self-rising flour	¼ cup buttermilk
1 tablespoon sugar	¾ cup corn kernels
1 teaspoon salt	¼ cup minced onion
1 large egg, lightly beaten	Cooking spray

1. Preheat the air fryer to 350ºF (177ºC). Line the air fryer basket with parchment paper. 2. In a medium bowl, whisk the flour, sugar, and salt until blended. Stir in the egg and buttermilk. Add the corn and minced onion. Mix well. Shape the corn fritter batter into 12 balls. 3. Place the fritters on the parchment and spritz with oil. Bake for 4 minutes. Flip the fritters, spritz them with oil, and bake for 4 minutes more until firm and lightly browned. 4. Serve immediately.

Simple and Easy Croutons

Prep time: 5 minutes | Cook time: 8 minutes | Serves 4

2 slices friendly bread	Hot soup, for serving
1 tablespoon olive oil	

1. Preheat the air fryer to 390ºF (199ºC). 2. Cut the slices of bread into medium-size chunks. 3. Brush the air fryer basket with the oil. 4. Place the chunks inside and air fry for at least 8 minutes. 5. Serve with hot soup.

Cheesy Baked Grits

Prep time: 10 minutes | Cook time: 12 minutes | Serves 6

¾ cup hot water	2 cloves garlic, minced
2 (1-ounce / 28-g) packages instant grits	½ to 1 teaspoon red pepper flakes
1 large egg, beaten	1 cup shredded Cheddar cheese
1 tablespoon butter, melted	or jalapeño Jack cheese

1. Preheat the air fryer to 400ºF (204ºC). 2. In a baking pan, combine the water, grits, egg, butter, garlic, and red pepper flakes. Stir until well combined. Stir in the shredded cheese. 3. Place the pan in the air fryer basket and air fry for 12 minutes, or until the grits have cooked through and a knife inserted near the center comes out clean. 4. Let stand for 5 minutes before serving.

Cheesy Chile Toast

Prep time: 5 minutes | Cook time: 5 minutes | Serves 1

2 tablespoons grated Parmesan cheese	room temperature
	10 to 15 thin slices serrano
2 tablespoons grated Mozzarella cheese	chile or jalapeño
	2 slices sourdough bread
2 teaspoons salted butter, at	½ teaspoon black pepper

1. Preheat the air fryer to 325ºF (163ºC). 2. In a small bowl, stir together the Parmesan, Mozzarella, butter, and chiles. 3. Spread half the mixture onto one side of each slice of bread. Sprinkle with the pepper. Place the slices, cheese-side up, in the air fryer basket. Bake for 5 minutes, or until the cheese has melted and started to brown slightly. 4. Serve immediately.

Garlicky Knots with Parsley

Prep time: 10 minutes | Cook time: 10 minutes | Makes 8 knots

1 teaspoon dried parsley	1 (11-ounce / 312-g) tube
¼ cup melted butter	refrigerated French bread
2 teaspoons garlic powder	dough, cut into 8 slices

1. Preheat the air fryer to 350ºF (177ºC). 2. Combine the parsley, butter, and garlic powder in a bowl. Stir to mix well. 3. Place the French bread dough slices on a clean work surface, then roll each slice into a 6-inch long rope. Tie the ropes into knots and arrange them on a plate. Brush the knots with butter mixture. 4. Transfer the knots into the air fryer. You need to work in batches to avoid overcrowding. 5. Air fry for 5 minutes or until the knots are golden brown. Flip the knots halfway through the cooking time. 6. Serve immediately.

Simple Pea Delight

Prep time: 5 minutes | Cook time: 15 minutes | Serves 2 to 4

1 cup flour	3 tablespoons pea protein
1 teaspoon baking powder	½ cup chicken or turkey strips
3 eggs	Pinch of sea salt
1 cup coconut milk	1 cup Mozzarella cheese
1 cup cream cheese	

1. Preheat the air fryer to 390°F (199°C). 2. In a large bowl, mix all ingredients together using a large wooden spoon. 3. Spoon equal amounts of the mixture into muffin cups and bake for 15 minutes. 4. Serve immediately.

Simple Baked Green Beans

Prep time: 5 minutes | Cook time: 10 minutes | Makes 2 cups

½ teaspoon lemon pepper	1 tablespoon olive oil
2 teaspoons granulated garlic	2 cups fresh green beans,
½ teaspoon salt	trimmed and snapped in half

1. Preheat the air fryer to 370°F (188°C). 2. Combine the lemon pepper, garlic, salt, and olive oil in a bowl. Stir to mix well. 3. Add the green beans to the bowl of mixture and toss to coat well. 4. Arrange the green beans in the preheated air fryer. Bake for 10 minutes or until tender and crispy. Shake the basket halfway through to make sure the green beans are cooked evenly. 5. Serve immediately.

Garlicky Baked Cherry Tomatoes

Prep time: 5 minutes | Cook time: 4 to 6 minutes | Serves 2

2 cups cherry tomatoes	1 tablespoon freshly chopped
1 clove garlic, thinly sliced	basil, for topping
1 teaspoon olive oil	Cooking spray
⅛ teaspoon kosher salt	

1. Preheat the air fryer to 360°F (182°C). Spritz the air fryer baking pan with cooking spray and set aside. 2. In a large bowl, toss together the cherry tomatoes, sliced garlic, olive oil, and kosher salt. Spread the mixture in an even layer in the prepared pan. 3. Bake in the preheated air fryer for 4 to 6 minutes, or until the tomatoes become soft and wilted. 4. Transfer to a bowl and rest for 5 minutes. Top with the chopped basil and serve warm.

Easy Devils on Horseback

Prep time: 5 minutes | Cook time: 7 minutes | Serves 12

24 petite pitted prunes (4½ ounces / 128 g)	divided
¼ cup crumbled blue cheese,	8 slices center-cut bacon, cut crosswise into thirds

1. Preheat the air fryer to 400°F (204°C). 2. Halve the prunes lengthwise, but don't cut them all the way through. Place ½ teaspoon of cheese in the center of each prune. Wrap a piece of bacon around each prune and secure the bacon with a toothpick. 3. Working in batches, arrange a single layer of the prunes in the air fryer basket. Air fry for about 7 minutes, flipping halfway, until the bacon is cooked through and crisp. 4. Let cool slightly and serve warm.

Classic Poutine

Prep time: 15 minutes | Cook time: 25 minutes | Serves 2

2 russet potatoes, scrubbed and cut into ½-inch sticks	1 teaspoon tomato paste
2 teaspoons vegetable oil	1½ cups beef stock
2 tablespoons butter	2 teaspoons Worcestershire sauce
¼ onion, minced	Salt and freshly ground black pepper, to taste
¼ teaspoon dried thyme	⅔ cup chopped string cheese
1 clove garlic, smashed	
3 tablespoons all-purpose flour	

1. Bring a pot of water to a boil, then put in the potato sticks and blanch for 4 minutes. 2. Preheat the air fryer to 400°F (204°C). 3. Drain the potato sticks and rinse under running cold water, then pat dry with paper towels. 4. Transfer the sticks in a large bowl and drizzle with vegetable oil. Toss to coat well. 5. Place the potato sticks in the preheated air fryer. Air fry for 25 minutes or until the sticks are golden brown. Shake the basket at least three times during the frying. 6. Meanwhile, make the gravy: Heat the butter in a saucepan over medium heat until melted. 7. Add the onion, thyme, and garlic and sauté for 5 minutes or until the onion is translucent. 8. Add the flour and sauté for an additional 2 minutes. Pour in the tomato paste and beef stock and cook for 1 more minute or until lightly thickened. 9. Drizzle the gravy with Worcestershire sauce and sprinkle with salt and ground black pepper. Reduce the heat to low to keep the gravy warm until ready to serve. 10. Transfer the fried potato sticks onto a plate, then sprinkle with salt and ground black pepper. Scatter with string cheese and pour the gravy over. Serve warm.

Spinach and Carrot Balls

Prep time: 10 minutes | Cook time: 10 minutes |
Serves 4

2 slices toasted bread	½ teaspoon garlic powder
1 carrot, peeled and grated	1 teaspoon minced garlic
1 package fresh spinach,	1 teaspoon salt
blanched and chopped	½ teaspoon black pepper
½ onion, chopped	1 tablespoon nutritional yeast
1 egg, beaten	1 tablespoon flour

1. Preheat the air fryer to 390ºF (199ºC). 2. In a food processor, pulse the toasted bread to form bread crumbs. Transfer into a shallow dish or bowl. 3. In a bowl, mix together all the other ingredients. 4. Use your hands to shape the mixture into small-sized balls. Roll the balls in the bread crumbs, ensuring to cover them well. 5. Put in the air fryer basket and air fry for 10 minutes. 6. Serve immediately.

Spicy Air Fried Old Bay Shrimp

Prep time: 7 minutes | Cook time: 10 minutes |
Makes 2 cups

½ teaspoon Old Bay Seasoning	⅛ teaspoon salt
1 teaspoon ground cayenne pepper	½ pound (227 g) shrimps, peeled and deveined
½ teaspoon paprika	Juice of half a lemon
1 tablespoon olive oil	

1. Preheat the air fryer to 390ºF (199ºC). 2. Combine the Old Bay Seasoning, cayenne pepper, paprika, olive oil, and salt in a large bowl, then add the shrimps and toss to coat well. 3. Put the shrimps in the preheated air fryer. Air fry for 10 minutes or until opaque. Flip the shrimps halfway through. 4. Serve the shrimps with lemon juice on top.

Lemony and Garlicky Asparagus

Prep time: 5 minutes | Cook time: 10 minutes |
Makes 10 spears

10 spears asparagus (about ½ pound / 227 g in total), snap the ends off	½ teaspoon salt
	¼ teaspoon ground black pepper
1 tablespoon lemon juice	Cooking spray
2 teaspoons minced garlic	

1. Preheat the air fryer to 400ºF (204ºC). Line a parchment paper in the air fryer basket. 2. Put the asparagus spears in a large bowl. Drizzle with lemon juice and sprinkle with minced garlic, salt, and ground black pepper. Toss to coat well. 3. Transfer the asparagus in the preheated air fryer and spritz with cooking spray. Air fryer for 10 minutes or until wilted and soft. Flip the asparagus halfway through. 4. Serve immediately.

Golden Salmon and Carrot Croquettes

Prep time: 15 minutes | Cook time: 10 minutes |
Serves 6

2 egg whites	2 tablespoons minced garlic cloves
1 cup almond flour	
1 cup panko breadcrumbs	½ cup chopped onion
1 pound (454 g) chopped salmon fillet	2 tablespoons chopped chives
	Cooking spray
⅔ cup grated carrots	

1. Preheat the air fryer to 350ºF (177ºC). Spritz the air fryer basket with cooking spray. 2. Whisk the egg whites in a bowl. Put the flour in a second bowl. Pour the breadcrumbs in a third bowl. Set aside. 3. Combine the salmon, carrots, garlic, onion, and chives in a large bowl. Stir to mix well. 4. Form the mixture into balls with your hands. Dredge the balls into the flour, then egg, and then breadcrumbs to coat well. 5. Arrange the salmon balls in the preheated air fryer and spritz with cooking spray. 6. Air fry for 10 minutes or until crispy and browned. Shake the basket halfway through. 7. Serve immediately.

Peppery Brown Rice Fritters

Prep time: 10 minutes | Cook time: 8 to 10 minutes |
Serves 4

1 (10-ounce / 284-g) bag frozen cooked brown rice, thawed	2 tablespoons minced fresh basil
1 egg	3 tablespoons grated Parmesan cheese
3 tablespoons brown rice flour	
⅓ cup finely grated carrots	2 teaspoons olive oil
⅓ cup minced red bell pepper	

1. Preheat the air fryer to 380ºF (193ºC). 2. In a small bowl, combine the thawed rice, egg, and flour and mix to blend. 3. Stir in the carrots, bell pepper, basil, and Parmesan cheese. 4. Form the mixture into 8 fritters and drizzle with the olive oil. 5. Put the fritters carefully into the air fryer basket. Air fry for 8 to 10 minutes, or until the fritters are golden brown and cooked through. 6. Serve immediately.

Baked Halloumi with Greek Salsa

Prep time: 15 minutes | Cook time: 6 minutes | Serves 4

Salsa:
1 small shallot, finely diced
3 garlic cloves, minced
2 tablespoons fresh lemon juice
2 tablespoons extra-virgin olive oil
1 teaspoon freshly cracked black pepper
Pinch of kosher salt
½ cup finely diced English cucumber
1 plum tomato, deseeded and finely diced
2 teaspoons chopped fresh parsley
1 teaspoon snipped fresh dill
1 teaspoon snipped fresh oregano
Cheese:
8 ounces (227 g) Halloumi cheese, sliced into ½-inch-thick pieces
1 tablespoon extra-virgin olive oil

1. Preheat the air fryer to 375°F (191°C). 2. For the salsa: Combine the shallot, garlic, lemon juice, olive oil, pepper, and salt in a medium bowl. Add the cucumber, tomato, parsley, dill, and oregano. Toss gently to combine; set aside. 3. For the cheese: Place the cheese slices in a medium bowl. Drizzle with the olive oil. Toss gently to coat. Arrange the cheese in a single layer in the air fryer basket. Bake for 6 minutes. 4. Divide the cheese among four serving plates. Top with the salsa and serve immediately.

Baked Chorizo Scotch Eggs

Prep time: 5 minutes | Cook time: 15 to 20 minutes | Makes 4 eggs

1 pound (454 g) Mexican chorizo or other seasoned sausage meat
4 soft-boiled eggs plus 1 raw egg
1 tablespoon water
½ cup all-purpose flour
1 cup panko bread crumbs
Cooking spray

1. Divide the chorizo into 4 equal portions. Flatten each portion into a disc. Place a soft-boiled egg in the center of each disc. Wrap the chorizo around the egg, encasing it completely. Place the encased eggs on a plate and chill for at least 30 minutes. 2. Preheat the air fryer to 360°F (182°C). 3. Beat the raw egg with 1 tablespoon of water. Place the flour on a small plate and the panko on a second plate. Working with 1 egg at a time, roll the encased egg in the flour, then dip it in the egg mixture. Dredge the egg in the panko and place on a plate. Repeat with the remaining eggs. 4. Spray the eggs with oil and place in the air fryer basket. Bake for 10 minutes. Turn and bake for an additional 5 to 10 minutes, or until browned and crisp on all sides. 5. Serve immediately.

Bacon Pinwheels

Prep time: 10 minutes | Cook time: 10 minutes | Makes 8 pinwheels

1 sheet puff pastry
2 tablespoons maple syrup
¼ cup brown sugar
8 slices bacon
Ground black pepper, to taste
Cooking spray

1. Preheat the air fryer to 360°F (182°C). Spritz the air fryer basket with cooking spray. 2. Roll the puff pastry into a 10-inch square with a rolling pin on a clean work surface, then cut the pastry into 8 strips. 3. Brush the strips with maple syrup and sprinkle with sugar, leaving a 1-inch far end uncovered. 4. Arrange each slice of bacon on each strip, leaving a ⅛-inch length of bacon hang over the end close to you. Sprinkle with black pepper. 5. From the end close to you, roll the strips into pinwheels, then dab the uncovered end with water and seal the rolls. 6. Arrange the pinwheels in the preheated air fryer and spritz with cooking spray. 7. Air fry for 10 minutes or until golden brown. Flip the pinwheels halfway through. 8. Serve immediately.

South Carolina Shrimp and Corn Bake

Prep time: 10 minutes | Cook time: 18 minutes | Serves 2

1 ear corn, husk and silk removed, cut into 2-inch rounds
8 ounces (227 g) red potatoes, unpeeled, cut into 1-inch pieces
2 teaspoons Old Bay Seasoning, divided
2 teaspoons vegetable oil, divided
¼ teaspoon ground black pepper
8 ounces (227 g) large shrimps (about 12 shrimps), deveined
6 ounces (170 g) andouille or chorizo sausage, cut into 1-inch pieces
2 garlic cloves, minced
1 tablespoon chopped fresh parsley

1. Preheat the air fryer to 400°F (204°C). 2. Put the corn rounds and potatoes in a large bowl. Sprinkle with 1 teaspoon of Old Bay seasoning and drizzle with vegetable oil. Toss to coat well. 3. Transfer the corn rounds and potatoes on a baking sheet, then put in the preheated air fryer. 4. Bake for 12 minutes or until soft and browned. Shake the basket halfway through the cooking time. 5. Meanwhile, cut slits into the shrimps but be careful not to cut them through. Combine the shrimps, sausage, remaining Old Bay seasoning, and remaining vegetable oil in the large bowl. Toss to coat well. 6. When the baking of the potatoes and corn rounds is complete, add the shrimps and sausage and bake for 6 more minutes or until the shrimps are opaque. Shake the basket halfway through the cooking time. 7. When the baking is finished, serve them on a plate and spread with parsley before serving.

Cheesy Potato Patties

Prep time: 5 minutes | Cook time: 10 minutes |
Serves 8

2 pounds (907 g) white potatoes	½ teaspoon hot paprika
½ cup finely chopped scallions	2 cups shredded Colby cheese
½ teaspoon freshly ground	¼ cup canola oil
black pepper, or more to taste	1 cup crushed crackers
1 tablespoon fine sea salt	

1. Preheat the air fryer to 360ºF (182ºC). 2. Boil the potatoes until soft. Dry them off and peel them before mashing thoroughly, leaving no lumps. 3. Combine the mashed potatoes with scallions, pepper, salt, paprika, and cheese. 4. Mold the mixture into balls with your hands and press with your palm to flatten them into patties. 5. In a shallow dish, combine the canola oil and crushed crackers. Coat the patties in the crumb mixture. 6. Bake the patties for about 10 minutes, in multiple batches if necessary. 7. Serve hot.

Easy Air Fried Edamame

Prep time: 5 minutes | Cook time: 7 minutes | Serves 6

1½ pounds (680 g) unshelled	2 tablespoons olive oil
edamame	1 teaspoon sea salt

1. Preheat the air fryer to 400ºF (204ºC). 2. Place the edamame in a large bowl, then drizzle with olive oil. Toss to coat well. 3. Transfer the edamame to the preheated air fryer. Cook for 7 minutes or until tender and warmed through. Shake the basket at least three times during the cooking. 4. Transfer the cooked edamame onto a plate and sprinkle with salt. Toss to combine well and set aside for 3 minutes to infuse before serving.

Beery and Crunchy Onion Rings

Prep time: 10 minutes | Cook time: 16 minutes |
Serves 2 to 4

⅔ cup all-purpose flour	¾ cup beer
1 teaspoon paprika	1½ cups breadcrumbs
½ teaspoon baking soda	1 tablespoons olive oil
1 teaspoon salt	1 large Vidalia onion, peeled
½ teaspoon freshly ground	and sliced into ½-inch rings
black pepper	Cooking spray
1 egg, beaten	

1. Preheat the air fryer to 360ºF (182ºC). Spritz the air fryer basket with cooking spray. 2. Combine the flour, paprika, baking soda, salt, and ground black pepper in a bowl. Stir to mix well. 3. Combine the egg and beer in a separate bowl. Stir to mix well. 4. Make a well in the center of the flour mixture, then pour the egg mixture in the well. Stir to mix everything well. 5. Pour the breadcrumbs and olive oil in a shallow plate. Stir to mix well. 6. Dredge the onion rings gently into the flour and egg mixture, then shake the excess off and put into the plate of breadcrumbs. Flip to coat the both sides well. 7. Arrange the onion rings in the preheated air fryer. Air fry in batches for 16 minutes or until golden brown and crunchy. Flip the rings and put the bottom rings to the top halfway through. 8. Serve immediately.

Easy Roasted Asparagus

Prep time: 5 minutes | Cook time: 6 minutes | Serves 4

1 pound (454 g) asparagus,	Salt and pepper, to taste
trimmed and halved crosswise	Lemon wedges, for serving
1 teaspoon extra-virgin olive oil	

1. Preheat the air fryer to 400ºF (204ºC). 2. Toss the asparagus with the oil, ⅛ teaspoon salt, and ⅛ teaspoon pepper in bowl. Transfer to air fryer basket. 3. Place the basket in air fryer and roast for 6 to 8 minutes, or until tender and bright green, tossing halfway through cooking. 4. Season with salt and pepper and serve with lemon wedges.

Southwest Corn and Bell Pepper Roast

Prep time: 10 minutes | Cook time: 10 minutes |
Serves 4

For the Corn:	1 teaspoon ground cumin
1½ cups thawed frozen corn	½ teaspoon kosher salt
kernels	Cooking spray
1 cup mixed diced bell peppers	For Serving:
1 jalapeño, diced	¼ cup feta cheese
1 cup diced yellow onion	¼ cup chopped fresh cilantro
½ teaspoon ancho chile powder	1 tablespoon fresh lemon juice
1 tablespoon fresh lemon juice	

1. Preheat the air fryer to 375ºF (191ºC). Spritz the air fryer with cooking spray. 2. Combine the ingredients for the corn in a large bowl. Stir to mix well. 3. Pout the mixture into the air fryer. Air fry for 10 minutes or until the corn and bell peppers are soft. Shake the basket halfway through the cooking time. 4. Transfer them onto a large plate, then spread with feta cheese and cilantro. Drizzle with lemon juice and serve.

Cheesy Jalapeño Cornbread

Prep time: 10 minutes | Cook time: 20 minutes |
Serves 8

⅔ cup cornmeal
⅓ cup all-purpose flour
¾ teaspoon baking powder
2 tablespoons buttery spread, melted
½ teaspoon kosher salt
1 tablespoon granulated sugar

¾ cup whole milk
1 large egg, beaten
1 jalapeño pepper, thinly sliced
⅓ cup shredded sharp Cheddar cheese
Cooking spray

1. Preheat the air fryer to 300ºF (149ºC). Spritz the air fryer basket with cooking spray. 2. Combine all the ingredients in a large bowl. Stir to mix well. Pour the mixture in a baking pan. 3. Arrange the pan in the preheated air fryer. Bake for 20 minutes or until a toothpick inserted in the center of the bread comes out clean. 4. When the cooking is complete, remove the baking pan from the air fryer and allow the bread to cool for a few minutes before slicing to serve.

Air Fried Tortilla Chips

Prep time: 5 minutes | Cook time: 10 minutes |
Serves 4

4 six-inch corn tortillas, cut in half and slice into thirds
1 tablespoon canola oil

¼ teaspoon kosher salt
Cooking spray

1. Preheat the air fryer to 360ºF (182ºC). Spritz the air fryer basket with cooking spray. 2. On a clean work surface, brush the tortilla chips with canola oil, then transfer the chips in the preheated air fryer. 3. Air fry for 10 minutes or until crunchy and lightly browned. Shake the basket and sprinkle with salt halfway through the cooking time. 4. Transfer the chips onto a plate lined with paper towels. Serve immediately.

Air Fried Butternut Squash with Chopped Hazelnuts

Prep time: 10 minutes | Cook time: 20 minutes |
Makes 3 cups

2 tablespoons whole hazelnuts
3 cups butternut squash, peeled, deseeded, and cubed
¼ teaspoon kosher salt

¼ teaspoon freshly ground black pepper
2 teaspoons olive oil
Cooking spray

1. Preheat the air fryer to 300ºF (149ºC). Spritz the air fryer basket with cooking spray. 2. Arrange the hazelnuts in the preheated air fryer. Air fry for 3 minutes or until soft. 3. Chopped the hazelnuts roughly and transfer to a small bowl. Set aside. 4. Set the air fryer temperature to 360ºF (182ºC). Spritz with cooking spray. 5. Put the butternut squash in a large bowl, then sprinkle with salt and pepper and drizzle with olive oil. Toss to coat well. 6. Transfer the squash in the air fryer. Air fry for 20 minutes or until the squash is soft. Shake the basket halfway through the frying time. 7. When the frying is complete, transfer the squash onto a plate and sprinkle with chopped hazelnuts before serving.

Air Fried Shishito Peppers

Prep time: 5 minutes | Cook time: 5 minutes | Serves 4

½ pound (227 g) shishito peppers (about 24)
1 tablespoon olive oil

Coarse sea salt, to taste
Lemon wedges, for serving
Cooking spray

1. Preheat the air fryer to 400ºF (204ºC). Spritz the air fryer basket with cooking spray. 2. Toss the peppers with olive oil in a large bowl to coat well. 3. Arrange the peppers in the preheated air fryer. 4. Air fryer for 5 minutes or until blistered and lightly charred. Shake the basket and sprinkle the peppers with salt halfway through the cooking time. 5. Transfer the peppers onto a plate and squeeze the lemon wedges on top before serving.

Purple Potato Chips with Rosemary

Prep time: 10 minutes | Cook time: 9 to 14 minutes |
Serves 6

1 cup Greek yogurt
2 chipotle chiles, minced
2 tablespoons adobo sauce
1 teaspoon paprika
1 tablespoon lemon juice
10 purple fingerling potatoes

1 teaspoon olive oil
2 teaspoons minced fresh rosemary leaves
⅛ teaspoon cayenne pepper
¼ teaspoon coarse sea salt

1. Preheat the air fryer to 400ºF (204ºC). 2. In a medium bowl, combine the yogurt, minced chiles, adobo sauce, paprika, and lemon juice. Mix well and refrigerate. 3. Wash the potatoes and dry them with paper towels. Slice the potatoes lengthwise, as thinly as possible. You can use a mandoline, a vegetable peeler, or a very sharp knife. 4. Combine the potato slices in a medium bowl and drizzle with the olive oil; toss to coat. 5. Air fry the chips, in batches, in the air fryer basket, for 9 to 14 minutes. Use tongs to gently rearrange the chips halfway during cooking time. 6. Sprinkle the chips with the rosemary, cayenne pepper, and sea salt. Serve with the chipotle sauce for dipping.

Easy Cinnamon Toast

Prep time: 5 minutes | Cook time: 20 minutes | Serves 6

1½ teaspoons cinnamon
1½ teaspoons vanilla extract
½ cup sugar

2 teaspoons ground black pepper
2 tablespoons melted coconut oil
12 slices whole wheat bread

1. Preheat the air fryer to 400°F (204°C). 2. Combine all the ingredients, except for the bread, in a large bowl. Stir to mix well. 3. Dunk the bread in the bowl of mixture gently to coat and infuse well. Shake the excess off. 4. Arrange the bread slices in the preheated air fryer. Air fry for 5 minutes or until golden brown. Flip the bread halfway through. You may need to cook in batches to avoid overcrowding. 5. Remove the bread slices from the air fryer and slice to serve.

Chapter 4 Poultry

Crunchy Chicken Tenders

Prep time: 5 minutes | Cook time: 12 minutes |
Serves 4

1 egg	½ teaspoon black pepper
¼ cup unsweetened almond milk	½ teaspoon dried thyme
¼ cup whole wheat flour	½ teaspoon dried sage
¼ cup whole wheat bread crumbs	½ teaspoon garlic powder
½ teaspoon salt	1 pound (454 g) chicken tenderloins
	1 lemon, quartered

1. Preheat the air fryer to 360°F(182°C). 2. In a shallow bowl, beat together the egg and almond milk until frothy. 3. In a separate shallow bowl, whisk together the flour, bread crumbs, salt, pepper, thyme, sage, and garlic powder. 4. Dip each chicken tenderloin into the egg mixture, then into the bread crumb mixture, coating the outside with the crumbs. Place the breaded chicken tenderloins into the bottom of the air fryer basket in an even layer, making sure that they don't touch each other. 5. Cook for 6 minutes, then turn and cook for an additional 5 to 6 minutes. Serve with lemon slices.

Chicken and Broccoli Casserole

Prep time: 5 minutes | Cook time: 20 to 25 minutes |
Serves 4

½ pound (227 g) broccoli, chopped into florets	½ teaspoon garlic powder
2 cups shredded cooked chicken	Salt and freshly ground black pepper, to taste
4 ounces (113 g) cream cheese	2 tablespoons chopped fresh basil
⅓ cup heavy cream	1 cup shredded Cheddar cheese
1½ teaspoons Dijon mustard	

1. Preheat the air fryer to 390°F (199°C). Lightly coat a casserole dish that will fit in air fryer, with olive oil and set aside. 2. Place the broccoli in a large glass bowl with 1 tablespoon of water and cover with a microwavable plate. Microwave on high for 2 to 3 minutes until the broccoli is bright green but not mushy. Drain if necessary and add to another large bowl along with the shredded chicken. 3. In the same glass bowl used to microwave the broccoli, combine the cream cheese and cream. Microwave for 30 seconds to 1 minute on high and stir until smooth. Add the mustard and garlic powder and season to taste with salt and freshly ground black pepper. Whisk until the sauce is smooth. 4. Pour the warm sauce over the broccoli and chicken mixture and then add the basil. Using a silicone spatula, gently fold the mixture until thoroughly combined. 5. Transfer the chicken mixture to the prepared casserole dish and top with the cheese. Air fry for 20 to 25 minutes until warmed through and the cheese has browned.

Teriyaki Chicken Thighs with Lemony Snow Peas

Prep time: 30 minutes | Cook time: 34 minutes |
Serves 4

¼ cup chicken broth	1 tablespoon sugar
½ teaspoon grated fresh ginger	6 ounces (170 g) snow peas, strings removed
⅛ teaspoon red pepper flakes	⅛ teaspoon lemon zest
1½ tablespoons soy sauce	1 garlic clove, minced
4 (5-ounce / 142-g) bone-in chicken thighs, trimmed	¼ teaspoon salt
1 tablespoon mirin	Ground black pepper, to taste
½ teaspoon cornstarch	½ teaspoon lemon juice

1. Combine the broth, ginger, pepper flakes, and soy sauce in a large bowl. Stir to mix well. 2. Pierce 10 to 15 holes into the chicken skin. Put the chicken in the broth mixture and toss to coat well. Let sit for 10 minutes to marinate. 3. Preheat the air fryer to 400°F (205°C). 4. Transfer the marinated chicken on a plate and pat dry with paper towels. 5. Scoop 2 tablespoons of marinade in a microwave-safe bowl and combine with mirin, cornstarch and sugar. Stir to mix well. Microwave for 1 minute or until frothy and has a thick consistency. Set aside. 6. Arrange the chicken in the preheated air fryer, skin side up, and air fry for 25 minutes or until the internal temperature of the chicken reaches at least 165°F (74°C). Gently turn the chicken over halfway through. 7. When the frying is complete, brush the chicken skin with marinade mixture. Air fryer the chicken for 5 more minutes or until glazed. 8. Remove the chicken from the air fryer and reserve ½ teaspoon of chicken fat remains in the air fryer. Allow the chicken to cool for 10 minutes. 9. Meanwhile, combine the reserved chicken fat, snow peas, lemon zest, garlic, salt, and ground black pepper in a small bowl. Toss to coat well. 10. Transfer the snow peas in the air fryer and air fry for 3 minutes or until soft. Remove the peas from the air fryer and toss with lemon juice. 11. Serve the chicken with lemony snow peas.

Tandoori Chicken

Prep time: 30 minutes | Cook time: 15 minutes |

Serves 4

1 pound (454 g) chicken tenders, halved crosswise	1 teaspoon ground turmeric
¼ cup plain Greek yogurt	1 teaspoon garam masala
1 tablespoon minced fresh ginger	1 teaspoon sweet smoked paprika
1 tablespoon minced garlic	1 tablespoon vegetable oil or melted ghee
¼ cup chopped fresh cilantro or parsley	2 teaspoons fresh lemon juice
1 teaspoon kosher salt	2 tablespoons chopped fresh cilantro
½ to 1 teaspoon cayenne pepper	

1. In a large glass bowl, toss together the chicken, yogurt, ginger, garlic, cilantro, salt, cayenne, turmeric, garam masala, and paprika to coat. Marinate at room temperature for 30 minutes, or cover and refrigerate for up to 24 hours. 2. Place the chicken in a single layer in the air fryer basket. (Discard remaining marinade.) Spray the chicken with oil. Set the air fryer to 350ºF (177ºC) for 15 minutes. Halfway through the cooking time, spray the chicken with more vegetable oil spray, and toss gently to coat. Cook for 5 minutes more. 3. Transfer the chicken to a serving platter. Sprinkle with lemon juice and toss to coat. Sprinkle with the cilantro and serve.

African Piri-Piri Chicken Drumsticks

Prep time: 30 minutes | Cook time: 20 minutes |

Serves 2

Chicken:	1 teaspoon smoked paprika
1 tablespoon chopped fresh thyme leaves	½ teaspoon kosher salt
1 tablespoon minced fresh ginger	½ teaspoon black pepper
	4 chicken drumsticks
1 small shallot, finely chopped	Glaze:
2 garlic cloves, minced	2 tablespoons butter or ghee
⅓ cup piri-piri sauce or hot sauce	1 teaspoon chopped fresh thyme leaves
3 tablespoons extra-virgin olive oil	1 garlic clove, minced
Zest and juice of 1 lemon	1 tablespoon piri-piri sauce
	1 tablespoon fresh lemon juice

1. For the chicken: In a small bowl, stir together all the ingredients except the chicken. Place the chicken and the marinade in a gallon-size resealable plastic bag. Seal the bag and massage to coat. Refrigerate for at least 2 hours or up to 24 hours, turning the bag occasionally. 2. Place the chicken legs in the air fryer basket. Set the air fryer to 400ºF (204ºC) for 20 minutes, turning the chicken halfway through the cooking time. 3. Meanwhile, for the glaze:

Melt the butter in a small saucepan over medium-high heat. Add the thyme and garlic. Cook, stirring, until the garlic just begins to brown, 1 to 2 minutes. Add the piri-piri sauce and lemon juice. Reduce the heat to medium-low and simmer for 1 to 2 minutes. 4. Transfer the chicken to a serving platter. Pour the glaze over the chicken. Serve immediately.

Cajun-Breaded Chicken Bites

Prep time: 10 minutes | Cook time: 12 minutes |

Serves 4

1 pound (454 g) boneless, skinless chicken breasts, cut into 1-inch cubes	pepper
	1 ounce (28 g) plain pork rinds, finely crushed
½ cup heavy whipping cream	¼ cup unflavored whey protein powder
½ teaspoon salt	
¼ teaspoon ground black	½ teaspoon Cajun seasoning

1. Place chicken in a medium bowl and pour in cream. Stir to coat. Sprinkle with salt and pepper. 2. In a separate large bowl, combine pork rinds, protein powder, and Cajun seasoning. Remove chicken from cream, shaking off any excess, and toss in dry mix until fully coated. 3. Place bites into ungreased air fryer basket. Adjust the temperature to 400ºF (204ºC) and air fry for 12 minutes, shaking the basket twice during cooking. Bites will be done when golden brown and have an internal temperature of at least 165ºF (74ºC). Serve warm.

Celery Chicken

Prep time: 10 minutes | Cook time: 15 minutes |

Serves 4

½ cup soy sauce	8 boneless, skinless chicken tenderloins
2 tablespoons hoisin sauce	
4 teaspoons minced garlic	1 cup chopped celery
1 teaspoon freshly ground black pepper	1 medium red bell pepper, diced
	Olive oil spray

1. Preheat the air fryer to 375ºF (191ºC). Spray the air fryer basket lightly with olive oil spray. 2. In a large bowl, mix together the soy sauce, hoisin sauce, garlic, and black pepper to make a marinade. Add the chicken, celery, and bell pepper and toss to coat. 3. Shake the excess marinade off the chicken, place it and the vegetables in the air fryer basket, and lightly spray with olive oil spray. You may need to cook them in batches. Reserve the remaining marinade. 4. Air fry for 8 minutes. Turn the chicken over and brush with some of the remaining marinade. Air fry for an additional 5 to 7 minutes, or until the chicken reaches an internal temperature of at least 165ºF (74ºC). Serve.

South Indian Pepper Chicken

Prep time: 30 minutes | Cook time: 15 minutes | Serves 4

Spice Mix:
1 dried red chile, or ½ teaspoon dried red pepper flakes
1-inch piece cinnamon or cassia bark
1½ teaspoons coriander seeds
1 teaspoon fennel seeds
1 teaspoon cumin seeds
1 teaspoon black peppercorns
½ teaspoon cardamom seeds
¼ teaspoon ground turmeric

1 teaspoon kosher salt
Chicken:
1 pound (454 g) boneless, skinless chicken thighs, cut crosswise into thirds
2 medium onions, cut into ½-inch-thick slices
¼ cup olive oil
Cauliflower rice, steamed rice, or naan bread, for serving

1. For the spice mix: Combine the dried chile, cinnamon, coriander, fennel, cumin, peppercorns, and cardamom in a clean coffee or spice grinder. Grind, shaking the grinder lightly so all the seeds and bits get into the blades, until the mixture is broken down to a fine powder. Stir in the turmeric and salt. 2. For the chicken: Place the chicken and onions in resealable plastic bag. Add the oil and 1½ tablespoons of the spice mix. Seal the bag and massage until the chicken is well coated. Marinate at room temperature for 30 minutes or in the refrigerator for up to 24 hours. 3. Place the chicken and onions in the air fryer basket. Set the air fryer to 350ºF (177ºC) for 10 minutes, stirring once halfway through the cooking time. Increase the temperature to 400ºF (204ºC) for 5 minutes. Use a meat thermometer to ensure the chicken has reached an internal temperature of 165ºF (74ºC). 4. Serve with steamed rice, cauliflower rice, or naan.

Spinach and Feta Stuffed Chicken Breasts

Prep time: 10 minutes | Cook time: 27 minutes | Serves 4

1 (10-ounce / 283-g) package frozen spinach, thawed and drained well
1 cup feta cheese, crumbled
½ teaspoon freshly ground

black pepper
4 boneless chicken breasts
Salt and freshly ground black pepper, to taste
1 tablespoon olive oil

1. Prepare the filling. Squeeze out as much liquid as possible from the thawed spinach. Rough chop the spinach and transfer it to a mixing bowl with the feta cheese and the freshly ground black pepper. 2. Prepare the chicken breast. Place the chicken breast on a cutting board and press down on the chicken breast with one hand to keep it stabilized. Make an incision about 1-inch long in the fattest side of the breast. Move the knife up and down inside the chicken breast, without poking through either the top or the bottom, or the other side of the breast. The inside pocket should be about 3-inches long, but the opening should only be about 1-inch wide. If this is too difficult, you can make the incision longer, but you will have to be more careful when cooking the chicken breast since this will expose more of the stuffing. 3. Once you have prepared the chicken breasts, use your fingers to stuff the filling into each pocket, spreading the mixture down as far as you can. 4. Preheat the air fryer to 380ºF (193ºC). 5. Lightly brush or spray the air fryer basket and the chicken breasts with olive oil. Transfer two of the stuffed chicken breasts to the air fryer. Air fry for 12 minutes, turning the chicken breasts over halfway through the cooking time. Remove the chicken to a resting plate and air fry the second two breasts for 12 minutes. Return the first batch of chicken to the air fryer with the second batch and air fry for 3 more minutes. When the chicken is cooked, an instant read thermometer should register 165ºF (74ºC) in the thickest part of the chicken, as well as in the stuffing. 6. Remove the chicken breasts and let them rest on a cutting board for 2 to 3 minutes. Slice the chicken on the bias and serve with the slices fanned out.

Herbed Roast Chicken Breast

Prep time: 10 minutes | Cook time: 25 minutes | Serves 2 to 4

2 tablespoons salted butter or ghee, at room temperature
1 teaspoon dried Italian seasoning, crushed
½ teaspoon kosher salt
½ teaspoon smoked paprika

¼ teaspoon black pepper
2 bone-in, skin-on chicken breast halves (about 10 ounces / 283 g each)
Lemon wedges, for serving

1. In a small bowl, stir together the butter, Italian seasoning, salt, paprika, and pepper until thoroughly combined. 2. Using a small sharp knife, carefully loosen the skin on each chicken breast half, starting at the thin end of each. Very carefully separate the skin from the flesh, leaving the skin attached at the thick end of each breast. Divide the herb butter into quarters. Rub one-quarter of the butter onto the flesh of each breast. Fold and lightly press the skin back onto each breast. Rub the remaining butter onto the skin of each breast. 3. Place the chicken in the air fryer basket. Set the air fryer to 375ºF (191ºC) for 25 minutes. Use a meat thermometer to ensure the chicken breasts have reached an internal temperature of 165ºF (74ºC). 4. Transfer the chicken to a cutting board. Lightly cover with aluminum foil and let rest for 5 to 10 minutes. 5. Serve with lemon wedges.

Ginger Turmeric Chicken Thighs

Prep time: 5 minutes | Cook time: 25 minutes |
Serves 4

4 (4-ounce / 113-g) boneless, skin-on chicken thighs	½ teaspoon salt
2 tablespoons coconut oil, melted	½ teaspoon garlic powder
½ teaspoon ground turmeric	½ teaspoon ground ginger
	¼ teaspoon ground black pepper

1. Place chicken thighs in a large bowl and drizzle with coconut oil. Sprinkle with remaining ingredients and toss to coat both sides of thighs. 2. Place thighs skin side up into ungreased air fryer basket. Adjust the temperature to 400°F (204°C) and air fry for 25 minutes. After 10 minutes, turn thighs. When 5 minutes remain, flip thighs once more. Chicken will be done when skin is golden brown and the internal temperature is at least 165°F (74°C). Serve warm.

Chicken and Gruyère Cordon Bleu

Prep time: 15 minutes | Cook time: 15 minutes |
Serves 4

4 chicken breast filets	Freshly ground black pepper, to taste
¼ cup chopped ham	
⅓ cup grated Swiss cheese, or Gruyère cheese	½ teaspoon dried marjoram
¼ cup all-purpose flour	1 egg
Pinch salt	1 cup panko bread crumbs
	Olive oil spray

1. Put the chicken breast filets on a work surface and gently press them with the palm of your hand to make them a bit thinner. Don't tear the meat. 2. In a small bowl, combine the ham and cheese. Divide this mixture among the chicken filets. Wrap the chicken around the filling to enclose it, using toothpicks to hold the chicken together. 3. In a shallow bowl, stir together the flour, salt, pepper, and marjoram. 4. In another bowl, beat the egg. 5. Spread the panko on a plate. 6. Dip the chicken in the flour mixture, in the egg, and in the panko to coat thoroughly. Press the crumbs into the chicken so they stick well. 7. Insert the crisper plate into the basket and the basket into the unit. Preheat the unit by selecting BAKE, setting the temperature to 375°F (191°C), and setting the time to 3 minutes. Select START/STOP to begin. 8. Once the unit is preheated, spray the crisper plate with olive oil. Place the chicken into the basket and spray it with olive oil. 9. Select BAKE, set the temperature to 375°F (191°C), and set the time to 15 minutes. Select START/STOP to begin. 10. When the cooking is complete, the chicken should be cooked through and a food thermometer inserted into the chicken should register 165°F (74°C). Carefully remove the toothpicks and serve.

Crisp Paprika Chicken Drumsticks

Prep time: 5 minutes | Cook time: 22 minutes |
Serves 2

2 teaspoons paprika	4 (5-ounce / 142-g) chicken drumsticks, trimmed
1 teaspoon packed brown sugar	
1 teaspoon garlic powder	1 teaspoon vegetable oil
½ teaspoon dry mustard	1 scallion, green part only, sliced thin on bias
½ teaspoon salt	
Pinch pepper	

1. Preheat the air fryer to 400°F (204°C). 2. Combine paprika, sugar, garlic powder, mustard, salt, and pepper in a bowl. Pat drumsticks dry with paper towels. Using metal skewer, poke 10 to 15 holes in skin of each drumstick. Rub with oil and sprinkle evenly with spice mixture. 3. Arrange drumsticks in air fryer basket, spaced evenly apart, alternating ends. Air fry until chicken is crisp and registers 195°F (91°C), 22 to 25 minutes, flipping chicken halfway through cooking. 4. Transfer chicken to serving platter, tent loosely with aluminum foil, and let rest for 5 minutes. Sprinkle with scallion and serve.

Chicken Hand Pies

Prep time: 30 minutes | Cook time: 10 minutes per
batch | Makes 8 pies

¾ cup chicken broth	1 tablespoon milk
¾ cup frozen mixed peas and carrots	Salt and pepper, to taste
	1 (8-count) can organic flaky biscuits
1 cup cooked chicken, chopped	
1 tablespoon cornstarch	Oil for misting or cooking spray

1. In a medium saucepan, bring chicken broth to a boil. Stir in the frozen peas and carrots and cook for 5 minutes over medium heat. Stir in chicken. 2. Mix the cornstarch into the milk until it dissolves. Stir it into the simmering chicken broth mixture and cook just until thickened. 3. Remove from heat, add salt and pepper to taste, and let cool slightly. 4. Lay biscuits out on wax paper. Peel each biscuit apart in the middle to make 2 rounds so you have 16 rounds total. Using your hands or a rolling pin, flatten each biscuit round slightly to make it larger and thinner. 5. Divide chicken filling among 8 of the biscuit rounds. Place remaining biscuit rounds on top and press edges all around. Use the tines of a fork to crimp biscuit edges and make sure they are sealed well. 6. Spray both sides lightly with oil or cooking spray. 7. Cook in a single layer, 4 at a time, at 330°F (166°C) for 10 minutes or until biscuit dough is cooked through and golden brown.

Sriracha-Honey Chicken Nuggets

Prep time: 15 minutes | Cook time: 19 minutes |
Serves 6

Oil, for spraying	½ teaspoon freshly ground
1 large egg	black pepper
¾ cup milk	2 boneless, skinless chicken
1 cup all-purpose flour	breasts, cut into bite-size pieces
2 tablespoons confectioners'	½ cup barbecue sauce
sugar	2 tablespoons honey
½ teaspoon paprika	1 tablespoon Sriracha
½ teaspoon salt	

1. Line the air fryer basket with parchment and spray lightly with oil. 2. In a small bowl, whisk together the egg and milk. 3. In a medium bowl, combine the flour, confectioners' sugar, paprika, salt, and black pepper and stir. 4. Coat the chicken in the egg mixture, then dredge in the flour mixture until evenly coated. 5. Place the chicken in the prepared basket and spray liberally with oil. 6. Air fry at 390°F (199°C) for 8 minutes, flip, spray with more oil, and cook for another 6 to 8 minutes, or until the internal temperature reaches 165°F (74°C) and the juices run clear. 7. In a large bowl, mix together the barbecue sauce, honey, and Sriracha. 8. Transfer the chicken to the bowl and toss until well coated with the barbecue sauce mixture. 9. Line the air fryer basket with fresh parchment, return the chicken to the basket, and cook for another 2 to 3 minutes, until browned and crispy.

Buttermilk Breaded Chicken

Prep time: 7 minutes | Cook time: 20 to 25 minutes |
Serves 4

1 cup all-purpose flour	2 tablespoons extra-virgin olive
2 teaspoons paprika	oil
Pinch salt	1½ cups bread crumbs
Freshly ground black pepper, to	6 chicken pieces, drumsticks,
taste	breasts, and thighs, patted dry
⅓ cup buttermilk	Cooking oil spray
2 eggs	

1. In a shallow bowl, stir together the flour, paprika, salt, and pepper. 2. In another bowl, beat the buttermilk and eggs until smooth. 3. In a third bowl, stir together the olive oil and bread crumbs until mixed. 4. Dredge the chicken in the flour, dip in the eggs to coat, and finally press into the bread crumbs, patting the crumbs firmly onto the chicken skin. 5. Insert the crisper plate into the basket and the basket into the unit. Preheat the unit by selecting AIR FRY, setting the temperature to 375°F (191°C), and setting the time to 3 minutes. Select START/STOP to begin. 6. Once the unit is preheated, spray the crisper plate with cooking oil. Place the

chicken into the basket. 7. Select AIR FRY, set the temperature to 375°F (191°C), and set the time to 25 minutes. Select START/STOP to begin. 8. After 10 minutes, flip the chicken. Resume cooking. After 10 minutes more, check the chicken. If a food thermometer inserted into the chicken registers 165°F (74°C) and the chicken is brown and crisp, it is done. Otherwise, resume cooking for up to 5 minutes longer. 9. When the cooking is complete, let cool for 5 minutes, then serve.

Barbecue Chicken Bites

Prep time: 5 minutes | Cook time: 19 minutes |
Serves 4

Oil, for spraying	½ cup all-purpose flour
2 (6-ounce / 170-g) boneless,	1 tablespoon granulated garlic
skinless chicken breasts, cut	2 teaspoons seasoned salt
into bite-size pieces	1 cup barbecue sauce

1. Line the air fryer basket with parchment and spray lightly with oil. 2. Place the chicken, flour, garlic, and seasoned salt in a zip-top plastic bag, seal, and shake well until evenly coated. 3. Place the chicken in an even layer in the prepared basket and spray liberally with oil. You may need to work in batches, depending on the size of your air fryer. 4. Roast at 390°F (199°C) for 8 minutes, flip, spray with more oil, and cook for another 8 minutes, or until the internal temperature reaches 165°F (74°C) and the juices run clear. 5. Transfer the chicken to a large bowl and toss with the barbecue sauce. 6. Line the air fryer basket with fresh parchment, return the chicken to the basket, and cook for another 3 minutes.

Jalapeño Popper Hasselback Chicken

Prep time: 10 minutes | Cook time: 19 minutes |
Serves 2

Oil, for spraying	¼ cup bacon bits
2 (8-ounce / 227-g) boneless,	¼ cup chopped pickled
skinless chicken breasts	jalapeños
2 ounces (57 g) cream cheese,	½ cup shredded Cheddar
softened	cheese, divided

1. Line the air fryer basket with parchment and spray lightly with oil. 2. Make multiple cuts across the top of each chicken breast, cutting only halfway through. 3. In a medium bowl, mix together the cream cheese, bacon bits, jalapeños, and ¼ cup of Cheddar cheese. Spoon some of the mixture into each cut. 4. Place the chicken in the prepared basket. 5. Air fry at 350°F (177°C) for 14 minutes. Scatter the remaining ¼ cup of cheese on top of the chicken and cook for another 2 to 5 minutes, or until the cheese is melted and the internal temperature reaches 165°F (74°C).

Chicken Croquettes with Creole Sauce

Prep time: 30 minutes | Cook time: 10 minutes |

Serves 4

2 cups shredded cooked chicken	Creole Sauce:
½ cup shredded Cheddar cheese	¼ cup mayonnaise
2 eggs	¼ cup sour cream
¼ cup finely chopped onion	1½ teaspoons Dijon mustard
¼ cup almond meal	1½ teaspoons fresh lemon juice
1 tablespoon poultry seasoning	½ teaspoon garlic powder
Olive oil	½ teaspoon Creole seasoning

1. In a large bowl, combine the chicken, Cheddar, eggs, onion, almond meal, and poultry seasoning. Stir gently until thoroughly combined. Cover and refrigerate for 30 minutes. 2. Meanwhile, to make the Creole sauce: In a small bowl, whisk together the mayonnaise, sour cream, Dijon mustard, lemon juice, garlic powder, and Creole seasoning until thoroughly combined. Cover and refrigerate until ready to serve. 3. Preheat the air fryer to 400ºF (204ºC). Divide the chicken mixture into 8 portions and shape into patties. 4. Working in batches if necessary, arrange the patties in a single layer in the air fryer basket and coat both sides lightly with olive oil. Pausing halfway through the cooking time to flip the patties, air fry for 10 minutes, or until lightly browned and the cheese is melted. Serve with the Creole sauce.

Simply Terrific Turkey Meatballs

Prep time: 10 minutes | Cook time: 7 to 10 minutes |

Serves 4

1 red bell pepper, seeded and coarsely chopped	ground turkey
2 cloves garlic, coarsely chopped	1 egg, lightly beaten
	½ cup grated Parmesan cheese
¼ cup chopped fresh parsley	1 teaspoon salt
1½ pounds (680 g) 85% lean	½ teaspoon freshly ground black pepper

1. Preheat the air fryer to 400ºF (204ºC). 2. In a food processor fitted with a metal blade, combine the bell pepper, garlic, and parsley. Pulse until finely chopped. Transfer the vegetables to a large mixing bowl. 3. Add the turkey, egg, Parmesan, salt, and black pepper. Mix gently until thoroughly combined. Shape the mixture into 1¼-inch meatballs. 4. Working in batches if necessary, arrange the meatballs in a single layer in the air fryer basket; coat lightly with olive oil spray. Pausing halfway through the cooking time to shake the basket, air fry for 7 to 10 minutes, until lightly browned and a thermometer inserted into the center of a meatball registers 165ºF (74ºC).

Ranch Chicken Wings

Prep time: 10 minutes | Cook time: 40 minutes |

Serves 4

2 tablespoons water	1 (1-ounce / 28-g) envelope
2 tablespoons hot pepper sauce	ranch salad dressing mix
2 tablespoons unsalted butter, melted	1 teaspoon paprika
2 tablespoons apple cider vinegar	4 pounds (1.8 kg) chicken wings, tips removed
	Cooking oil spray

1. In a large bowl, whisk the water, hot pepper sauce, melted butter, vinegar, salad dressing mix, and paprika until combined. 2. Add the wings and toss to coat. At this point, you can cover the bowl and marinate the wings in the refrigerator for 4 to 24 hours for best results. However, you can just let the wings stand for 30 minutes in the refrigerator. 3. Insert the crisper plate into the basket and the basket into the unit. Preheat the unit by selecting AIR FRY, setting the temperature to 400ºF (204ºC), and setting the time to 3 minutes. Select START/STOP to begin. 4. Once the unit is preheated, spray the crisper plate with cooking oil. Working in batches, put half the wings into the basket; it is okay to stack them. Refrigerate the remaining wings. 5. Select AIR FRY, set the temperature to 400ºF (204ºC), and set the time to 20 minutes. Select START/STOP to begin. 6. After 5 minutes, remove the basket and shake it. Reinsert the basket to resume cooking. Remove and shake the basket every 5 minutes, three more times, until the chicken is browned and glazed and a food thermometer inserted into the wings registers 165ºF (74ºC). 7. Repeat steps 4, 5, and 6 with the remaining wings. 8. When the cooking is complete, serve warm.

Chipotle Aioli Wings

Prep time: 5 minutes | Cook time: 25 minutes |

Serves 6

2 pounds (907 g) bone-in chicken wings	pepper
	2 tablespoons mayonnaise
½ teaspoon salt	2 teaspoons chipotle powder
¼ teaspoon ground black	2 tablespoons lemon juice

1. In a large bowl, toss wings in salt and pepper, then place into ungreased air fryer basket. Adjust the temperature to 400ºF (204ºC) and air fry for 25 minutes, shaking the basket twice while cooking. Wings will be done when golden and have an internal temperature of at least 165ºF (74ºC). 2. In a small bowl, whisk together mayonnaise, chipotle powder, and lemon juice. Place cooked wings into a large serving bowl and drizzle with aioli. Toss to coat. Serve warm.

Chicken Schnitzel Dogs

Prep time: 15 minutes | Cook time: 8 to 10 minutes | Serves 4

½ cup flour	4 chicken tenders, pounded thin
½ teaspoon salt	Oil for misting or cooking spray
1 teaspoon marjoram	4 whole-grain hotdog buns
1 teaspoon dried parsley flakes	4 slices Gouda cheese
½ teaspoon thyme	1 small Granny Smith apple,
1 egg	thinly sliced
1 teaspoon lemon juice	½ cup shredded Napa cabbage
1 teaspoon water	Coleslaw dressing
1 cup bread crumbs	

1. In a shallow dish, mix together the flour, salt, marjoram, parsley, and thyme. 2. In another shallow dish, beat together egg, lemon juice, and water. 3. Place bread crumbs in a third shallow dish. 4. Cut each of the flattened chicken tenders in half lengthwise. 5. Dip flattened chicken strips in flour mixture, then egg wash. Let excess egg drip off and roll in bread crumbs. Spray both sides with oil or cooking spray. 6. Air fry at 390°F (199°C) for 5 minutes. Spray with oil, turn over, and spray other side. 7. Cook for 3 to 5 minutes more, until well done and crispy brown. 8. To serve, place 2 schnitzel strips on bottom of each hotdog bun. Top with cheese, sliced apple, and cabbage. Drizzle with coleslaw dressing and top with other half of bun.

Korean Honey Wings

Prep time: 10 minutes | Cook time: 25 minutes per batch | Serves 4

¼ cup gochujang, or red pepper paste	2 teaspoons ground ginger
¼ cup mayonnaise	3 pounds (1.4 kg) whole chicken wings
2 tablespoons honey	Olive oil spray
1 tablespoon sesame oil	1 teaspoon salt
2 teaspoons minced garlic	½ teaspoon freshly ground black pepper
1 tablespoon sugar	

1. In a large bowl, whisk the gochujang, mayonnaise, honey, sesame oil, garlic, sugar, and ginger. Set aside. 2. Insert the crisper plate into the basket and the basket into the unit. Preheat the unit by selecting AIR FRY, setting the temperature to 400°F (204°C), and setting the time to 3 minutes. Select START/STOP to begin. 3. To prepare the chicken wings, cut the wings in half. The meatier part is the drumette. Cut off and discard the wing tip from the flat part (or save the wing tips in the freezer to make chicken stock). 4. Once the unit is preheated, spray the crisper plate with olive oil. Working in batches, place half the chicken wings into the basket, spray

them with olive oil, and sprinkle with the salt and pepper. 5. Select AIR FRY, set the temperature to 400°F (204°C), and set the time to 20 minutes. Select START/STOP to begin. 6. After 10 minutes, remove the basket, flip the wings, and spray them with more olive oil. Reinsert the basket to resume cooking. 7. Cook the wings to an internal temperature of 165°F (74°C), then transfer them to the bowl with the prepared sauce and toss to coat. 8. Repeat steps 4, 5, 6, and 7 for the remaining chicken wings. 9. Return the coated wings to the basket and air fry for 4 to 6 minutes more until the sauce has glazed the wings and the chicken is crisp. After 3 minutes, check the wings to make sure they aren't burning. Serve hot.

Spice-Rubbed Turkey Breast

Prep time: 5 minutes | Cook time: 45 to 55 minutes | Serves 10

1 tablespoon sea salt	black pepper
1 teaspoon paprika	4 pounds (1.8 kg) bone-in, skin-
1 teaspoon onion powder	on turkey breast
1 teaspoon garlic powder	2 tablespoons unsalted butter,
½ teaspoon freshly ground	melted

1. In a small bowl, combine the salt, paprika, onion powder, garlic powder, and pepper. 2. Sprinkle the seasonings all over the turkey. Brush the turkey with some of the melted butter. 3. Set the air fryer to 350°F (177°C). Place the turkey in the air fryer basket, skin-side down, and roast for 25 minutes. 4. Flip the turkey and brush it with the remaining butter. Continue cooking for another 20 to 30 minutes, until an instant-read thermometer reads 160°F (71°C). 5. Remove the turkey breast from the air fryer. Tent a piece of aluminum foil over the turkey, and allow it to rest for about 5 minutes before serving.

Cheesy Pepperoni and Chicken Pizza

Prep time: 15 minutes | Cook time: 15 minutes | Serves 6

2 cups cooked chicken, cubed	1 cup shredded Mozzarella
1 cup pizza sauce	cheese
20 slices pepperoni	Cooking spray
¼ cup grated Parmesan cheese	

1. Preheat the air fryer to 375°F (191°C). Spritz a baking pan with cooking spray. 2. Arrange the chicken cubes in the prepared baking pan, then top the cubes with pizza sauce and pepperoni. Stir to coat the cubes and pepperoni with sauce. 3. Scatter the cheeses on top, then place the baking pan in the preheated air fryer. Air fryer for 15 minutes or until frothy and the cheeses melt. 4. Serve immediately.

Turkey Meatloaf

Prep time: 10 minutes | Cook time: 50 minutes | Serves 4

8 ounces (227 g) sliced mushrooms
1 small onion, coarsely chopped
2 cloves garlic
1½ pounds (680 g) 85% lean ground turkey
2 eggs, lightly beaten
1 tablespoon tomato paste
¼ cup almond meal
2 tablespoons almond milk
1 tablespoon dried oregano
1 teaspoon salt
½ teaspoon freshly ground black pepper
1 Roma tomato, thinly sliced

1. Preheat the air fryer to 350ºF (177ºC). Lightly coat a round pan with olive oil and set aside. 2. In a food processor fitted with a metal blade, combine the mushrooms, onion, and garlic. Pulse until finely chopped. Transfer the vegetables to a large mixing bowl. 3. Add the turkey, eggs, tomato paste, almond meal, milk, oregano, salt, and black pepper. Mix gently until thoroughly combined. Transfer the mixture to the prepared pan and shape into a loaf. Arrange the tomato slices on top. 4. Air fry for 50 minutes or until the meatloaf is nicely browned and a thermometer inserted into the thickest part registers 165ºF (74ºC). Remove from the air fryer and let rest for about 10 minutes before slicing.

Bacon Lovers' Stuffed Chicken

Prep time: 10 minutes | Cook time: 20 minutes | Serves 4

4 (5-ounce / 142-g) boneless, skinless chicken breasts, pounded to ¼ inch thick
2 (5.2-ounce / 147-g) packages Boursin cheese (or Kite Hill brand chive cream cheese style
spread, softened, for dairy-free)
8 slices thin-cut bacon or beef bacon
Sprig of fresh cilantro, for garnish (optional)

1. Spray the air fryer basket with avocado oil. Preheat the air fryer to 400ºF (204ºC). 2. Place one of the chicken breasts on a cutting board. With a sharp knife held parallel to the cutting board, make a 1-inch-wide incision at the top of the breast. Carefully cut into the breast to form a large pocket, leaving a ½-inch border along the sides and bottom. Repeat with the other 3 chicken breasts. 3. Snip the corner of a large resealable plastic bag to form a ¾-inch hole. Place the Boursin cheese in the bag and pipe the cheese into the pockets in the chicken breasts, dividing the cheese evenly among them. 4. Wrap 2 slices of bacon around each chicken breast and secure the ends with toothpicks. Place the bacon-wrapped chicken in the air fryer basket and air fry until the bacon is crisp and the chicken's internal temperature reaches 165ºF (74ºC), about 18 to 20

minutes, flipping after 10 minutes. Garnish with a sprig of cilantro before serving, if desired. 5. Store leftovers in an airtight container in the refrigerator for up to 4 days. Reheat in a preheated 400ºF (204ºC) air fryer for 5 minutes, or until warmed through.

Tex-Mex Chicken Roll-Ups

Prep time: 10 minutes | Cook time: 14 to 17 minutes | Serves 8

2 pounds (907 g) boneless, skinless chicken breasts or thighs
1 teaspoon chili powder
½ teaspoon smoked paprika
½ teaspoon ground cumin
Sea salt and freshly ground
black pepper, to taste
6 ounces (170 g) Monterey Jack cheese, shredded
4 ounces (113 g) canned diced green chiles
Avocado oil spray

1. Place the chicken in a large zip-top bag or between two pieces of plastic wrap. Using a meat mallet or heavy skillet, pound the chicken until it is about ¼ inch thick. 2. In a small bowl, combine the chili powder, smoked paprika, cumin, and salt and pepper to taste. Sprinkle both sides of the chicken with the seasonings. 3. Sprinkle the chicken with the Monterey Jack cheese, then the diced green chiles. 4. Roll up each piece of chicken from the long side, tucking in the ends as you go. Secure the roll-up with a toothpick. 5. Set the air fryer to 350ºF (177ºC). Spray the outside of the chicken with avocado oil. Place the chicken in a single layer in the basket, working in batches if necessary, and roast for 7 minutes. Flip and cook for another 7 to 10 minutes, until an instant-read thermometer reads 160ºF (71ºC). 6. Remove the chicken from the air fryer and allow it to rest for about 5 minutes before serving.

Cilantro Lime Chicken Thighs

Prep time: 15 minutes | Cook time: 22 minutes | Serves 4

4 bone-in, skin-on chicken thighs
1 teaspoon baking powder
½ teaspoon garlic powder
2 teaspoons chili powder
1 teaspoon cumin
2 medium limes
¼ cup chopped fresh cilantro

1. Pat chicken thighs dry and sprinkle with baking powder. 2. In a small bowl, mix garlic powder, chili powder, and cumin and sprinkle evenly over thighs, gently rubbing on and under chicken skin. 3. Cut one lime in half and squeeze juice over thighs. Place chicken into the air fryer basket. 4. Adjust the temperature to 380ºF (193ºC) and roast for 22 minutes. 5. Cut other lime into four wedges for serving and garnish cooked chicken with wedges and cilantro.

Nacho Chicken Fries

Prep time: 20 minutes | Cook time: 6 to 7 minutes per batch | Serves 4 to 6

1 pound (454 g) chicken tenders
Salt, to taste
¼ cup flour
2 eggs
¾ cup panko bread crumbs
¾ cup crushed organic nacho cheese tortilla chips

Oil for misting or cooking spray
Seasoning Mix:
1 tablespoon chili powder
1 teaspoon ground cumin
½ teaspoon garlic powder
½ teaspoon onion powder

1. Stir together all seasonings in a small cup and set aside. 2. Cut chicken tenders in half crosswise, then cut into strips no wider than about ½ inch. 3. Preheat the air fryer to 390ºF (199ºC). 4. Salt chicken to taste. Place strips in large bowl and sprinkle with 1 tablespoon of the seasoning mix. Stir well to distribute seasonings. 5. Add flour to chicken and stir well to coat all sides. 6. Beat eggs together in a shallow dish. 7. In a second shallow dish, combine the panko, crushed chips, and the remaining 2 teaspoons of seasoning mix. 8. Dip chicken strips in eggs, then roll in crumbs. Mist with oil or cooking spray. 9. Chicken strips will cook best if done in two batches. They can be crowded and overlapping a little but not stacked in double or triple layers. 10. Cook for 4 minutes. Shake basket, mist with oil, and cook 2 to 3 more minutes, until chicken juices run clear and outside is crispy. 11. Repeat step 10 to cook remaining chicken fries.

Classic Chicken Kebab

Prep time: 35 minutes | Cook time: 25 minutes | Serves 4

¼ cup olive oil
1 teaspoon garlic powder
1 teaspoon onion powder
1 teaspoon ground cumin
½ teaspoon dried oregano
½ teaspoon dried basil
¼ cup lemon juice
1 tablespoon apple cider vinegar
Olive oil cooking spray

1 pound (454 g) boneless skinless chicken thighs, cut into 1-inch pieces
1 red bell pepper, cut into 1-inch pieces
1 red onion, cut into 1-inch pieces
1 zucchini, cut into 1-inch pieces
12 cherry tomatoes

1. In a large bowl, mix together the olive oil, garlic powder, onion powder, cumin, oregano, basil, lemon juice, and apple cider vinegar. 2. Spray six skewers with olive oil cooking spray. 3. On each skewer, slide on a piece of chicken, then a piece of bell pepper, onion, zucchini, and finally a tomato and then repeat. Each skewer should have at least two pieces of each item. 4. Once all of the skewers are prepared, place them in a 9-by-13-inch baking dish and pour the olive oil marinade over the top of the skewers. Turn each skewer so that all sides of the chicken and vegetables are coated. 5. Cover the dish with plastic wrap and place it in the refrigerator for 30 minutes. 6. After 30 minutes, preheat the air fryer to 380ºF(193ºC). (If using a grill attachment, make sure it is inside the air fryer during preheating.) 7. Remove the skewers from the marinade and lay them in a single layer in the air fryer basket. If the air fryer has a grill attachment, you can also lay them on this instead. 8. Cook for 10 minutes. Rotate the kebabs, then cook them for 15 minutes more. 9. Remove the skewers from the air fryer and let them rest for 5 minutes before serving.

Chicken Rochambeau

Prep time: 15 minutes | Cook time: 20 minutes | Serves 4

1 tablespoon butter
4 chicken tenders, cut in half crosswise
Salt and pepper, to taste
¼ cup flour
Oil for misting
4 slices ham, ¼- to ⅜-inches thick and large enough to cover an English muffin
2 English muffins, split

Sauce:
2 tablespoons butter
½ cup chopped green onions
½ cup chopped mushrooms
2 tablespoons flour
1 cup chicken broth
¼ teaspoon garlic powder
1½ teaspoons Worcestershire sauce

1. Place 1 tablespoon of butter in a baking pan and air fry at 390ºF (199ºC) for 2 minutes to melt. 2. Sprinkle chicken tenders with salt and pepper to taste, then roll in the ¼ cup of flour. 3. Place chicken in baking pan, turning pieces to coat with melted butter. 4. Air fry at 390ºF (199ºC) for 5 minutes. Turn chicken pieces over, and spray tops lightly with olive oil. Cook 5 minutes longer or until juices run clear. The chicken will not brown. 5. While chicken is cooking, make the sauce: In a medium saucepan, melt the 2 tablespoons of butter. 6. Add onions and mushrooms and sauté until tender, about 3 minutes. 7. Stir in the flour. Gradually add broth, stirring constantly until you have a smooth gravy. 8. Add garlic powder and Worcestershire sauce and simmer on low heat until sauce thickens, about 5 minutes. 9. When chicken is cooked, remove baking pan from air fryer and set aside. 10. Place ham slices directly into air fryer basket and air fry at 390ºF (199ºC) for 5 minutes or until hot and beginning to sizzle a little. Remove and set aside on top of the chicken for now. 11. Place the English muffin halves in air fryer basket and air fry at 390ºF (199ºC) for 1 minute. 12. Open air fryer and place a ham slice on top of each English muffin half. Stack 2 pieces of chicken on top of each ham slice. Air fry for 1 to 2 minutes to heat through. 13. Place each English muffin stack on a serving plate and top with plenty of sauce.

Chicken Drumsticks with Barbecue-Honey Sauce

Prep time: 5 minutes | Cook time: 40 minutes |

Serves 5

1 tablespoon olive oil	Salt and ground black pepper,
10 chicken drumsticks	to taste
Chicken seasoning or rub, to	1 cup barbecue sauce
taste	¼ cup honey

1. Preheat the air fryer to 390°F (199°C). Grease the air fryer basket with olive oil. 2. Rub the chicken drumsticks with chicken seasoning or rub, salt and ground black pepper on a clean work surface. 3. Arrange the chicken drumsticks in a single layer in the air fryer, then air fry for 18 minutes or until lightly browned. Flip the drumsticks halfway through. You may need to work in batches to avoid overcrowding. 4. Meanwhile, combine the barbecue sauce and honey in a small bowl. Stir to mix well. 5. Remove the drumsticks from the air fryer and baste with the sauce mixture to serve.

Herb-Buttermilk Chicken Breast

Prep time: 5 minutes | Cook time: 40 minutes |

Serves 2

1 large bone-in, skin-on chicken	½ teaspoon dried dill
breast	½ teaspoon onion powder
1 cup buttermilk	¼ teaspoon garlic powder
1½ teaspoons dried parsley	¼ teaspoon dried tarragon
1½ teaspoons dried chives	Cooking spray
¾ teaspoon kosher salt	

1. Place the chicken breast in a bowl and pour over the buttermilk, turning the chicken in it to make sure it's completely covered. Let the chicken stand at room temperature for at least 20 minutes or in the refrigerator for up to 4 hours. 2. Meanwhile, in a bowl, stir together the parsley, chives, salt, dill, onion powder, garlic powder, and tarragon. 3. Preheat the air fryer to 300°F (149°C). 4. Remove the chicken from the buttermilk, letting the excess drip off, then place the chicken skin-side up directly in the air fryer. Sprinkle the seasoning mix all over the top of the chicken breast, then let stand until the herb mix soaks into the buttermilk, at least 5 minutes. 5. Spray the top of the chicken with cooking spray. Bake for 10 minutes, then increase the temperature to 350°F (177°C) and bake until an instant-read thermometer inserted into the thickest part of the breast reads 160°F (71°C) and the chicken is deep golden brown, 30 to 35 minutes. 6. Transfer the chicken breast to a cutting board, let rest for 10 minutes, then cut the meat off the bone and cut into thick slices for serving.

Butter and Bacon Chicken

Prep time: 10 minutes | Cook time: 65 minutes |

Serves 6

1 (4-pound / 1.8-kg) whole	½ teaspoon garlic powder
chicken	1 teaspoon salt
2 tablespoons salted butter,	½ teaspoon ground black
softened	pepper
1 teaspoon dried thyme	6 slices sugar-free bacon

1. Pat chicken dry with a paper towel, then rub with butter on all sides. Sprinkle thyme, garlic powder, salt, and pepper over chicken. 2. Place chicken into ungreased air fryer basket, breast side up. Lay strips of bacon over chicken and secure with toothpicks. 3. Adjust the temperature to 350°F (177°C) and air fry for 65 minutes. Halfway through cooking, remove and set aside bacon and flip chicken over. Chicken will be done when the skin is golden and crispy and the internal temperature is at least 165°F (74°C). Serve warm with bacon.

Hawaiian Huli Huli Chicken

Prep time: 30 minutes | Cook time: 15 minutes |

Serves 4

4 boneless, skinless chicken	¼ cup sugar
thighs (about 1½ pounds / 680	2 tablespoons ketchup
g)	1 tablespoon minced fresh
1 (8-ounce / 227-g) can	ginger
pineapple chunks in juice,	1 tablespoon minced garlic
drained, ¼ cup juice reserved	¼ cup chopped scallions
¼ cup soy sauce	

1. Use a fork to pierce the chicken all over to allow the marinade to penetrate better. Place the chicken in a large bowl or large resealable plastic bag. 2. Set the drained pineapple chunks aside. In a small microwave-safe bowl, combine the pineapple juice, soy sauce, sugar, ketchup, ginger, and garlic. Pour half the sauce over the chicken; toss to coat. Reserve the remaining sauce. Marinate the chicken at room temperature for 30 minutes, or cover and refrigerate for up to 24 hours. 3. Place the chicken in the air fryer basket. (Discard marinade.) Set the air fryer to 350°F (177°C) for 15 minutes, turning halfway through the cooking time. 4. Meanwhile, microwave the reserved sauce on high for 45 to 60 seconds, stirring every 15 seconds, until the sauce has the consistency of a thick glaze. 5. At the end of the cooking time, use a meat thermometer to ensure the chicken has reached an internal temperature of 165°F (74°C). 6. Transfer the chicken to a serving platter. Pour the sauce over the chicken. Garnish with the pineapple chunks and scallions.

Piri-Piri Chicken Thighs

Prep time: 5 minutes | Cook time: 25 minutes |
Serves 4

¼ cup piri-piri sauce	oil
1 tablespoon freshly squeezed lemon juice	4 bone-in, skin-on chicken thighs, each weighing
2 tablespoons brown sugar, divided	approximately 7 to 8 ounces (198 to 227 g)
2 cloves garlic, minced	½ teaspoon cornstarch
1 tablespoon extra-virgin olive	

1. To make the marinade, whisk together the piri-piri sauce, lemon juice, 1 tablespoon of brown sugar, and the garlic in a small bowl. While whisking, slowly pour in the oil in a steady stream and continue to whisk until emulsified. Using a skewer, poke holes in the chicken thighs and place them in a small glass dish. Pour the marinade over the chicken and turn the thighs to coat them with the sauce. Cover the dish and refrigerate for at least 15 minutes and up to 1 hour. 2. Preheat the air fryer to 375°F (191°C). Remove the chicken thighs from the dish, reserving the marinade, and place them skin-side down in the air fryer basket. Air fry until the internal temperature reaches 165°F (74°C), 15 to 20 minutes. 3. Meanwhile, whisk the remaining brown sugar and the cornstarch into the marinade and microwave it on high power for 1 minute until it is bubbling and thickened to a glaze. 4. Once the chicken is cooked, turn the thighs over and brush them with the glaze. Air fry for a few additional minutes until the glaze browns and begins to char in spots. 5. Remove the chicken to a platter and serve with additional piri-piri sauce, if desired.

Fajita-Stuffed Chicken Breast

Prep time: 15 minutes | Cook time: 25 minutes |
Serves 4

2 (6-ounce / 170-g) boneless, skinless chicken breasts	seeded and sliced
¼ medium white onion, peeled and sliced	1 tablespoon coconut oil
1 medium green bell pepper,	2 teaspoons chili powder
	1 teaspoon ground cumin
	½ teaspoon garlic powder

1. Slice each chicken breast completely in half lengthwise into two even pieces. Using a meat tenderizer, pound out the chicken until it's about ¼-inch thickness. 2. Lay each slice of chicken out and place three slices of onion and four slices of green pepper on the end closest to you. Begin rolling the peppers and onions tightly into the chicken. Secure the roll with either toothpicks or a couple pieces of butcher's twine. 3. Drizzle coconut oil over chicken. Sprinkle each side with chili powder, cumin, and garlic powder.

Place each roll into the air fryer basket. 4. Adjust the temperature to 350°F (177°C) and air fry for 25 minutes. 5. Serve warm.

Lemon Thyme Roasted Chicken

Prep time: 10 minutes | Cook time: 60 minutes |
Serves 6

1 (4-pound / 1.8-kg) chicken	1 teaspoon baking powder
2 teaspoons dried thyme	1 medium lemon
1 teaspoon garlic powder	2 tablespoons salted butter,
½ teaspoon onion powder	melted
2 teaspoons dried parsley	

1. Rub chicken with thyme, garlic powder, onion powder, parsley, and baking powder. 2. Slice lemon and place four slices on top of chicken, breast side up, and secure with toothpicks. Place remaining slices inside of the chicken. 3. Place entire chicken into the air fryer basket, breast side down. 4. Adjust the temperature to 350°F (177°C) and air fry for 60 minutes. 5. After 30 minutes, flip chicken so breast side is up. 6. When done, internal temperature should be 165°F (74°C) and the skin golden and crispy. To serve, pour melted butter over entire chicken.

Chicken Enchiladas

Prep time: 10 minutes | Cook time: 8 minutes |
Serves 4

Oil, for spraying	rinsed and drained
3 cups shredded cooked chicken	1 (4-ounce / 113-g) can diced green chiles, drained
1 package taco seasoning	
8 flour tortillas, at room temperature	1 (10-ounce / 283-g) can red or green enchilada sauce
½ cup canned black beans,	1 cup shredded Cheddar cheese

1. Line the air fryer basket with parchment and spray lightly with oil. (Do not skip the step of lining the basket; the parchment will keep the sauce and cheese from dripping through the holes.) 2. In a small bowl, mix together the chicken and taco seasoning. 3. Divide the mixture among the tortillas. Top with the black beans and green chiles. Carefully roll up each tortilla. 4. Place the enchiladas, seam-side down, in the prepared basket. You may need to work in batches, depending on the size of your air fryer. 5. Spoon the enchilada sauce over the enchiladas. Use just enough sauce to keep them from drying out. You can add more sauce when serving. Sprinkle the cheese on top. 6. Air fry at 360°F (182°C) for 5 to 8 minutes, or until heated through and the cheese is melted. 7. Place 2 enchiladas on each plate and top with more enchilada sauce, if desired.

Garlic Soy Chicken Thighs

Prep time: 10 minutes | Cook time: 30 minutes | Serves 1 to 2

2 tablespoons chicken stock

2 tablespoons reduced-sodium soy sauce

1½ tablespoons sugar

4 garlic cloves, smashed and peeled

2 large scallions, cut into 2- to 3-inch batons, plus more, thinly sliced, for garnish

2 bone-in, skin-on chicken thighs (7 to 8 ounces / 198 to 227 g each)

1. Preheat the air fryer to 375°F (191°C). 2. In a metal cake pan, combine the chicken stock, soy sauce, and sugar and stir until the sugar dissolves. Add the garlic cloves, scallions, and chicken thighs, turning the thighs to coat them in the marinade, then resting them skin-side up. Place the pan in the air fryer and bake, flipping the thighs every 5 minutes after the first 10 minutes, until the chicken is cooked through and the marinade is reduced to a sticky glaze over the chicken, about 30 minutes. 3. Remove the pan from the air fryer and serve the chicken thighs warm, with any remaining glaze spooned over top and sprinkled with more sliced scallions.

Honey-Glazed Chicken Thighs

Prep time: 5 minutes | Cook time: 14 minutes | Serves 4

Oil, for spraying

4 boneless, skinless chicken thighs, fat trimmed

3 tablespoons soy sauce

1 tablespoon balsamic vinegar

2 teaspoons honey

2 teaspoons minced garlic

1 teaspoon ground ginger

1. Preheat the air fryer to 400°F (204°C). Line the air fryer basket with parchment and spray lightly with oil. 2. Place the chicken in the prepared basket. 3. Cook for 7 minutes, flip, and cook for another 7 minutes, or until the internal temperature reaches 165°F (74°C) and the juices run clear. 4. In a small saucepan, combine the soy sauce, balsamic vinegar, honey, garlic, and ginger and cook over low heat for 1 to 2 minutes, until warmed through. 5. Transfer the chicken to a serving plate and drizzle with the sauce just before serving.

Stuffed Turkey Roulade

Prep time: 10 minutes | Cook time: 45 minutes | Serves 4

1 (2-pound / 907-g) boneless turkey breast, skin removed

1 teaspoon salt

½ teaspoon black pepper

4 ounces (113 g) goat cheese

1 tablespoon fresh thyme

1 tablespoon fresh sage

2 garlic cloves, minced

2 tablespoons olive oil

Fresh chopped parsley, for garnish

1. Preheat the air fryer to 380°F(193°C). 2. Using a sharp knife, butterfly the turkey breast, and season both sides with salt and pepper and set aside. 3. In a small bowl, mix together the goat cheese, thyme, sage, and garlic. 4. Spread the cheese mixture over the turkey breast, then roll it up tightly, tucking the ends underneath. 5. Place the turkey breast roulade onto a piece of aluminum foil, wrap it up, and place it into the air fryer. 6. Bake for 30 minutes. Remove the foil from the turkey breast and brush the top with oil, then continue cooking for another 10 to 15 minutes, or until the outside has browned and the internal temperature reaches 165°F(74°C). 7. Remove and cut into 1-inch-wide slices and serve with a sprinkle of parsley on top.

Chapter 5 Beef, Pork, and Lamb

Sausage-Stuffed Peppers

Prep time: 15 minutes | Cook time: 28 to 30 minutes | Serves 6

Avocado oil spray
8 ounces (227 g) Italian sausage, casings removed
½ cup chopped mushrooms
¼ cup diced onion
1 teaspoon Italian seasoning
Sea salt and freshly ground

black pepper, to taste
1 cup keto-friendly marinara sauce
3 bell peppers, halved and seeded
3 ounces (85 g) provolone cheese, shredded

1. Spray a large skillet with oil and place it over medium-high heat. Add the sausage and cook for 5 minutes, breaking up the meat with a wooden spoon. Add the mushrooms, onion, and Italian seasoning, and season with salt and pepper. Cook for 5 minutes more. Stir in the marinara sauce and cook until heated through. 2. Scoop the sausage filling into the bell pepper halves. 3. Set the air fryer to 350ºF (177ºC). Arrange the peppers in a single layer in the air fryer basket, working in batches if necessary. Air fry for 15 minutes. 4. Top the stuffed peppers with the cheese and air fry for 3 to 5 minutes more, until the cheese is melted and the peppers are tender.

Bacon-Wrapped Pork Tenderloin

Prep time: 30 minutes | Cook time: 22 to 25 minutes | Serves 6

½ cup minced onion
½ cup hard apple cider, or apple juice
¼ cup honey
1 tablespoon minced garlic
¼ teaspoon salt

¼ teaspoon freshly ground black pepper
2 pounds (907 g) pork tenderloin
1 to 2 tablespoons oil
8 uncooked bacon slices

1. In a medium bowl, stir together the onion, hard cider, honey, garlic, salt, and pepper. Transfer to a large resealable bag or airtight container and add the pork. Seal the bag. Refrigerate to marinate for at least 2 hours. 2. Preheat the air fryer to 400ºF (204ºC). Line the air fryer basket with parchment paper. 3. Remove the pork from the marinade and place it on the parchment. Spritz with oil. 4. Cook for 15 minutes. 5. Wrap the bacon slices around the pork and secure

them with toothpicks. Turn the pork roast and spritz with oil. Cook for 7 to 10 minutes more until the internal temperature reaches 145ºF (63ºC), depending on how well-done you like pork loin. It will continue cooking after it's removed from the fryer, so let it sit for 5 minutes before serving.

Swedish Meatballs

Prep time: 25 minutes | Cook time: 20 minutes | Serves 4

Meatballs:
¾ cup fresh bread crumbs
¼ cup heavy cream
¼ cup finely chopped onion
½ teaspoon dried parsley flakes
½ teaspoon kosher salt
¼ teaspoon ground allspice
¼ teaspoon freshly grated nutmeg
¼ teaspoon white pepper
½ pound (227 g) 85% lean ground beef
½ pound (227 g) ground pork
1 large egg, beaten

1 egg white, lightly beaten
Gravy:
2 tablespoons salted butter
2 tablespoons all-purpose flour
1½ cups low-sodium beef broth
1 teaspoon Worcestershire sauce
¼ cup heavy cream
Kosher salt and black pepper, to taste
For Serving:
Chopped fresh parsley
Lingonberry jam

1. For the meatballs: In a large bowl, mix the bread crumbs and cream until well combined; let stand for 5 minutes. Add the onion, parsley flakes, salt, allspice, nutmeg, and white pepper. Stir to make a thick paste. Add the ground beef, ground pork, egg, and egg white. Mix until evenly combined. 2. Form into 1-inch meatballs. Place in a single layer in the air fryer basket. Set the air fryer to 350ºF (177ºC) for 20 minutes, turning halfway through the cooking time. 3. Meanwhile, for the gravy: In a medium saucepan, melt the butter over medium heat. Add the flour and cook, whisking, until smooth. Whisk in the broth and Worcestershire. Bring to a simmer. Add the cream. Reduce the heat to medium-low and simmer until the gravy thickens, about 10 minutes. Season with salt and black pepper. 4. At the end of the cooking time, use a meat thermometer to ensure the meatballs have reached an internal temperature of 160ºF / 71ºC (medium). 5. Transfer the meatballs to a serving bowl. Ladle the gravy over the meatballs and sprinkle with parsley. Serve with lingonberry jam.

Spaghetti Zoodles and Meatballs

Prep time: 30 minutes | Cook time: 11 to 13 minutes | Serves 6

1 pound (454 g) ground beef	Freshly ground black pepper, to
1½ teaspoons sea salt, plus	taste
more for seasoning	Avocado oil spray
1 large egg, beaten	Keto-friendly marinara sauce,
1 teaspoon gelatin	for serving
¾ cup Parmesan cheese	6 ounces (170 g) zucchini
2 teaspoons minced garlic	noodles, made using a spiralizer
1 teaspoon Italian seasoning	or store-bought

1. Place the ground beef in a large bowl, and season with the salt. 2. Place the egg in a separate bowl and sprinkle with the gelatin. Allow to sit for 5 minutes. 3. Stir the gelatin mixture, then pour it over the ground beef. Add the Parmesan, garlic, and Italian seasoning. Season with salt and pepper. 4. Form the mixture into 1½-inch meatballs and place them on a plate; cover with plastic wrap and refrigerate for at least 1 hour or overnight. 5. Spray the meatballs with oil. Set the air fryer to 400ºF (204ºC) and arrange the meatballs in a single layer in the air fryer basket. Air fry for 4 minutes. Flip the meatballs and spray them with more oil. Air fry for 4 minutes more, until an instant-read thermometer reads 160ºF (71ºC). Transfer the meatballs to a plate and allow them to rest. 6. While the meatballs are resting, heat the marinara in a saucepan on the stove over medium heat. 7. Place the zucchini noodles in the air fryer, and cook at 400ºF (204ºC) for 3 to 5 minutes. 8. To serve, place the zucchini noodles in serving bowls. Top with meatballs and warm marinara.

Ham with Sweet Potatoes

Prep time: 20 minutes | Cook time: 15 to 17 minutes | Serves 4

1 cup freshly squeezed orange	black pepper
juice	3 sweet potatoes, cut into small
½ cup packed light brown sugar	wedges
1 tablespoon Dijon mustard	2 ham steaks (8 ounces / 227 g
½ teaspoon salt	each), halved
½ teaspoon freshly ground	1 to 2 tablespoons oil

1. In a large bowl, whisk the orange juice, brown sugar, Dijon, salt, and pepper until blended. Toss the sweet potato wedges with the brown sugar mixture. 2. Preheat the air fryer to 400ºF (204ºC). Line the air fryer basket with parchment paper and spritz with oil. 3. Place the sweet potato wedges on the parchment. 4. Cook for 10 minutes. 5. Place ham steaks on top of the sweet potatoes and brush everything with more of the orange juice mixture. 6. Cook for 3 minutes. Flip the ham and cook or 2 to 4 minutes more until the sweet potatoes are soft and the glaze has thickened. Cut the ham steaks in half to serve.

Indian Mint and Chile Kebabs

Prep time: 30 minutes | Cook time: 15 minutes | Serves 4

1 pound (454 g) ground lamb	½ teaspoon ground turmeric
½ cup finely minced onion	½ teaspoon cayenne pepper
¼ cup chopped fresh mint	¼ teaspoon ground cardamom
¼ cup chopped fresh cilantro	¼ teaspoon ground cinnamon
1 tablespoon minced garlic	1 teaspoon kosher salt

1. In the bowl of a stand mixer fitted with the paddle attachment, combine the lamb, onion, mint, cilantro, garlic, turmeric, cayenne, cardamom, cinnamon, and salt. Mix on low speed until you have a sticky mess of spiced meat. If you have time, let the mixture stand at room temperature for 30 minutes (or cover and refrigerate for up to a day or two, until you're ready to make the kebabs). 2. Divide the meat into eight equal portions. Form each into a long sausage shape. Place the kebabs in a single layer in the air fryer basket. Set the air fryer to 350ºF (177ºC) for 10 minutes. Increase the air fryer temperature to 400ºF (204ºC) and cook for 3 to 4 minutes more to brown the kebabs. Use a meat thermometer to ensure the kebabs have reached an internal temperature of 160ºF / 71ºC (medium).

Cheese Crusted Chops

Prep time: 10 minutes | Cook time: 12 minutes | Serves 4 to 6

¼ teaspoon pepper	1 teaspoon smoked paprika
½ teaspoons salt	2 beaten eggs
4 to 6 thick boneless pork chops	3 tablespoons grated Parmesan
1 cup pork rind crumbs	cheese
¼ teaspoon chili powder	Cooking spray
½ teaspoons onion powder	

1. Preheat the air fryer to 400ºF (205ºC). 2. Rub the pepper and salt on both sides of pork chops. 3. In a food processor, pulse pork rinds into crumbs. Mix crumbs with chili powder, onion powder, and paprika in a bowl. 4. Beat eggs in another bowl. 5. Dip pork chops into eggs then into pork rind crumb mixture. 6. Spritz the air fryer basket with cooking spray and add pork chops to the basket. 7. Air fry for 12 minutes. 8. Serve garnished with the Parmesan cheese.

Sichuan Cumin Lamb

Prep time: 30 minutes | Cook time: 10 minutes |
Serves 4

Lamb:
2 tablespoons cumin seeds
1 teaspoon Sichuan
peppercorns, or ½ teaspoon
cayenne pepper
1 pound (454 g) lamb
(preferably shoulder), cut into
½ by 2-inch pieces
2 tablespoons vegetable oil

1 tablespoon light soy sauce
1 tablespoon minced garlic
2 fresh red chiles, chopped
1 teaspoon kosher salt
¼ teaspoon sugar
For Serving:
2 scallions, chopped
Large handful of chopped fresh
cilantro

1. For the lamb: In a dry skillet, toast the cumin seeds and Sichuan peppercorns (if using) over medium heat, stirring frequently, until fragrant, 1 to 2 minutes. Remove from the heat and let cool. Use a mortar and pestle to coarsely grind the toasted spices. 2. Use a fork to pierce the lamb pieces to allow the marinade to penetrate better. In a large bowl or resealable plastic bag, combine the toasted spices, vegetable oil, soy sauce, garlic, chiles, salt, and sugar. Add the lamb to the bag. Seal and massage to coat. Marinate at room temperature for 30 minutes. 3. Place the lamb in a single layer in the air fryer basket. Set the air fryer to 350°F (177°C) for 10 minutes. Use a meat thermometer to ensure the lamb has reached an internal temperature of 145°F (63°C) (medium-rare). 4. Transfer the lamb to a serving bowl. Stir in the scallions and cilantro and serve.

Chicken Fried Steak with Cream Gravy

Prep time: 5 minutes | Cook time: 10 minutes |
Serves 4

4 small thin cube steaks (about
1 pound / 454 g)
½ teaspoon salt
½ teaspoon freshly ground
black pepper
¼ teaspoon garlic powder
1 egg, lightly beaten
1 cup crushed pork rinds (about
3 ounces / 85 g)

Cream Gravy:
½ cup heavy cream
2 ounces (57 g) cream cheese
¼ cup bacon grease
2 to 3 tablespoons water
2 to 3 dashes Worcestershire
sauce
Salt and freshly ground black
pepper, to taste

1. Preheat the air fryer to 400°F (204°C). 2. Working one at a time, place the steak between two sheets of parchment paper and use a meat mallet to pound to an even thickness. 3. In a small bowl, combine the salt, pepper, and garlic power. Season both sides of each steak with the mixture. 4. Place the egg in a small shallow dish and the pork rinds in another small shallow dish. Dip each steak first in the egg wash, followed by the pork rinds, pressing lightly to form an even coating. Working in batches if necessary, arrange the steaks in a single layer in the air fryer basket. Air fry for 10 minutes until crispy and cooked through. 5. To make the cream gravy: In a heavy-bottomed pot, warm the cream, cream cheese, and bacon grease over medium heat, whisking until smooth. Lower the heat if the mixture begins to boil. Continue whisking as you slowly add the water, 1 tablespoon at a time, until the sauce reaches the desired consistency. Season with the Worcestershire sauce and salt and pepper to taste. Serve over the chicken fried steaks.

Cheese Pork Chops

Prep time: 15 minutes | Cook time: 9 to 14 minutes |
Serves 4

2 large eggs
½ cup finely grated Parmesan
cheese
½ cup finely ground blanched
almond flour or finely crushed
pork rinds
1 teaspoon paprika

½ teaspoon dried oregano
½ teaspoon garlic powder
Salt and freshly ground black
pepper, to taste
1¼ pounds (567 g) (1-inch-
thick) boneless pork chops
Avocado oil spray

1. Beat the eggs in a shallow bowl. In a separate bowl, combine the Parmesan cheese, almond flour, paprika, oregano, garlic powder, and salt and pepper to taste. 2. Dip the pork chops into the eggs, then coat them with the Parmesan mixture, gently pressing the coating onto the meat. Spray the breaded pork chops with oil. 3. Set the air fryer to 400°F (204°C). Place the pork chops in the air fryer basket in a single layer, working in batches if necessary. Cook for 6 minutes. Flip the chops and spray them with more oil. Cook for another 3 to 8 minutes, until an instant-read thermometer reads 145°F (63°C). 4. Allow the pork chops to rest for at least 5 minutes, then serve.

Beef Flank Steak with Sage

Prep time: 13 minutes | Cook time: 7 minutes |
Serves 2

⅓ cup sour cream
½ cup green onion, chopped
1 tablespoon mayonnaise
3 cloves garlic, smashed
1 pound (454 g) beef flank
steak, trimmed and cubed

2 tablespoons fresh sage,
minced
½ teaspoon salt
⅓ teaspoon black pepper, or to
taste

1. Season your meat with salt and pepper; arrange beef cubes on the bottom of a baking dish that fits in your air fryer. 2. Stir in green onions and garlic; air fry for about 7 minutes at 385°F (196°C). 3. Once your beef starts to tender, add the cream, mayonnaise, and sage; air fry an additional 8 minutes. Bon appétit!

Lemony Pork Loin Chop Schnitzel

Prep time: 15 minutes | Cook time: 15 minutes |
Serves 4

4 thin boneless pork loin chops	1 cup panko breadcrumbs
2 tablespoons lemon juice	2 eggs
½ cup flour	Lemon wedges, for serving
¼ teaspoon marjoram	Cooking spray
1 teaspoon salt	

1. Preheat the air fryer to 390ºF (199ºC) and spritz with cooking spray. 2. On a clean work surface, drizzle the pork chops with lemon juice on both sides. 3. Combine the flour with marjoram and salt on a shallow plate. Pour the breadcrumbs on a separate shallow dish. Beat the eggs in a large bowl. 4. Dredge the pork chops in the flour, then dunk in the beaten eggs to coat well. Shake the excess off and roll over the breadcrumbs. 5. Arrange the chops in the preheated air fryer and spritz with cooking spray. Air fry for 15 minutes or until the chops are golden and crispy. Flip the chops halfway through. Squeeze the lemon wedges over the fried chops and serve immediately.

Lamb and Cucumber Burgers

Prep time: 8 minutes | Cook time: 15 to 18 minutes |
Serves 4

1 teaspoon ground ginger	yogurt
½ teaspoon ground coriander	1 pound (454 g) ground lamb
¼ teaspoon freshly ground white pepper	1 teaspoon garlic paste
½ teaspoon ground cinnamon	¼ teaspoon salt
½ teaspoon dried oregano	¼ teaspoon freshly ground
¼ teaspoon ground allspice	black pepper
¼ teaspoon ground turmeric	Cooking oil spray
½ cup low-fat plain Greek	4 hamburger buns
	½ cucumber, thinly sliced

1. In a small bowl, stir together the ginger, coriander, white pepper, cinnamon, oregano, allspice, and turmeric. 2. Put the yogurt in a small bowl and add half the spice mixture. Mix well and refrigerate. 3. Insert the crisper plate into the basket and the basket into the unit. Preheat the unit by selecting AIR FRY, setting the temperature to 360ºF (182ºC), and setting the time to 3 minutes. Select START/STOP to begin. 4. In a large bowl, combine the lamb, garlic paste, remaining spice mix, salt, and pepper. Gently but thoroughly mix the ingredients with your hands. Form the meat into 4 patties. 5. Once the unit is preheated, spray the crisper plate with cooking oil, and place the patties into the basket. 6. Select AIR FRY, set the temperature to 360ºF (182ºC), and set the time to 18 minutes. Select START/STOP to begin. 7. After 15 minutes, check the burgers. If a food thermometer inserted into the burgers registers 160ºF (71ºC), the burgers are done. If not, resume cooking. 8. When the cooking is complete, assemble the burgers on the buns with cucumber slices and a dollop of the yogurt dip.

Fajita Meatball Lettuce Wraps

Prep time: 10 minutes | Cook time: 10 minutes |
Serves 4

1 pound (454 g) ground beef (85% lean)	1 teaspoon fine sea salt
½ cup salsa, plus more for serving if desired	½ teaspoon chili powder
	½ teaspoon ground cumin
¼ cup chopped onions	1 clove garlic, minced
¼ cup diced green or red bell peppers	For Serving (Optional):
	8 leaves Boston lettuce
1 large egg, beaten	Pico de gallo or salsa
	Lime slices

1. Spray the air fryer basket with avocado oil. Preheat the air fryer to 350ºF (177ºC). 2. In a large bowl, mix together all the ingredients until well combined. 3. Shape the meat mixture into eight 1-inch balls. Place the meatballs in the air fryer basket, leaving a little space between them. Air fry for 10 minutes, or until cooked through and no longer pink inside and the internal temperature reaches 145ºF (63ºC). 4. Serve each meatball on a lettuce leaf, topped with pico de gallo or salsa, if desired. Serve with lime slices if desired. 5. Store leftovers in an airtight container in the fridge for 3 days or in the freezer for up to a month. Reheat in a preheated 350ºF (177ºC) air fryer for 4 minutes, or until heated through.

Beef Burger

Prep time: 20 minutes | Cook time: 12 minutes |
Serves 4

1¼ pounds (567 g) lean ground beef	½ teaspoon cumin powder
	¼ cup scallions, minced
1 tablespoon coconut aminos	⅓ teaspoon sea salt flakes
1 teaspoon Dijon mustard	⅓ teaspoon freshly cracked
A few dashes of liquid smoke	mixed peppercorns
1 teaspoon shallot powder	1 teaspoon celery seeds
1 clove garlic, minced	1 teaspoon parsley flakes

1. Mix all of the above ingredients in a bowl; knead until everything is well incorporated. 2. Shape the mixture into four patties. Next, make a shallow dip in the center of each patty to prevent them puffing up during air frying. 3. Spritz the patties on all sides using nonstick cooking spray. Cook approximately 12 minutes at 360ºF (182ºC). 4. Check for doneness, an instant-read thermometer should read 160ºF (71ºC). Bon appétit!

Spinach and Provolone Steak Rolls

Prep time: 10 minutes | Cook time: 12 minutes |
Makes 8 rolls

1 (1-pound / 454-g) flank steak, butterflied	1 cup fresh spinach leaves
8 (1-ounce / 28-g, ¼-inch-thick) deli slices provolone cheese	½ teaspoon salt
	¼ teaspoon ground black pepper

1. Place steak on a large plate. Place provolone slices to cover steak, leaving 1-inch at the edges. Lay spinach leaves over cheese. Gently roll steak and tie with kitchen twine or secure with toothpicks. Carefully slice into eight pieces. Sprinkle each with salt and pepper. 2. Place rolls into ungreased air fryer basket, cut side up. Adjust the temperature to 400°F (204°C) and air fry for 12 minutes. Steak rolls will be browned and cheese will be melted when done and have an internal temperature of at least 150°F (66°C) for medium steak and 180°F (82°C) for well-done steak. Serve warm.

Herbed Beef

Prep time: 5 minutes | Cook time: 22 minutes |
Serves 6

1 teaspoon dried dill	2 pounds (907 g) beef steak
1 teaspoon dried thyme	3 tablespoons butter
1 teaspoon garlic powder	

1. Preheat the air fryer to 360°F (182°C). 2. Combine the dill, thyme, and garlic powder in a small bowl, and massage into the steak. 3. Air fry the steak in the air fryer for 20 minutes, then remove, shred, and return to the air fryer. 4. Add the butter and air fry the shredded steak for a further 2 minutes at 365°F (185°C). Make sure the beef is coated in the butter before serving.

Chorizo and Beef Burger

Prep time: 10 minutes | Cook time: 15 minutes |
Serves 4

¾ pound (340 g) 80/20 ground beef	5 slices pickled jalapeños, chopped
¼ pound (113 g) Mexican-style ground chorizo	2 teaspoons chili powder
¼ cup chopped onion	1 teaspoon minced garlic
	¼ teaspoon cumin

1. In a large bowl, mix all ingredients. Divide the mixture into four sections and form them into burger patties. 2. Place burger patties into the air fryer basket, working in batches if necessary. 3. Adjust the temperature to 375°F (191°C) and air fry for 15 minutes. 4. Flip the patties halfway through the cooking time. Serve warm.

London Broil with Herb Butter

Prep time: 30 minutes | Cook time: 20 to 25 minutes | Serves 4

1½ pounds (680 g) London broil top round steak	softened
¼ cup olive oil	1 tablespoon chopped fresh parsley
2 tablespoons balsamic vinegar	¼ teaspoon salt
1 tablespoon Worcestershire sauce	¼ teaspoon dried ground rosemary or thyme
4 cloves garlic, minced	¼ teaspoon garlic powder
Herb Butter:	Pinch of red pepper flakes
6 tablespoons unsalted butter,	

1. Place the beef in a gallon-size resealable bag. In a small bowl, whisk together the olive oil, balsamic vinegar, Worcestershire sauce, and garlic. Pour the marinade over the beef, massaging gently to coat, and seal the bag. Let sit at room temperature for an hour or refrigerate overnight. 2. To make the herb butter: In a small bowl, mix the butter with the parsley, salt, rosemary, garlic powder, and red pepper flakes until smooth. Cover and refrigerate until ready to use. 3. Preheat the air fryer to 400°F (204°C). 4. Remove the beef from the marinade (discard the marinade) and place the beef in the air fryer basket. Pausing halfway through the cooking time to turn the meat, air fry for 20 to 25 minutes, until a thermometer inserted into the thickest part indicates the desired doneness, 125°F / 52°C (rare) to 150°F / 66°C (medium). Let the beef rest for 10 minutes before slicing. Serve topped with the herb butter.

Kale and Beef Omelet

Prep time: 15 minutes | Cook time: 16 minutes |
Serves 4

½ pound (227 g) leftover beef, coarsely chopped	4 eggs, beaten
2 garlic cloves, pressed	4 tablespoons heavy cream
1 cup kale, torn into pieces and wilted	½ teaspoon turmeric powder
1 tomato, chopped	Salt and ground black pepper, to taste
¼ teaspoon sugar	⅛ teaspoon ground allspice
	Cooking spray

1. Preheat the air fryer to 360°F (182°C). Spritz four ramekins with cooking spray. 2. Put equal amounts of each of the ingredients into each ramekin and mix well. 3. Air fry for 16 minutes. Serve immediately.

Garlic Balsamic London Broil

Prep time: 30 minutes | Cook time: 8 to 10 minutes |
Serves 8

2 pounds (907 g) London broil	2 tablespoons olive oil
3 large garlic cloves, minced	Sea salt and ground black
3 tablespoons balsamic vinegar	pepper, to taste
3 tablespoons whole-grain	½ teaspoon dried hot red pepper
mustard	flakes

1. Score both sides of the cleaned London broil. 2. Thoroughly combine the remaining ingredients; massage this mixture into the meat to coat it on all sides. Let it marinate for at least 3 hours. 3. Set the air fryer to 400ºF (204ºC); Then cook the London broil for 15 minutes. Flip it over and cook another 10 to 12 minutes. Bon appétit!

Herb-Crusted Lamb Chops

Prep time: 10 minutes | Cook time: 5 minutes |
Serves 2

1 large egg	leaves
2 cloves garlic, minced	½ teaspoon ground black
¼ cup pork dust	pepper
¼ cup powdered Parmesan	4 (1-inch-thick) lamb chops
cheese	For Garnish/Serving (Optional):
1 tablespoon chopped fresh	Sprigs of fresh oregano
oregano leaves	Sprigs of fresh rosemary
1 tablespoon chopped fresh	Sprigs of fresh thyme
rosemary leaves	Lavender flowers
1 teaspoon chopped fresh thyme	Lemon slices

1. Spray the air fryer basket with avocado oil. Preheat the air fryer to 400ºF (204ºC). 2. Beat the egg in a shallow bowl, add the garlic, and stir well to combine. In another shallow bowl, mix together the pork dust, Parmesan, herbs, and pepper. 3. One at a time, dip the lamb chops into the egg mixture, shake off the excess egg, and then dredge them in the Parmesan mixture. Use your hands to coat the chops well in the Parmesan mixture and form a nice crust on all sides; if necessary, dip the chops again in both the egg and the Parmesan mixture. 4. Place the lamb chops in the air fryer basket, leaving space between them, and air fry for 5 minutes, or until the internal temperature reaches 145ºF (63ºC) for medium doneness. Allow to rest for 10 minutes before serving. 5. Garnish with sprigs of oregano, rosemary, and thyme, and lavender flowers, if desired. Serve with lemon slices, if desired. 6. Best served fresh. Store leftovers in an airtight container in the fridge for up to 4 days. Serve chilled over a salad, or reheat in a 350ºF (177ºC) air fryer for 3 minutes, or until heated through.

Short Ribs with Chimichurri

Prep time: 30 minutes | Cook time: 13 minutes |
Serves 4

1 pound (454 g) boneless short	1 tablespoon freshly squeezed
ribs	lemon juice
1½ teaspoons sea salt, divided	½ teaspoon ground cumin
½ teaspoon freshly ground	¼ teaspoon red pepper flakes
black pepper, divided	2 tablespoons extra-virgin olive
½ cup fresh parsley leaves	oil
½ cup fresh cilantro leaves	Avocado oil spray
1 teaspoon minced garlic	

1. Pat the short ribs dry with paper towels. Sprinkle the ribs all over with 1 teaspoon salt and ¼ teaspoon black pepper. Let sit at room temperature for 45 minutes. 2. Meanwhile, place the parsley, cilantro, garlic, lemon juice, cumin, red pepper flakes, the remaining ½ teaspoon salt, and the remaining ¼ teaspoon black pepper in a blender or food processor. With the blender running, slowly drizzle in the olive oil. Blend for about 1 minute, until the mixture is smooth and well combined. 3. Set the air fryer to 400ºF (204ºC). Spray both sides of the ribs with oil. Place in the basket and air fry for 8 minutes. Flip and cook for another 5 minutes, until an instant-read thermometer reads 125ºF (52ºC) for medium-rare (or to your desired doneness). 4. Allow the meat to rest for 5 to 10 minutes, then slice. Serve warm with the chimichurri sauce.

Mushroom in Bacon-Wrapped Filets Mignons

Prep time: 10 minutes | Cook time: 13 minutes per batch | Serves 8

1 ounce (28 g) dried porcini	pepper
mushrooms	8 (4-ounce / 113-g) filets
½ teaspoon granulated white	mignons or beef tenderloin
sugar	steaks
½ teaspoon salt	8 thin-cut bacon strips
½ teaspoon ground white	

1. Preheat the air fryer to 400ºF (204ºC). 2. Put the mushrooms, sugar, salt, and white pepper in a spice grinder and grind to combine. 3. On a clean work surface, rub the filets mignons with the mushroom mixture, then wrap each filet with a bacon strip. Secure with toothpicks if necessary. 4. Arrange the bacon-wrapped filets mignons in the preheated air fryer basket, seam side down. Work in batches to avoid overcrowding. 5. Air fry for 13 minutes or until medium rare. Flip the filets halfway through. 6. Serve immediately.

Steaks with Walnut-Blue Cheese Butter

Prep time: 30 minutes | Cook time: 10 minutes |
Serves 6

½ cup unsalted butter, at room temperature
½ cup crumbled blue cheese
2 tablespoons finely chopped walnuts
1 tablespoon minced fresh rosemary

1 teaspoon minced garlic
¼ teaspoon cayenne pepper
Sea salt and freshly ground black pepper, to taste
1½ pounds (680 g) New York strip steaks, at room temperature

1. In a medium bowl, combine the butter, blue cheese, walnuts, rosemary, garlic, and cayenne pepper and salt and black pepper to taste. Use clean hands to ensure that everything is well combined. Place the mixture on a sheet of parchment paper and form it into a log. Wrap it tightly in plastic wrap. Refrigerate for at least 2 hours or freeze for 30 minutes. 2. Season the steaks generously with salt and pepper. 3. Place the air fryer basket or grill pan in the air fryer. Set the air fryer to 400°F (204°C) and let it preheat for 5 minutes. 4. Place the steaks in the basket in a single layer and air fry for 5 minutes. Flip the steaks, and cook for 5 minutes more, until an instant-read thermometer reads 120°F (49°C) for medium-rare (or as desired). 5. Transfer the steaks to a plate. Cut the butter into pieces and place the desired amount on top of the steaks. Tent a piece of aluminum foil over the steaks and allow to sit for 10 minutes before serving. 6. Store any remaining butter in a sealed container in the refrigerator for up to 2 weeks.

Bacon Wrapped Pork with Apple Gravy

Prep time: 10 minutes | Cook time: 25 minutes |
Serves 4

Pork:
1 tablespoons Dijon mustard
1 pork tenderloin
3 strips bacon
Apple Gravy:
3 tablespoons ghee, divided

1 small shallot, chopped
2 apples
1 tablespoon almond flour
1 cup vegetable broth
½ teaspoon Dijon mustard

1. Preheat the air fryer to 360°F (182°C). 2. Spread Dijon mustard all over tenderloin and wrap with strips of bacon. 3. Put into air fryer and air fry for 12 minutes. Use a meat thermometer to check for doneness. 4. To make sauce, heat 1 tablespoons of ghee in a pan and add shallots. Cook for 1 minute. 5. Then add apples, cooking for 4 minutes until softened. 6. Add flour and 2 tablespoons of ghee to make a roux. Add broth and mustard, stirring well to combine. 7.

When sauce starts to bubble, add 1 cup of sautéed apples, cooking until sauce thickens. 8. Once pork tenderloin is cooked, allow to sit 8 minutes to rest before slicing. 9. Serve topped with apple gravy.

Mustard Herb Pork Tenderloin

Prep time: 5 minutes | Cook time: 20 minutes |
Serves 6

¼ cup mayonnaise
2 tablespoons Dijon mustard
½ teaspoon dried thyme
¼ teaspoon dried rosemary
1 (1-pound / 454-g) pork

tenderloin
½ teaspoon salt
¼ teaspoon ground black pepper

1. In a small bowl, mix mayonnaise, mustard, thyme, and rosemary. Brush tenderloin with mixture on all sides, then sprinkle with salt and pepper on all sides. 2. Place tenderloin into ungreased air fryer basket. Adjust the temperature to 400°F (204°C) and air fry for 20 minutes, turning tenderloin halfway through cooking. Tenderloin will be golden and have an internal temperature of at least 145°F (63°C) when done. Serve warm.

Italian Sausages with Peppers and Onions

Prep time: 5 minutes | Cook time: 28 minutes |
Serves 3

1 medium onion, thinly sliced
1 yellow or orange bell pepper, thinly sliced
1 red bell pepper, thinly sliced
¼ cup avocado oil or melted

coconut oil
1 teaspoon fine sea salt
6 Italian sausages
Dijon mustard, for serving (optional)

1. Preheat the air fryer to 400°F (204°C). 2. Place the onion and peppers in a large bowl. Drizzle with the oil and toss well to coat the veggies. Season with the salt. 3. Place the onion and peppers in a pie pan and cook in the air fryer for 8 minutes, stirring halfway through. Remove from the air fryer and set aside. 4. Spray the air fryer basket with avocado oil. Place the sausages in the air fryer basket and air fry for 20 minutes, or until crispy and golden brown. During the last minute or two of cooking, add the onion and peppers to the basket with the sausages to warm them through. 5. Place the onion and peppers on a serving platter and arrange the sausages on top. Serve Dijon mustard on the side, if desired. 6. Store leftovers in an airtight container in the fridge for up to 7 days or in the freezer for up to a month. Reheat in a preheated 390°F (199°C) air fryer for 3 minutes, or until heated through.

Barbecue Ribs

Prep time: 5 minutes | Cook time: 30 minutes |
Serves 4

1 (2-pound / 907-g) rack baby back ribs	1 teaspoon dried oregano
1 teaspoon onion powder	Salt and freshly ground black pepper, to taste
1 teaspoon garlic powder	Cooking oil spray
1 teaspoon light brown sugar	½ cup barbecue sauce

1. Use a sharp knife to remove the thin membrane from the back of the ribs. Cut the rack in half, or as needed, so the ribs fit in the air fryer basket. The best way to do this is to cut the ribs into 4- or 5-rib sections. 2. In a small bowl, stir together the onion powder, garlic powder, brown sugar, and oregano and season with salt and pepper. Rub the spice seasoning onto the front and back of the ribs. 3. Cover the ribs with plastic wrap or foil and let sit at room temperature for 30 minutes. 4. Insert the crisper plate into the basket and the basket into the unit. Preheat the unit by selecting AIR ROAST, setting the temperature to 360ºF (182ºC), and setting the time to 3 minutes. Select START/STOP to begin. 5. Once the unit is preheated, spray the crisper plate with cooking oil. Place the ribs into the basket. It is okay to stack them. 6. Select AIR ROAST, set the temperature to 360ºF (182ºC), and set the time to 30 minutes. Select START/STOP to begin. 7. After 15 minutes, flip the ribs. Resume cooking for 15 minutes, or until a food thermometer registers 190ºF (88ºC). 8. When the cooking is complete, transfer the ribs to a serving dish. Drizzle the ribs with the barbecue sauce and serve.

Pork Loin Roast

Prep time: 30 minutes | Cook time: 55 minutes |
Serves 6

1½ pounds (680 g) boneless pork loin roast, washed	¾ teaspoon sea salt flakes
1 teaspoon mustard seeds	1 teaspoon red pepper flakes, crushed
1 teaspoon garlic powder	2 dried sprigs thyme, crushed
1 teaspoon porcini powder	2 tablespoons lime juice
1 teaspoon shallot powder	

1. Firstly, score the meat using a small knife; make sure to not cut too deep. 2. In a small-sized mixing dish, combine all seasonings in the order listed above; mix to combine well. 3. Massage the spice mix into the pork meat to evenly distribute. Drizzle with lemon juice. 4. Set the air fryer to 360ºF (182ºC). Place the pork in the air fryer basket; roast for 25 to 30 minutes. Pause the machine, check for doneness and cook for 25 minutes more.

Greek Lamb Pita Pockets

Prep time: 15 minutes | Cook time: 6 minutes |
Serves 4

Dressing:	¼ teaspoon oregano
1 cup plain yogurt	¼ teaspoon coriander
1 tablespoon lemon juice	¼ teaspoon ground cumin
1 teaspoon dried dill weed, crushed	¼ teaspoon salt
1 teaspoon ground oregano	4 pita halves
½ teaspoon salt	Suggested Toppings:
Meatballs:	1 red onion, slivered
½ pound (227 g) ground lamb	1 medium cucumber, deseeded, thinly sliced
1 tablespoon diced onion	Crumbled feta cheese
1 teaspoon dried parsley	Sliced black olives
1 teaspoon dried dill weed, crushed	Chopped fresh peppers

1. Preheat the air fryer to 390ºF (199ºC). 2. Stir the dressing ingredients together in a small bowl and refrigerate while preparing lamb. 3. Combine all meatball ingredients in a large bowl and stir to distribute seasonings. 4. Shape meat mixture into 12 small meatballs, rounded or slightly flattened if you prefer. 5. Transfer the meatballs in the preheated air fryer and air fry for 6 minutes, until well done. Remove and drain on paper towels. 6. To serve, pile meatballs and the choice of toppings in pita pockets and drizzle with dressing.

Cajun Bacon Pork Loin Fillet

Prep time: 30 minutes | Cook time: 20 minutes |
Serves 6

1½ pounds (680 g) pork loin fillet or pork tenderloin	Salt, to taste
3 tablespoons olive oil	6 slices bacon
2 tablespoons Cajun spice mix	Olive oil spray

1. Cut the pork in half so that it will fit in the air fryer basket. 2. Place both pieces of meat in a resealable plastic bag. Add the oil, Cajun seasoning, and salt to taste, if using. Seal the bag and massage to coat all of the meat with the oil and seasonings. Marinate in the refrigerator for at least 1 hour or up to 24 hours. 3. Remove the pork from the bag and wrap 3 bacon slices around each piece. Spray the air fryer basket with olive oil spray. Place the meat in the air fryer. Set the air fryer to 350ºF (177ºC) for 15 minutes. Increase the temperature to 400ºF (204ºC) for 5 minutes. Use a meat thermometer to ensure the meat has reached an internal temperature of 145ºF (63ºC). 4. Let the meat rest for 10 minutes. Slice into 6 medallions and serve.

Panko Crusted Calf's Liver Strips

Prep time: 15 minutes | Cook time: 23 to 25 minutes
| Serves 4

1 pound (454 g) sliced calf's liver, cut into ½-inch wide strips
2 eggs
2 tablespoons milk
½ cup whole wheat flour
2 cups panko breadcrumbs
Salt and ground black pepper, to taste
Cooking spray

1. Preheat the air fryer to 390°F (199°C) and spritz with cooking spray. 2. Rub the calf's liver strips with salt and ground black pepper on a clean work surface. 3. Whisk the eggs with milk in a large bowl. Pour the flour in a shallow dish. Pour the panko on a separate shallow dish. 4. Dunk the liver strips in the flour, then in the egg mixture. Shake the excess off and roll the strips over the panko to coat well. 5. Arrange half of the liver strips in a single layer in the preheated air fryer and spritz with cooking spray. 6. Air fry for 5 minutes or until browned. Flip the strips halfway through. Repeat with the remaining strips. 7. Serve immediately.

Hoisin BBQ Pork Chops

Prep time: 5 minutes | Cook time: 22 minutes |
Serves 2 to 3

3 tablespoons hoisin sauce
¼ cup honey
1 tablespoon soy sauce
3 tablespoons rice vinegar
2 tablespoons brown sugar
1½ teaspoons grated fresh ginger
1 to 2 teaspoons Sriracha sauce, to taste
2 to 3 bone-in center cut pork chops, 1-inch thick (about 1¼ pounds / 567 g)
Chopped scallions, for garnish

1. Combine the hoisin sauce, honey, soy sauce, rice vinegar, brown sugar, ginger, and Sriracha sauce in a small saucepan. Whisk the ingredients together and bring the mixture to a boil over medium-high heat on the stovetop. Reduce the heat and simmer the sauce until it has reduced in volume and thickened slightly, about 10 minutes. 2. Preheat the air fryer to 400°F (204°C). 3. Place the pork chops into the air fryer basket and pour half the hoisin BBQ sauce over the top. Air fry for 6 minutes. Then, flip the chops over, pour the remaining hoisin BBQ sauce on top and air fry for 5 to 6 more minutes, depending on the thickness of the pork chops. The internal temperature of the pork chops should be 155°F (68°C) when tested with an instant read thermometer. 4. Let the pork chops rest for 5 minutes before serving. You can spoon a little of the sauce from the bottom drawer of the air fryer over the top if desired. Sprinkle with chopped scallions and serve.

Korean Beef Tacos

Prep time: 30 minutes | Cook time: 12 minutes |
Serves 6

2 tablespoons gochujang (Korean red chile paste)
2 cloves garlic, minced
2 teaspoons minced fresh ginger
2 tablespoons toasted sesame oil
1 tablespoon soy sauce
2 tablespoons sesame seeds
2 teaspoons sugar
½ teaspoon kosher salt
1½ pounds (680 g) thinly sliced beef (chuck, rib eye, or sirloin)
1 medium red onion, sliced
12 (6-inch) flour tortillas, warmed; or lettuce leaves
½ cup chopped green onions
¼ cup chopped fresh cilantro (optional)
½ cup kimchi (optional)

1. In a small bowl, combine the gochujang, garlic, ginger, sesame oil, soy sauce, sesame seeds, sugar, and salt. Whisk until well combined. Place the beef and red onion in a resealable plastic bag and pour the marinade over. Seal the bag and massage to coat all of the meat and onion. Marinate at room temperature for 30 minutes or in the refrigerator for up to 24 hours. 2. Place the meat and onion in the air fryer basket, leaving behind as much of the marinade as possible; discard the marinade. Set the air fryer to 400°F (204°C) for 12 minutes, shaking halfway through the cooking time. 3. To serve, place meat and onion in the tortillas. Top with the green onions and the cilantro and kimchi, if using, and serve.

Honey-Baked Pork Loin

Prep time: 30 minutes | Cook time: 22 to 25 minutes
| Serves 6

¼ cup honey
¼ cup freshly squeezed lemon juice
2 tablespoons soy sauce
1 teaspoon garlic powder
1 (2-pound / 907-g) pork loin
2 tablespoons vegetable oil

1. In a medium bowl, whisk together the honey, lemon juice, soy sauce, and garlic powder. Reserve half of the mixture for basting during cooking. 2. Cut 5 slits in the pork loin and transfer it to a resealable bag. Add the remaining honey mixture. Seal the bag and refrigerate to marinate for at least 2 hours. 3. Preheat the air fryer to 400°F (204°C). Line the air fryer basket with parchment paper. 4. Remove the pork from the marinade, and place it on the parchment. Spritz with oil, then baste with the reserved marinade. 5. Cook for 15 minutes. Flip the pork, baste with more marinade and spritz with oil again. Cook for 7 to 10 minutes more until the internal temperature reaches 145°F (63°C). Let rest for 5 minutes before serving.

Bacon and Cheese Stuffed Pork Chops

Prep time: 10 minutes | Cook time: 12 minutes |
Serves 4

½ ounce (14 g) plain pork rinds, finely crushed
½ cup shredded sharp Cheddar cheese
4 slices cooked sugar-free bacon, crumbled

4 (4-ounce / 113-g) boneless pork chops
½ teaspoon salt
¼ teaspoon ground black pepper

1. In a small bowl, mix pork rinds, Cheddar, and bacon. 2. Make a 3-inch slit in the side of each pork chop and stuff with ¼ pork rind mixture. Sprinkle each side of pork chops with salt and pepper. 3. Place pork chops into ungreased air fryer basket, stuffed side up. Adjust the temperature to 400ºF (204ºC) and air fry for 12 minutes. Pork chops will be browned and have an internal temperature of at least 145ºF (63ºC) when done. Serve warm.

Tuscan Air Fried Veal Loin

Prep time: 1 hour 10 minutes | Cook time: 12 minutes | Makes 3 veal chops

1½ teaspoons crushed fennel seeds
1 tablespoon minced fresh rosemary leaves
1 tablespoon minced garlic
1½ teaspoons lemon zest

1½ teaspoons salt
½ teaspoon red pepper flakes
2 tablespoons olive oil
3 (10-ounce / 284-g) bone-in veal loin, about ½ inch thick

1. Combine all the ingredients, except for the veal loin, in a large bowl. Stir to mix well. 2. Dunk the loin in the mixture and press to submerge. Wrap the bowl in plastic and refrigerate for at least an hour to marinate. 3. Preheat the air fryer to 400ºF (204ºC). 4. Arrange the veal loin in the preheated air fryer and air fry for 12 minutes for medium-rare, or until it reaches your desired doneness. 5. Serve immediately.

Spicy Lamb Sirloin Chops

Prep time: 30 minutes | Cook time: 15 minutes |
Serves 4

½ yellow onion, coarsely chopped
4 coin-size slices peeled fresh ginger
5 garlic cloves

1 teaspoon garam masala
1 teaspoon ground fennel
1 teaspoon ground cinnamon
1 teaspoon ground turmeric
½ to 1 teaspoon cayenne pepper

½ teaspoon ground cardamom
1 teaspoon kosher salt

1 pound (454 g) lamb sirloin chops

1. In a blender, combine the onion, ginger, garlic, garam masala, fennel, cinnamon, turmeric, cayenne, cardamom, and salt. Pulse until the onion is finely minced and the mixture forms a thick paste, 3 to 4 minutes. 2. Place the lamb chops in a large bowl. Slash the meat and fat with a sharp knife several times to allow the marinade to penetrate better. Add the spice paste to the bowl and toss the lamb to coat. Marinate at room temperature for 30 minutes or cover and refrigerate for up to 24 hours. 3. Place the lamb chops in a single layer in the air fryer basket. Set the air fryer to 325ºF (163ºC) for 15 minutes, turning the chops halfway through the cooking time. Use a meat thermometer to ensure the lamb has reached an internal temperature of 145ºF (63ºC) (medium-rare).

Bo Luc Lac

Prep time: 50 minutes | Cook time: 8 minutes |
Serves 4

For the Meat:
2 teaspoons soy sauce
4 garlic cloves, minced
1 teaspoon kosher salt
2 teaspoons sugar
¼ teaspoon ground black pepper
1 teaspoon toasted sesame oil
1½ pounds (680 g) top sirloin steak, cut into 1-inch cubes
Cooking spray
For the Salad:
1 head Bibb lettuce, leaves separated and torn into large pieces
¼ cup fresh mint leaves

½ cup halved grape tomatoes
½ red onion, halved and thinly sliced
2 tablespoons apple cider vinegar
1 garlic clove, minced
2 teaspoons sugar
¼ teaspoon kosher salt
¼ teaspoon ground black pepper
2 tablespoons vegetable oil
For Serving:
Lime wedges, for garnish
Coarse salt and freshly cracked black pepper, to taste

1. Combine the ingredients for the meat, except for the steak, in a large bowl. Stir to mix well. 2. Dunk the steak cubes in the bowl and press to coat. Wrap the bowl in plastic and marinate under room temperature for at least 30 minutes. 3. Preheat the air fryer to 450ºF (232ºC). Spritz the air fryer basket with cooking spray. 4. Discard the marinade and transfer the steak cubes in the preheated air fryer basket. You need to air fry in batches to avoid overcrowding. 5. Air fry for 4 minutes or until the steak cubes are lightly browned but still have a little pink. Shake the basket halfway through the cooking time. 6. Meanwhile, combine the ingredients for the salad in a separate large bowl. Toss to mix well. 7. Pour the salad in a large serving bowl and top with the steak cubes. Squeeze the lime wedges over and sprinkle with salt and black pepper before serving.

Cheddar Bacon Burst with Spinach

Prep time: 5 minutes | Cook time: 60 minutes | Serves 8

30 slices bacon

1 tablespoon Chipotle seasoning

2 teaspoons Italian seasoning

2½ cups Cheddar cheese

4 cups raw spinach

1. Preheat the air fryer to 375°F (191°C). 2. Weave the bacon into 15 vertical pieces and 12 horizontal pieces. Cut the extra 3 in half to fill in the rest, horizontally. 3. Season the bacon with Chipotle seasoning and Italian seasoning. 4. Add the cheese to the bacon. 5. Add the spinach and press down to compress. 6. Tightly roll up the woven bacon. 7. Line a baking sheet with kitchen foil and add plenty of salt to it. 8. Put the bacon on top of a cooling rack and put that on top of the baking sheet. 9. Bake for 60 minutes. 10. Let cool for 15 minutes before slicing and serving.

Beefy Poppers

Prep time: 15 minutes | Cook time: 15 minutes | Makes 8 poppers

8 medium jalapeño peppers, stemmed, halved, and seeded

1 (8-ounce / 227-g) package cream cheese (or Kite Hill brand cream cheese style spread for dairy-free), softened

2 pounds (907 g) ground beef

(85% lean)

1 teaspoon fine sea salt

½ teaspoon ground black pepper

8 slices thin-cut bacon

Fresh cilantro leaves, for garnish

1. Spray the air fryer basket with avocado oil. Preheat the air fryer to 400°F (204°C). 2. Stuff each jalapeño half with a few tablespoons of cream cheese. Place the halves back together again to form 8 jalapeños. 3. Season the ground beef with the salt and pepper and mix with your hands to incorporate. Flatten about ¼ pound (113 g) of ground beef in the palm of your hand and place a stuffed jalapeño in the center. Fold the beef around the jalapeño, forming an egg shape. Wrap the beef-covered jalapeño with a slice of bacon and secure it with a toothpick. 4. Place the jalapeños in the air fryer basket, leaving space between them (if you're using a smaller air fryer, work in batches if necessary), and air fry for 15 minutes, or until the beef is cooked through and the bacon is crispy. Garnish

with cilantro before serving. 5. Store leftovers in an airtight container in the fridge for 3 days or in the freezer for up to a month. Reheat in a preheated 350°F (177°C) air fryer for 4 minutes, or until heated through and the bacon is crispy.

Pigs in a Blanket

Prep time: 10 minutes | Cook time: 7 minutes | Serves 2

½ cup shredded Mozzarella cheese

2 tablespoons blanched finely ground almond flour

1 ounce (28 g) full-fat cream

cheese

2 (2-ounce / 57-g) beef smoked sausages

½ teaspoon sesame seeds

1. Place Mozzarella, almond flour, and cream cheese in a large microwave-safe bowl. Microwave for 45 seconds and stir until smooth. Roll dough into a ball and cut in half. 2. Press each half out into a 4 × 5-inch rectangle. Roll one sausage up in each dough half and press seams closed. Sprinkle the top with sesame seeds. 3. Place each wrapped sausage into the air fryer basket. 4. Adjust the temperature to 400°F (204°C) and air fry for 7 minutes. 5. The outside will be golden when completely cooked. Serve immediately.

Parmesan-Crusted Pork Chops

Prep time: 5 minutes | Cook time: 12 minutes | Serves 4

1 large egg

½ cup grated Parmesan cheese

4 (4-ounce / 113-g) boneless pork chops

½ teaspoon salt

¼ teaspoon ground black pepper

1. Whisk egg in a medium bowl and place Parmesan in a separate medium bowl. 2. Sprinkle pork chops on both sides with salt and pepper. Dip each pork chop into egg, then press both sides into Parmesan. 3. Place pork chops into ungreased air fryer basket. Adjust the temperature to 400°F (204°C) and air fry for 12 minutes, turning chops halfway through cooking. Pork chops will be golden and have an internal temperature of at least 145°F (63°C) when done. Serve warm.

Carne Asada

Prep time: 5 minutes | Cook time: 15 minutes | Serves 4

3 chipotle peppers in adobo, chopped
⅓ cup chopped fresh oregano
⅓ cup chopped fresh parsley
4 cloves garlic, minced
Juice of 2 limes

1 teaspoon ground cumin seeds
⅓ cup olive oil
1 to 1½ pounds (454 g to 680 g) flank steak
Salt, to taste

1. Combine the chipotle, oregano, parsley, garlic, lime juice, cumin, and olive oil in a large bowl. Stir to mix well. 2. Dunk the flank steak in the mixture and press to coat well. Wrap the bowl in plastic and marinate under room temperature for at least 30 minutes. 3. Preheat the air fryer to 390ºF (199ºC). 4. Discard the marinade and place the steak in the preheated air fryer. Sprinkle with salt. 5. Air fry for 15 minutes or until the steak is medium-rare or it reaches your desired doneness. Flip the steak halfway through the cooking time. 6. Remove the steak from the air fryer and slice to serve.

Chapter 6 Fish and Seafood

Baked Tilapia with Garlic Aioli

Prep time: 5 minutes | Cook time: 15 minutes |
Serves 4

Tilapia:
4 tilapia fillets
1 tablespoon extra-virgin olive oil
1 teaspoon garlic powder
1 teaspoon paprika
1 teaspoon dried basil
A pinch of lemon-pepper

seasoning
Garlic Aioli:
2 garlic cloves, minced
1 tablespoon mayonnaise
Juice of ½ lemon
1 teaspoon extra-virgin olive oil
Salt and pepper, to taste

1. Preheat the air fryer to 400°F (204°C). 2. On a clean work surface, brush both sides of each fillet with the olive oil. Sprinkle with the garlic powder, paprika, basil, and lemon-pepper seasoning. 3. Place the fillets in the air fryer basket and bake for 15 minutes, flipping the fillets halfway through, or until the fish flakes easily and is no longer translucent in the center. 4. Meanwhile, make the garlic aioli: Whisk together the garlic, mayo, lemon juice, olive oil, salt, and pepper in a small bowl until smooth. 5. Remove the fish from the basket and serve with the garlic aioli on the side.

Swordfish Skewers with Caponata

Prep time: 15 minutes | Cook time: 20 minutes |
Serves 2

1 (10-ounce / 283-g) small
Italian eggplant, cut into 1-inch
pieces
6 ounces (170 g) cherry
tomatoes
3 scallions, cut into 2 inches
long
2 tablespoons extra-virgin olive
oil, divided
Salt and pepper, to taste
12 ounces (340 g) skinless
swordfish steaks, 1¼ inches

thick, cut into 1-inch pieces
2 teaspoons honey, divided
2 teaspoons ground coriander,
divided
1 teaspoon grated lemon zest,
divided
1 teaspoon juice
4 (6-inch) wooden skewers
1 garlic clove, minced
½ teaspoon ground cumin
1 tablespoon chopped fresh
basil

1. Preheat the air fryer to 400°F (204°C). 2. Toss eggplant, tomatoes, and scallions with 1 tablespoon oil, ¼ teaspoon salt,

and ⅛ teaspoon pepper in bowl; transfer to air fryer basket. Air fry until eggplant is softened and browned and tomatoes have begun to burst, about 14 minutes, tossing halfway through cooking. Transfer vegetables to cutting board and set aside to cool slightly. 3. Pat swordfish dry with paper towels. Combine 1 teaspoon oil, 1 teaspoon honey, 1 teaspoon coriander, ½ teaspoon lemon zest, ⅛ teaspoon salt, and pinch pepper in a clean bowl. Add swordfish and toss to coat. Thread swordfish onto skewers, leaving about ¼ inch between each piece (3 or 4 pieces per skewer). 4. Arrange skewers in air fryer basket, spaced evenly apart. (Skewers may overlap slightly.) Return basket to air fryer and air fry until swordfish is browned and registers 140°F (60°C), 6 to 8 minutes, flipping and rotating skewers halfway through cooking. 5. Meanwhile, combine remaining 2 teaspoons oil, remaining 1 teaspoon honey, remaining 1 teaspoon coriander, remaining ½ teaspoon lemon zest, lemon juice, garlic, cumin, ¼ teaspoon salt, and ⅛ teaspoon pepper in large bowl. Microwave, stirring once, until fragrant, about 30 seconds. Coarsely chop the cooked vegetables, transfer to bowl with dressing, along with any accumulated juices, and gently toss to combine. Stir in basil and season with salt and pepper to taste. Serve skewers with caponata.

Snapper with Shallot and Tomato

Prep time: 20 minutes | Cook time: 15 minutes |
Serves 2

2 snapper fillets
1 shallot, peeled and sliced
2 garlic cloves, halved
1 bell pepper, sliced
1 small-sized serrano pepper,
sliced
1 tomato, sliced

1 tablespoon olive oil
¼ teaspoon freshly ground
black pepper
½ teaspoon paprika
Sea salt, to taste
2 bay leaves

1. Place two parchment sheets on a working surface. Place the fish in the center of one side of the parchment paper. 2. Top with the shallot, garlic, peppers, and tomato. Drizzle olive oil over the fish and vegetables. Season with black pepper, paprika, and salt. Add the bay leaves. 3. Fold over the other half of the parchment. Now, fold the paper around the edges tightly and create a half moon shape, sealing the fish inside. 4. Cook in the preheated air fryer at 390°F (199°C) for 15 minutes. Serve warm.

Blackened Salmon

Prep time: 10 minutes | Cook time: 8 minutes |

Serves 2

10 ounces (283 g) salmon fillet
½ teaspoon ground coriander
1 teaspoon ground cumin

1 teaspoon dried basil
1 tablespoon avocado oil

1. In the shallow bowl, mix ground coriander, ground cumin, and dried basil. 2. Then coat the salmon fillet in the spices and sprinkle with avocado oil. 3. Put the fish in the air fryer basket and cook at 395°F (202°C) for 4 minutes per side.

Scallops in Lemon-Butter Sauce

Prep time: 10 minutes | Cook time: 6 minutes |

Serves 2

8 large dry sea scallops (about
¾ pound / 340 g)
Salt and freshly ground black
pepper, to taste
2 tablespoons olive oil
2 tablespoons unsalted butter,
melted

2 tablespoons chopped flat-leaf
parsley
1 tablespoon fresh lemon juice
2 teaspoons capers, drained and
chopped
1 teaspoon grated lemon zest
1 clove garlic, minced

1. Preheat the air fryer to 400°F (204°C). 2. Use a paper towel to pat the scallops dry. Sprinkle lightly with salt and pepper. Brush with the olive oil. Arrange the scallops in a single layer in the air fryer basket. Pausing halfway through the cooking time to turn the scallops, air fry for about 6 minutes until firm and opaque. 3. Meanwhile, in a small bowl, combine the oil, butter, parsley, lemon juice, capers, lemon zest, and garlic. Drizzle over the scallops just before serving.

Mackerel with Spinach

Prep time: 15 minutes | Cook time: 20 minutes |

Serves 5

1 pound (454 g) mackerel,
trimmed
1 bell pepper, chopped
½ cup spinach, chopped

1 tablespoon avocado oil
1 teaspoon ground black pepper
1 teaspoon keto tomato paste

1. In the mixing bowl, mix bell pepper with spinach, ground black pepper, and tomato paste. 2. Fill the mackerel with spinach mixture. 3. Then brush the fish with avocado oil and put it in the air fryer. 4. Cook the fish at 365°F (185°C) for 20 minutes.

Pesto Fish Pie

Prep time: 15 minutes | Cook time: 15 minutes |

Serves 4

2 tablespoons prepared pesto
¼ cup half-and-half
¼ cup grated Parmesan cheese
1 teaspoon kosher salt
1 teaspoon black pepper
Vegetable oil spray
1 (10-ounce / 283-g) package
frozen chopped spinach, thawed
and squeezed dry

1 pound (454 g) firm white fish,
cut into 2-inch chunks
½ cup cherry tomatoes,
quartered
All-purpose flour
½ sheet frozen puff pastry (from
a 17.3-ounce / 490-g package),
thawed

1. In a small bowl, combine the pesto, half-and-half, Parmesan, salt, and pepper. Stir until well combined; set aside. 2. Spray a baking pan with vegetable oil spray. Arrange the spinach evenly across the bottom of the pan. Top with the fish and tomatoes. Pour the pesto mixture evenly over everything. 3. On a lightly floured surface, roll the puff pastry sheet into a circle. Place the pastry on top of the pan and tuck it in around the edges of the pan. (Or, do what I do and stretch it with your hands and then pat it into place.) 4. Place the pan in the air fryer basket. Set the air fryer to 400°F (204°C) for 15 minutes, or until the pastry is well browned. Let stand 5 minutes before serving.

Lemony Shrimp and Zucchini

Prep time: 15 minutes | Cook time: 7 to 8 minutes |

Serves 4

1¼ pounds (567 g) extra-
large raw shrimp, peeled and
deveined
2 medium zucchini (about 8
ounces / 227 g each), halved
lengthwise and cut into ½-inch-
thick slices
1½ tablespoons olive oil

½ teaspoon garlic salt
1½ teaspoons dried oregano
⅛ teaspoon crushed red pepper
flakes (optional)
Juice of ½ lemon
1 tablespoon chopped fresh
mint
1 tablespoon chopped fresh dill

1. Preheat the air fryer to 350°F (177°C). 2. In a large bowl, combine the shrimp, zucchini, oil, garlic salt, oregano, and pepper flakes (if using) and toss to coat. 3. Working in batches, arrange a single layer of the shrimp and zucchini in the air fryer basket. Air fry for 7 to 8 minutes, shaking the basket halfway, until the zucchini is golden and the shrimp are cooked through. 4. Transfer to a serving dish and tent with foil while you air fry the remaining shrimp and zucchini. 5. Top with the lemon juice, mint, and dill and serve.

Crab Cake Sandwich

Prep time: 15 minutes | Cook time: 10 minutes | Serves 4

Crab Cakes:
½ cup panko bread crumbs
1 large egg, beaten
1 large egg white
1 tablespoon mayonnaise
1 teaspoon Dijon mustard
¼ cup minced fresh parsley
1 tablespoon fresh lemon juice
½ teaspoon Old Bay seasoning
⅛ teaspoon sweet paprika
⅛ teaspoon kosher salt
Freshly ground black pepper, to taste

10 ounces (283 g) lump crab meat
Cooking spray
Cajun Mayo:
¼ cup mayonnaise
1 tablespoon minced dill pickle
1 teaspoon fresh lemon juice
¾ teaspoon Cajun seasoning
For Serving:
4 Boston lettuce leaves
4 whole wheat potato buns or gluten-free buns

1. For the crab cakes: In a large bowl, combine the panko, whole egg, egg white, mayonnaise, mustard, parsley, lemon juice, Old Bay, paprika, salt, and pepper to taste and mix well. Fold in the crab meat, being careful not to over mix. Gently shape into 4 round patties, about ½ cup each, ¾ inch thick. Spray both sides with oil. 2. Preheat the air fryer to 370°F (188°C). 3. Working in batches, place the crab cakes in the air fryer basket. Air fry for about 10 minutes, flipping halfway, until the edges are golden. 4. Meanwhile, for the Cajun mayo: In a small bowl, combine the mayonnaise, pickle, lemon juice, and Cajun seasoning. 5. To serve: Place a lettuce leaf on each bun bottom and top with a crab cake and a generous tablespoon of Cajun mayonnaise. Add the bun top and serve.

Friday Night Fish Fry

Prep time: 10 minutes | Cook time: 10 minutes | Serves 4

1 large egg
½ cup powdered Parmesan cheese (about 1½ ounces / 43 g)
1 teaspoon smoked paprika
¼ teaspoon celery salt
¼ teaspoon ground black

pepper
4 (4-ounce / 113-g) cod fillets
Chopped fresh oregano or parsley, for garnish (optional)
Lemon slices, for serving (optional)

1. Spray the air fryer basket with avocado oil. Preheat the air fryer to 400°F (204°C). 2. Crack the egg in a shallow bowl and beat it lightly with a fork. Combine the Parmesan cheese, paprika, celery salt, and pepper in a separate shallow bowl. 3. One at a time, dip the fillets into the egg, then dredge them in the Parmesan mixture. Using your hands, press the Parmesan onto the fillets to form a nice crust. As you finish, place the fish in the air fryer basket. 4.

Air fry the fish in the air fryer for 10 minutes, or until it is cooked through and flakes easily with a fork. Garnish with fresh oregano or parsley and serve with lemon slices, if desired. 5. Store leftovers in an airtight container in the refrigerator for up to 3 days. Reheat in a preheated 400°F (204°C) air fryer for 5 minutes, or until warmed through.

Popcorn Crawfish

Prep time: 15 minutes | Cook time: 18 to 20 minutes | Serves 4

½ cup flour, plus 2 tablespoons
½ teaspoon garlic powder
1½ teaspoons Old Bay Seasoning
½ teaspoon onion powder
½ cup beer, plus 2 tablespoons
1 (12-ounce / 340-g) package frozen crawfish tail meat,

thawed and drained
Oil for misting or cooking spray
Coating:
1½ cups panko crumbs
1 teaspoon Old Bay Seasoning
½ teaspoon ground black pepper

1. In a large bowl, mix together the flour, garlic powder, Old Bay Seasoning, and onion powder. Stir in beer to blend. 2. Add crawfish meat to batter and stir to coat. 3. Combine the coating ingredients in food processor and pulse to finely crush the crumbs. Transfer crumbs to shallow dish. 4. Preheat the air fryer to 390°F (199°C). 5. Pour the crawfish and batter into a colander to drain. Stir with a spoon to drain excess batter. 6. Working with a handful of crawfish at a time, roll in crumbs and place on a cookie sheet. It's okay if some of the smaller pieces of crawfish meat stick together. 7. Spray breaded crawfish with oil or cooking spray and place all at once into air fryer basket. 8. Air fry at 390°F (199°C) for 5 minutes. Shake basket or stir and mist again with olive oil or spray. Cook 5 more minutes, shake basket again, and mist lightly again. Continue cooking 3 to 5 more minutes, until browned and crispy.

Sweet Tilapia Fillets

Prep time: 5 minutes | Cook time: 14 minutes | Serves 4

2 tablespoons erythritol
1 tablespoon apple cider vinegar

4 tilapia fillets, boneless
1 teaspoon olive oil

1. Mix apple cider vinegar with olive oil and erythritol. 2. Then rub the tilapia fillets with the sweet mixture and put in the air fryer basket in one layer. Cook the fish at 360°F (182°C) for 7 minutes per side.

Crab Cakes

Prep time: 10 minutes | Cook time: 10 minutes |

Serves 4

2 (6-ounce / 170-g) cans lump crab meat	½ teaspoon Dijon mustard
¼ cup blanched finely ground almond flour	½ tablespoon lemon juice
	½ medium green bell pepper, seeded and chopped
1 large egg	¼ cup chopped green onion
2 tablespoons full-fat mayonnaise	½ teaspoon Old Bay seasoning

1. In a large bowl, combine all ingredients. Form into four balls and flatten into patties. Place patties into the air fryer basket. 2. Adjust the temperature to 350ºF (177ºC) and air fry for 10 minutes. 3. Flip patties halfway through the cooking time. Serve warm.

Parmesan Mackerel with Coriander

Prep time: 10 minutes | Cook time: 7 minutes |

Serves 2

12 ounces (340 g) mackerel fillet	grated
	1 teaspoon ground coriander
2 ounces (57 g) Parmesan,	1 tablespoon olive oil

1. Sprinkle the mackerel fillet with olive oil and put it in the air fryer basket. 2. Top the fish with ground coriander and Parmesan. 3. Cook the fish at 390ºF (199ºC) for 7 minutes.

Roasted Fish with Almond-Lemon Crumbs

Prep time: 10 minutes | Cook time: 7 to 8 minutes |

Serves 4

½ cup raw whole almonds	Freshly ground black pepper, to taste
1 scallion, finely chopped	
Grated zest and juice of 1 lemon	4 (6 ounces / 170 g each) skinless fish fillets
½ tablespoon extra-virgin olive oil	Cooking spray
	1 teaspoon Dijon mustard
¾ teaspoon kosher salt, divided	

1. In a food processor, pulse the almonds to coarsely chop. Transfer to a small bowl and add the scallion, lemon zest, and olive oil. Season with ¼ teaspoon of the salt and pepper to taste and mix to combine. 2. Spray the top of the fish with oil and squeeze the lemon juice over the fish. Season with the remaining ½ teaspoon salt and pepper to taste. Spread the mustard on top of the fish. Dividing evenly, press the almond mixture onto the top of the fillets to adhere. 3. Preheat the air fryer to 375ºF (191ºC). 4. Working in batches, place the fillets in the air fryer basket in a single layer. Air fry for 7 to 8 minutes, until the crumbs start to brown and the fish is cooked through. 5. Serve immediately.

Air Fried Crab Bun

Prep time: 15 minutes | Cook time: 20 minutes |

Serves 2

5 ounces (142 g) crab meat, chopped	½ teaspoon coconut aminos
	½ teaspoon ground black pepper
2 eggs, beaten	
2 tablespoons coconut flour	1 tablespoon coconut oil, softened
¼ teaspoon baking powder	

1. In the mixing bowl, mix crab meat with eggs, coconut flour, baking powder, coconut aminos, ground black pepper, and coconut oil. 2. Knead the smooth dough and cut it into pieces. 3. Make the buns from the crab mixture and put them in the air fryer basket. 4. Cook the crab buns at 365ºF (185ºC) for 20 minutes.

Shrimp Curry

Prep time: 30 minutes | Cook time: 10 minutes |

Serves 4

¾ cup unsweetened full-fat coconut milk	1 teaspoon salt
¼ cup finely chopped yellow onion	¼ to ½ teaspoon cayenne pepper
2 teaspoons garam masala	1 pound (454 g) raw shrimp (21 to 25 count), peeled and deveined
1 tablespoon minced fresh ginger	
1 tablespoon minced garlic	2 teaspoons chopped fresh cilantro
1 teaspoon ground turmeric	

1. In a large bowl, stir together the coconut milk, onion, garam masala, ginger, garlic, turmeric, salt and cayenne, until well blended. 2. Add the shrimp and toss until coated with sauce on all sides. Marinate at room temperature for 30 minutes. 3. Transfer the shrimp and marinade to a baking pan. Place the pan in the air fryer basket. Set the air fryer to 375ºF (191ºC) for 10 minutes, stirring halfway through the cooking time. 4. Transfer the shrimp to a serving bowl or platter. Sprinkle with the cilantro and serve.

Shrimp Dejonghe Skewers

Prep time: 10 minutes | Cook time: 15 minutes | Serves 4

2 teaspoons sherry	1 teaspoon kosher salt
3 tablespoons unsalted butter, melted	Pinch of cayenne pepper
1 cup panko bread crumbs	1½ pounds (680 g) shrimp, peeled and deveined
3 cloves garlic, minced	Vegetable oil, for spraying
⅓ cup minced flat-leaf parsley, plus more for garnish	Lemon wedges, for serving

1. Stir the sherry and melted butter together in a shallow bowl or pie plate and whisk until combined. Set aside. Whisk together the panko, garlic, parsley, salt, and cayenne pepper on a large plate or shallow bowl. 2. Thread the shrimp onto metal skewers designed for the air fryer or bamboo skewers, 3 to 4 per skewer. Dip 1 shrimp skewer in the butter mixture, then dredge in the panko mixture until each shrimp is lightly coated. Place the skewer on a plate or rimmed baking sheet and repeat the process with the remaining skewers. 3. Preheat the air fryer to 350ºF (177ºC). Arrange 4 skewers in the air fryer basket. Spray the skewers with oil and air fry for 8 minutes, until the bread crumbs are golden brown and the shrimp are cooked through. Transfer the cooked skewers to a serving plate and keep warm while cooking the remaining 4 skewers in the air fryer. 4. Sprinkle the cooked skewers with additional fresh parsley and serve with lemon wedges if desired.

Crab and Bell Pepper Cakes

Prep time: 5 minutes | Cook time: 10 minutes | Serves 4

8 ounces (227 g) jumbo lump crabmeat	1 egg
1 tablespoon Old Bay seasoning	¼ cup mayonnaise
⅓ cup bread crumbs	Juice of ½ lemon
¼ cup diced red bell pepper	1 teaspoon all-purpose flour
¼ cup diced green bell pepper	Cooking oil spray

1. Sort through the crabmeat, picking out any bits of shell or cartilage. 2. In a large bowl, stir together the Old Bay seasoning, bread crumbs, red and green bell peppers, egg, mayonnaise, and lemon juice. Gently stir in the crabmeat. 3. Insert the crisper plate into the basket and the basket into the unit. Preheat the unit by selecting AIR FRY, setting the temperature to 375ºF (191ºC), and setting the time to 3 minutes. Select START/STOP to begin. 4. Form the mixture into 4 patties. Sprinkle ¼ teaspoon of flour on top of each patty. 5. Once the unit is preheated, spray the crisper plate with cooking oil. Place the crab cakes into the basket and spray them with cooking oil. 6. Select AIR FRY, set the temperature to 375ºF (191ºC), and set the time to 10 minutes. Select START/STOP to begin. 7. When the cooking is complete, the crab cakes will be golden brown and firm.

Cod with Creamy Mustard Sauce

Prep time: 10 minutes | Cook time: 10 minutes | Serves 4

Fish:	black pepper
Oil, for spraying	Mustard Sauce:
1 pound (454 g) cod fillets	½ cup heavy cream
2 tablespoons olive oil	3 tablespoons Dijon mustard
1 tablespoon lemon juice	1 tablespoon unsalted butter
1 teaspoon salt	1 teaspoon salt
½ teaspoon freshly ground	

Make the Fish 1. Line the air fryer basket with parchment and spray lightly with oil. 2. Rub the cod with the olive oil and lemon juice. Season with the salt and black pepper. 3. Place the cod in the prepared basket. You may need to work in batches, depending on the size of your air fryer. 4. Roast at 350ºF (177ºC) for 5 minutes. Increase the temperature to 400ºF (204ºC) and cook for another 5 minutes, until flaky and the internal temperature reaches 145ºF (63ºC). Make the Mustard Sauce 5. In a small saucepan, mix together the heavy cream, mustard, butter, and salt and bring to a simmer over low heat. Cook for 3 to 4 minutes, or until the sauce starts to thicken. 6. Transfer the cod to a serving plate and drizzle with the mustard sauce. Serve immediately.

Herbed Shrimp Pita

Prep time: 5 minutes | Cook time: 8 minutes | Serves 4

1 pound (454 g) medium shrimp, peeled and deveined	¼ teaspoon black pepper
2 tablespoons olive oil	4 whole wheat pitas
1 teaspoon dried oregano	4 ounces (113 g) feta cheese, crumbled
½ teaspoon dried thyme	1 cup shredded lettuce
½ teaspoon garlic powder	1 tomato, diced
¼ teaspoon onion powder	¼ cup black olives, sliced
½ teaspoon salt	1 lemon

1. Preheat the oven to 380°F(193°C). 2. In a medium bowl, combine the shrimp with the olive oil, oregano, thyme, garlic powder, onion powder, salt, and black pepper. 3. Pour shrimp in a single layer in the air fryer basket and roast for 6 to 8 minutes, or until cooked through. 4. Remove from the air fryer and divide into warmed pitas with feta, lettuce, tomato, olives, and a squeeze of lemon.

Italian Baked Cod

Prep time: 5 minutes | Cook time: 12 minutes |
Serves 4

4 (6-ounce / 170-g) cod fillets	1 teaspoon Italian seasoning
2 tablespoons salted butter, melted	¼ teaspoon salt
	½ cup low-carb marinara sauce

1. Place cod into an ungreased round nonstick baking dish. Pour butter over cod and sprinkle with Italian seasoning and salt. Top with marinara. 2. Place dish into air fryer basket. Adjust the temperature to 350°F (177°C) and bake for 12 minutes. Fillets will be lightly browned, easily flake, and have an internal temperature of at least 145°F (63°C) when done. Serve warm.

Lemon Mahi-Mahi

Prep time: 5 minutes | Cook time: 14 minutes |
Serves 2

Oil, for spraying	¼ teaspoon salt
2 (6-ounce / 170-g) mahi-mahi fillets	¼ teaspoon freshly ground black pepper
1 tablespoon lemon juice	1 tablespoon chopped fresh dill
1 tablespoon olive oil	2 lemon slices

1. Line the air fryer basket with parchment and spray lightly with oil. 2. Place the mahi-mahi in the prepared basket. 3. In a small bowl, whisk together the lemon juice and olive oil. Brush the mixture evenly over the mahi-mahi. 4. Sprinkle the mahi-mahi with the salt and black pepper and top with the dill. 5. Air fry at 400°F (204°C) for 12 to 14 minutes, depending on the thickness of the fillets, until they flake easily. 6. Transfer to plates, top each with a lemon slice, and serve.

Fried Catfish with Dijon Sauce

Prep time: 20 minutes | Cook time: 7 minutes |
Serves 4

4 tablespoons butter, melted	4 (4-ounce / 113-g) catfish fillets
2 teaspoons Worcestershire sauce, divided	Cooking spray
1 teaspoon lemon pepper	½ cup sour cream
1 cup panko bread crumbs	1 tablespoon Dijon mustard

1. In a shallow bowl, stir together the melted butter, 1 teaspoon of Worcestershire sauce, and the lemon pepper. Place the bread crumbs in another shallow bowl. 2. One at a time, dip both sides of the fillets in the butter mixture, then the bread crumbs, coating thoroughly. 3. Preheat the air fryer to 300°F (149°C). Line the air fryer basket with parchment paper. 4. Place the coated fish on the parchment and spritz with oil. 5. Bake for 4 minutes. Flip the fish, spritz it with oil, and bake for 3 to 6 minutes more, depending on the thickness of the fillets, until the fish flakes easily with a fork. 6. In a small bowl, stir together the sour cream, Dijon, and remaining 1 teaspoon of Worcestershire sauce. This sauce can be made 1 day in advance and refrigerated before serving. Serve with the fried fish.

Asian Swordfish

Prep time: 10 minutes | Cook time: 6 to 11 minutes |
Serves 4

4 (4-ounce / 113-g) swordfish steaks	½ teaspoon Chinese five-spice powder
½ teaspoon toasted sesame oil	⅛ teaspoon freshly ground black pepper
1 jalapeño pepper, finely minced	2 tablespoons freshly squeezed lemon juice
2 garlic cloves, grated	
1 tablespoon grated fresh ginger	

1. Place the swordfish steaks on a work surface and drizzle with the sesame oil. 2. In a small bowl, mix the jalapeño, garlic, ginger, five-spice powder, pepper, and lemon juice. Rub this mixture into the fish and let it stand for 10 minutes. 3. Roast the swordfish in the air fryer at 380°F (193°C) for 6 to 11 minutes, or until the swordfish reaches an internal temperature of at least 140°F (60°C) on a meat thermometer. Serve immediately.

Baked Salmon with Tomatoes and Olives

Prep time: 5 minutes | Cook time: 8 minutes | Serves 4

2 tablespoons olive oil	1 teaspoon chopped fresh dill
4 (1½-inch-thick) salmon fillets	2 Roma tomatoes, diced
½ teaspoon salt	¼ cup sliced Kalamata olives
¼ teaspoon cayenne	4 lemon slices

1. Preheat the air fryer to 380°F(193°C). 2. Brush the olive oil on both sides of the salmon fillets, and then season them lightly with salt, cayenne, and dill. 3. Place the fillets in a single layer in the basket of the air fryer, then layer the tomatoes and olives over the top. Top each fillet with a lemon slice. 4. Bake for 8 minutes, or until the salmon has reached an internal temperature of 145°F(63°C).

Salmon with Cauliflower

Prep time: 10 minutes | Cook time: 25 minutes | Serves 4

1 pound (454 g) salmon fillet, diced	1 tablespoon coconut oil, melted
1 cup cauliflower, shredded	1 teaspoon ground turmeric
1 tablespoon dried cilantro	¼ cup coconut cream

1. Mix salmon with cauliflower, dried cilantro, ground turmeric, coconut cream, and coconut oil. 2. Transfer the salmon mixture into the air fryer and cook the meal at 350ºF (177ºC) for 25 minutes. Stir the meal every 5 minutes to avoid the burning.

Mouthwatering Cod over Creamy Leek Noodles

Prep time: 10 minutes | Cook time: 24 minutes | Serves 4

1 small leek, sliced into long thin noodles (about 2 cups)	Coating:
½ cup heavy cream	¼ cup grated Parmesan cheese
2 cloves garlic, minced	2 tablespoons mayonnaise
1 teaspoon fine sea salt, divided	2 tablespoons unsalted butter, softened
4 (4-ounce / 113-g) cod fillets (about 1 inch thick)	1 tablespoon chopped fresh thyme, or ½ teaspoon dried
½ teaspoon ground black pepper	thyme leaves, plus more for garnish

1. Preheat the air fryer to 350ºF (177ºC). 2. Place the leek noodles in a casserole dish or a pan that will fit in your air fryer. 3. In a small bowl, stir together the cream, garlic, and ½ teaspoon of the salt. Pour the mixture over the leeks and cook in the air fryer for 10 minutes, or until the leeks are very tender. 4. Pat the fish dry and season with the remaining ½ teaspoon of salt and the pepper. When the leeks are ready, open the air fryer and place the fish fillets on top of the leeks. Air fry for 8 to 10 minutes, until the fish flakes easily with a fork (the thicker the fillets, the longer this will take). 5. While the fish cooks, make the coating: In a small bowl, combine the Parmesan, mayo, butter, and thyme. 6. When the fish is ready, remove it from the air fryer and increase the heat to 425ºF (218ºC) (or as high as your air fryer can go). Spread the fillets with a ½-inch-thick to ¾-inch-thick layer of the coating. 7. Place the fish back in the air fryer and air fry for 3 to 4 minutes, until the coating browns. 8. Garnish with fresh or dried thyme, if desired. Store leftovers in an airtight container in the refrigerator for up to 3 days. Reheat in a casserole dish in a preheated 350ºF (177ºC) air fryer for 6 minutes, or until heated through.

Cod Tacos with Mango Salsa

Prep time: 15 minutes | Cook time: 17 minutes | Serves 4

1 mango, peeled and diced	1 egg
1 small jalapeño pepper, diced	¾ cup cornstarch
½ red bell pepper, diced	¾ cup all-purpose flour
½ red onion, minced	½ teaspoon ground cumin
Pinch chopped fresh cilantro	¼ teaspoon chili powder
Juice of ½ lime	1 pound (454 g) cod, cut into 4
¼ teaspoon salt	pieces
¼ teaspoon ground black pepper	Olive oil spray
½ cup Mexican beer	4 corn tortillas, or flour tortillas, at room temperature

1. In a small bowl, stir together the mango, jalapeño, red bell pepper, red onion, cilantro, lime juice, salt, and pepper. Set aside. 2. In a medium bowl, whisk the beer and egg. 3. In another medium bowl, stir together the cornstarch, flour, cumin, and chili powder. 4. Insert the crisper plate into the basket and the basket into the unit. Preheat the unit by selecting AIR FRY, setting the temperature to 375ºF (191ºC), and setting the time to 3 minutes. Select START/ STOP to begin. 5. Dip the fish pieces into the egg mixture and in the flour mixture to coat completely. 6. Once the unit is preheated, place a parchment paper liner into the basket. Place the fish on the liner in a single layer. 7. Select AIR FRY, set the temperature to 375ºF (191ºC), and set the time to 17 minutes. Select START/ STOP to begin. 8. After about 9 minutes, spray the fish with olive oil. Reinsert the basket to resume cooking. 9. When the cooking is complete, the fish should be golden and crispy. Place the pieces in the tortillas, top with the mango salsa, and serve.

Almond-Crusted Fish

Prep time: 15 minutes | Cook time: 10 minutes | Serves 4

4 (4-ounce / 113-g) fish fillets	Salt and pepper, to taste
¾ cup bread crumbs	¾ cup flour
¼ cup sliced almonds, crushed	1 egg, beaten with 1 tablespoon
2 tablespoons lemon juice	water
⅛ teaspoon cayenne	Oil for misting or cooking spray

1. Split fish fillets lengthwise down the center to create 8 pieces. 2. Mix bread crumbs and almonds together and set aside. 3. Mix the lemon juice and cayenne together. Brush on all sides of fish. 4. Season fish to taste with salt and pepper. 5. Place the flour on a sheet of wax paper. 6. Roll fillets in flour, dip in egg wash, and roll in the crumb mixture. 7. Mist both sides of fish with oil or cooking spray. 8. Spray the air fryer basket and lay fillets inside. 9. Roast at 390ºF (199ºC) for 5 minutes, turn fish over, and cook for an additional 5 minutes or until fish is done and flakes easily.

Tandoori Shrimp

Prep time: 25 minutes | Cook time: 6 minutes |

Serves 4

1 pound (454 g) jumbo raw shrimp (21 to 25 count), peeled and deveined	1 teaspoon ground turmeric
	1 teaspoon garam masala
	1 teaspoon smoked paprika
1 tablespoon minced fresh ginger	1 teaspoon kosher salt
3 cloves garlic, minced	½ to 1 teaspoon cayenne pepper
¼ cup chopped fresh cilantro or parsley, plus more for garnish	2 tablespoons olive oil (for Paleo) or melted ghee
	2 teaspoons fresh lemon juice

1. In a large bowl, combine the shrimp, ginger, garlic, cilantro, turmeric, garam masala, paprika, salt, and cayenne. Toss well to coat. Add the oil or ghee and toss again. Marinate at room temperature for 15 minutes, or cover and refrigerate for up to 8 hours. 2. Place the shrimp in a single layer in the air fryer basket. Set the air fryer to 325ºF (163ºC) for 6 minutes. Transfer the shrimp to a serving platter. Cover and let the shrimp finish cooking in the residual heat, about 5 minutes. 3. Sprinkle the shrimp with the lemon juice and toss to coat. Garnish with additional cilantro and serve.

Roasted Cod with Lemon-Garlic Potatoes

Prep time: 10 minutes | Cook time: 28 minutes |

Serves 2

3 tablespoons unsalted butter, softened, divided	340-g), unpeeled, sliced ¼ inch thick
2 garlic cloves, minced	1 tablespoon minced fresh parsley, chives, or tarragon
1 lemon, grated to yield 2 teaspoons zest and sliced ¼ inch thick	2 (8-ounce / 227-g) skinless cod fillets, 1¼ inches thick
Salt and pepper, to taste	Vegetable oil spray
1 large russet potato (12 ounce /	

1. Preheat the air fryer to 400ºF (204ºC). 2. Make foil sling for air fryer basket by folding 1 long sheet of aluminum foil so it is 4 inches wide. Lay sheet of foil widthwise across basket, pressing foil into and up sides of basket. Fold excess foil as needed so that edges of foil are flush with top of basket. Lightly spray the foil and basket with vegetable oil spray. 3. Microwave 1 tablespoon butter, garlic, 1 teaspoon lemon zest, ¼ teaspoon salt, and ⅛ teaspoon pepper in a medium bowl, stirring once, until the butter is melted and the mixture is fragrant, about 30 seconds. Add the potato slices and toss to coat. Shingle the potato slices on sling in prepared basket to create 2 even layers. Air fry until potato slices are spotty brown and just tender, 16 to 18 minutes, using a sling to rotate potatoes halfway through cooking. 4. Combine the remaining 2 tablespoons butter, remaining 1 teaspoon lemon zest, and parsley in a small bowl. Pat the cod dry with paper towels and season with salt and pepper. Place the fillets, skinned-side down, on top of potato slices, spaced evenly apart. (Tuck thinner tail ends of fillets under themselves as needed to create uniform pieces.) Dot the fillets with the butter mixture and top with the lemon slices. Return the basket to the air fryer and air fry until the cod flakes apart when gently prodded with a paring knife and registers 140ºF (60ºC), 12 to 15 minutes, using a sling to rotate the potato slices and cod halfway through cooking. 5. Using a sling, carefully remove potatoes and cod from air fryer. Cut the potato slices into 2 portions between fillets using fish spatula. Slide spatula along underside of potato slices and transfer with cod to individual plates. Serve.

Firecracker Shrimp

Prep time: 10 minutes | Cook time: 7 minutes |

Serves 4

1 pound (454 g) medium shelled and deveined shrimp	2 tablespoons sriracha
	¼ teaspoon powdered erythritol
2 tablespoons salted butter, melted	¼ cup full-fat mayonnaise
½ teaspoon Old Bay seasoning	⅛ teaspoon ground black pepper
¼ teaspoon garlic powder	

1. In a large bowl, toss shrimp in butter, Old Bay seasoning, and garlic powder. Place shrimp into the air fryer basket. 2. Adjust the temperature to 400ºF (204ºC) and set the timer for 7 minutes. 3. Flip the shrimp halfway through the cooking time. Shrimp will be bright pink when fully cooked. 4. In another large bowl, mix sriracha, powdered erythritol, mayonnaise, and pepper. Toss shrimp in the spicy mixture and serve immediately.

Lime Lobster Tails

Prep time: 10 minutes | Cook time: 6 minutes |

Serves 4

4 lobster tails, peeled	½ teaspoon dried basil
2 tablespoons lime juice	½ teaspoon coconut oil, melted

1. Mix lobster tails with lime juice, dried basil, and coconut oil. 2. Put the lobster tails in the air fryer and cook at 380ºF (193ºC) for 6 minutes.

Tuna Casserole

Prep time: 15 minutes | Cook time: 15 minutes |
Serves 4

2 tablespoons salted butter	mayonnaise
¼ cup diced white onion	¼ teaspoon xanthan gum
¼ cup chopped white	½ teaspoon red pepper flakes
mushrooms	2 medium zucchini, spiralized
2 stalks celery, finely chopped	2 (5-ounce / 142-g) cans
½ cup heavy cream	albacore tuna
½ cup vegetable broth	1 ounce (28 g) pork rinds, finely
2 tablespoons full-fat	ground

1. In a large saucepan over medium heat, melt butter. Add onion, mushrooms, and celery and sauté until fragrant, about 3 to 5 minutes. 2. Pour in heavy cream, vegetable broth, mayonnaise, and xanthan gum. Reduce heat and continue cooking an additional 3 minutes, until the mixture begins to thicken. 3. Add red pepper flakes, zucchini, and tuna. Turn off heat and stir until zucchini noodles are coated. 4. Pour into a round baking dish. Top with ground pork rinds and cover the top of the dish with foil. Place into the air fryer basket. 5. Adjust the temperature to 370ºF (188ºC) and set the timer for 15 minutes. 6. When 3 minutes remain, remove the foil to brown the top of the casserole. Serve warm.

Orange-Mustard Glazed Salmon

Prep time: 10 minutes | Cook time: 10 minutes |
Serves 2

1 tablespoon orange marmalade	2 (8-ounce / 227 -g) skin-on
¼ teaspoon grated orange zest	salmon fillets, 1½ inches thick
plus 1 tablespoon juice	Salt and pepper, to taste
2 teaspoons whole-grain	Vegetable oil spray
mustard	

1. Preheat the air fryer to 400ºF (204ºC). 2. Make foil sling for air fryer basket by folding 1 long sheet of aluminum foil so it is 4 inches wide. Lay sheet of foil widthwise across basket, pressing foil into and up sides of basket. Fold excess foil as needed so that edges of foil are flush with top of basket. Lightly spray foil and basket with vegetable oil spray. 3. Combine marmalade, orange zest and juice, and mustard in bowl. Pat salmon dry with paper towels and season with salt and pepper. Brush tops and sides of fillets evenly with glaze. Arrange fillets skin side down on sling in prepared basket, spaced evenly apart. Air fry salmon until center is still translucent when checked with the tip of a paring knife and registers 125ºF (52ºC) (for medium-rare), 10 to 14 minutes, using sling to rotate fillets halfway through cooking. 4. Using the sling, carefully remove salmon from air fryer. Slide fish spatula along underside of fillets and transfer to individual serving plates, leaving skin behind. Serve.

Crab Cakes with Bell Peppers

Prep time: 5 minutes | Cook time: 10 minutes |
Serves 4

8 ounces (227 g) jumbo lump	¼ cup diced red bell pepper
crab meat	¼ cup mayonnaise
1 egg, beaten	1 tablespoon Old Bay seasoning
Juice of ½ lemon	1 teaspoon flour
⅓ cup bread crumbs	Cooking spray
¼ cup diced green bell pepper	

1. Preheat the air fryer to 375ºF (190ºC). 2. Make the crab cakes: Place all the ingredients except the flour and oil in a large bowl and stir until well incorporated. 3. Divide the crab mixture into four equal portions and shape each portion into a patty with your hands. Top each patty with a sprinkle of ¼ teaspoon of flour. 4. Arrange the crab cakes in the air fryer basket and spritz them with cooking spray. 5. Air fry for 10 minutes, flipping the crab cakes halfway through, or until they are cooked through. 6. Divide the crab cakes among four plates and serve.

Marinated Salmon Fillets

Prep time: 10 minutes | Cook time: 15 to 20 minutes |
Serves 4

¼ cup soy sauce	½ teaspoon freshly ground
¼ cup rice wine vinegar	black pepper
1 tablespoon brown sugar	½ teaspoon minced garlic
1 tablespoon olive oil	4 (6-ounce / 170-g) salmon
1 teaspoon mustard powder	fillets, skin-on
1 teaspoon ground ginger	Cooking spray

1. In a small bowl, combine the soy sauce, rice wine vinegar, brown sugar, olive oil, mustard powder, ginger, black pepper, and garlic to make a marinade. 2. Place the fillets in a shallow baking dish and pour the marinade over them. Cover the baking dish and marinate for at least 1 hour in the refrigerator, turning the fillets occasionally to keep them coated in the marinade. 3. Preheat the air fryer to 370ºF (188ºC). Spray the air fryer basket lightly with cooking spray. 4. Shake off as much marinade as possible from the fillets and place them, skin-side down, in the air fryer basket in a single layer. You may need to cook the fillets in batches. 5. Air fry for 15 to 20 minutes for well done. The minimum internal temperature should be 145ºF (63ºC) at the thickest part of the fillets. 6. Serve hot.

Crab Cakes with Sriracha Mayonnaise

Prep time: 15 minutes | Cook time: 10 minutes |

Serves 4

Sriracha Mayonnaise:	¼ cup diced celery
1 cup mayonnaise	1 pound (454 g) lump crab meat
1 tablespoon sriracha	1 teaspoon Old Bay seasoning
1½ teaspoons freshly squeezed	1 egg
lemon juice	1½ teaspoons freshly squeezed
Crab Cakes:	lemon juice
1 teaspoon extra-virgin olive oil	1¾ cups panko bread crumbs,
¼ cup finely diced red bell	divided
pepper	Vegetable oil, for spraying
¼ cup diced onion	

1. Mix the mayonnaise, sriracha, and lemon juice in a small bowl. Place ⅔ cup of the mixture in a separate bowl to form the base of the crab cakes. Cover the remaining sriracha mayonnaise and refrigerate. (This will become dipping sauce for the crab cakes once they are cooked.) 2. Heat the olive oil in a heavy-bottomed, medium skillet over medium-high heat. Add the bell pepper, onion, and celery and sauté for 3 minutes. Transfer the vegetables to the bowl with the reserved ⅔ cup of sriracha mayonnaise. Mix in the crab, Old Bay seasoning, egg, and lemon juice. Add 1 cup of the panko. Form the crab mixture into 8 cakes. Dredge the cakes in the remaining ¾ cup of panko, turning to coat. Place on a baking sheet. Cover and refrigerate for at least 1 hour and up to 8 hours. 3. Preheat the air fryer to 375ºF (191ºC). Spray the air fryer basket with oil. Working in batches as needed so as not to overcrowd the basket, place the chilled crab cakes in a single layer in the basket. Spray the crab cakes with oil. Bake until golden brown, 8 to 10 minutes, carefully turning halfway through cooking. Remove to a platter and keep warm. Repeat with the remaining crab cakes as needed. Serve the crab cakes immediately with sriracha mayonnaise dipping sauce.

New Orleans-Style Crab Cakes

Prep time: 10 minutes | Cook time: 8 to 10 minutes |

Serves 4

1¼ cups bread crumbs	1½ cups crab meat
2 teaspoons Creole Seasoning	2 large eggs, beaten
1 teaspoon dry mustard	1 teaspoon butter, melted
1 teaspoon salt	⅓ cup minced onion
1 teaspoon freshly ground black	Cooking spray
pepper	Pecan Tartar Sauce, for serving

1. Preheat the air fryer to 350ºF (177ºC). Line the air fryer basket with parchment paper. 2. In a medium bowl, whisk the bread crumbs, Creole Seasoning, dry mustard, salt, and pepper until blended. Add the crab meat, eggs, butter, and onion. Stir until blended. Shape the crab mixture into 8 patties. 3. Place the crab cakes on the parchment and spritz with oil. 4. Air fry for 4 minutes. Flip the cakes, spritz them with oil, and air fry for 4 to 6 minutes more until the outsides are firm and a fork inserted into the center comes out clean. Serve with the Pecan Tartar Sauce.

Almond Pesto Salmon

Prep time: 5 minutes | Cook time: 12 minutes |

Serves 2

¼ cup pesto	(about 4 ounces / 113 g each)
¼ cup sliced almonds, roughly	2 tablespoons unsalted butter,
chopped	melted
2 (1½-inch-thick) salmon fillets	

1. In a small bowl, mix pesto and almonds. Set aside. 2. Place fillets into a round baking dish. 3. Brush each fillet with butter and place half of the pesto mixture on the top of each fillet. Place dish into the air fryer basket. 4. Adjust the temperature to 390ºF (199ºC) and set the timer for 12 minutes. 5. Salmon will easily flake when fully cooked and reach an internal temperature of at least 145ºF (63ºC). Serve warm.

Crawfish Creole Casserole

Prep time: 20 minutes | Cook time: 25 minutes |

Serves 4

1½ cups crawfish meat	1 tablespoon cornstarch
½ cup chopped celery	1 teaspoon Creole seasoning
½ cup chopped onion	¾ teaspoon salt
½ cup chopped green bell	½ teaspoon freshly ground
pepper	black pepper
2 large eggs, beaten	1 cup shredded Cheddar cheese
1 cup half-and-half	Cooking spray
1 tablespoon butter, melted	

1. In a medium bowl, stir together the crawfish, celery, onion, and green pepper. 2. In another medium bowl, whisk the eggs, half-and-half, butter, cornstarch, Creole seasoning, salt, and pepper until blended. Stir the egg mixture into the crawfish mixture. Add the cheese and stir to combine. 3. Preheat the air fryer to 300ºF (149ºC). Spritz a baking pan with oil. 4. Transfer the crawfish mixture to the prepared pan and place it in the air fryer basket. 5. Bake for 25 minutes, stirring every 10 minutes, until a knife inserted into the center comes out clean. 6. Serve immediately.

Cod with Jalapeño

Prep time: 5 minutes | Cook time: 14 minutes | Serves 4

4 cod fillets, boneless

1 jalapeño, minced

1 tablespoon avocado oil

½ teaspoon minced garlic

1. In the shallow bowl, mix minced jalapeño, avocado oil, and minced garlic. 2. Put the cod fillets in the air fryer basket in one layer and top with minced jalapeño mixture. 3. Cook the fish at 365°F (185°C) for 7 minutes per side.

South Indian Fried Fish

Prep time: 20 minutes | Cook time: 8 minutes | Serves 4

2 tablespoons olive oil

2 tablespoons fresh lime or lemon juice

1 teaspoon minced fresh ginger

1 clove garlic, minced

1 teaspoon ground turmeric

½ teaspoon kosher salt

¼ to ½ teaspoon cayenne pepper

1 pound (454 g) tilapia fillets (2 to 3 fillets)

Olive oil spray

Lime or lemon wedges (optional)

1. In a large bowl, combine the oil, lime juice, ginger, garlic, turmeric, salt, and cayenne. Stir until well combined; set aside. 2. Cut each tilapia fillet into three or four equal-size pieces. Add the fish to the bowl and gently mix until all of the fish is coated in the marinade. Marinate for 10 to 15 minutes at room temperature. (Don't marinate any longer or the acid in the lime juice will "cook" the fish.) 3. Spray the air fryer basket with olive oil spray. Place the fish in the basket and spray the fish. Set the air fryer to 325°F (163°C) for 3 minutes to partially cook the fish. Set the air fryer to 400°F (204°C) for 5 minutes to finish cooking and crisp up the fish. (Thinner pieces of fish will cook faster so you may want to check at the 3-minute mark of the second cooking time and remove those that are cooked through, and then add them back toward the end of the second cooking time to crisp.) 4. Carefully remove the fish from the basket. Serve hot, with lemon wedges if desired.

Chili Lime Shrimp

Prep time: 5 minutes | Cook time: 5 minutes | Serves 4

1 pound (454 g) medium shrimp, peeled and deveined

1 tablespoon salted butter, melted

2 teaspoons chili powder

¼ teaspoon garlic powder

¼ teaspoon salt

¼ teaspoon ground black pepper

½ small lime, zested and juiced, divided

1. In a medium bowl, toss shrimp with butter, then sprinkle with chili powder, garlic powder, salt, pepper, and lime zest. 2. Place shrimp into ungreased air fryer basket. Adjust the temperature to 400°F (204°C) and air fry for 5 minutes. Shrimp will be firm and form a "C" shape when done. 3. Transfer shrimp to a large serving dish and drizzle with lime juice. Serve warm.

Chapter 7 Snacks and Appetizers

Sweet Potato Fries with Mayonnaise

Prep time: 5 minutes | Cook time: 20 minutes |
Serves 2 to 3

1 large sweet potato (about 1 pound / 454 g), scrubbed
1 teaspoon vegetable or canola oil
Salt, to taste
Dipping Sauce:

¼ cup light mayonnaise
½ teaspoon sriracha sauce
1 tablespoon spicy brown mustard
1 tablespoon sweet Thai chili sauce

1. Preheat the air fryer to 200ºF (93ºC). 2. On a flat work surface, cut the sweet potato into fry-shaped strips about ¼ inch wide and ¼ inch thick. You can use a mandoline to slice the sweet potato quickly and uniformly. 3. In a medium bowl, drizzle the sweet potato strips with the oil and toss well. 4. Transfer to the air fryer basket and air fry for 10 minutes, shaking the basket twice during cooking. 5. Remove the air fryer basket and sprinkle with the salt and toss to coat. 6. Increase the air fryer temperature to 400ºF (204ºC) and air fry for an additional 10 minutes, or until the fries are crispy and tender. Shake the basket a few times during cooking. 7. Meanwhile, whisk together all the ingredients for the sauce in a small bowl. 8. Remove the sweet potato fries from the basket to a plate and serve warm alongside the dipping sauce.

String Bean Fries

Prep time: 15 minutes | Cook time: 5 to 6 minutes |
Serves 4

½ pound (227 g) fresh string beans
2 eggs
4 teaspoons water
½ cup white flour
½ cup bread crumbs

¼ teaspoon salt
¼ teaspoon ground black pepper
¼ teaspoon dry mustard (optional)
Oil for misting or cooking spray

1. Preheat the air fryer to 360ºF (182ºC). 2. Trim stem ends from string beans, wash, and pat dry. 3. In a shallow dish, beat eggs and water together until well blended. 4. Place flour in a second shallow dish. 5. In a third shallow dish, stir together the bread crumbs, salt, pepper, and dry mustard if using. 6. Dip each string bean in egg mixture, flour, egg mixture again, then bread crumbs. 7. When you finish coating all the string beans, open air fryer and place them in basket. 8. Cook for 3 minutes. 9. Stop and mist string beans with oil or cooking spray. 10. Cook for 2 to 3 more minutes or until string beans are crispy and nicely browned.

Beef and Mango Skewers

Prep time: 10 minutes | Cook time: 4 to 7 minutes |
Serves 4

¾ pound (340 g) beef sirloin tip, cut into 1-inch cubes
2 tablespoons balsamic vinegar
1 tablespoon olive oil
1 tablespoon honey

½ teaspoon dried marjoram
Pinch of salt
Freshly ground black pepper, to taste
1 mango

1. Preheat the air fryer to 390ºF (199ºC). 2. Put the beef cubes in a medium bowl and add the balsamic vinegar, olive oil, honey, marjoram, salt, and pepper. Mix well, then massage the marinade into the beef with your hands. Set aside. 3. To prepare the mango, stand it on end and cut the skin off, using a sharp knife. Then carefully cut around the oval pit to remove the flesh. Cut the mango into 1-inch cubes. 4. Thread metal skewers alternating with three beef cubes and two mango cubes. 5. Roast the skewers in the air fryer basket for 4 to 7 minutes, or until the beef is browned and at least 145ºF (63ºC). 6. Serve hot.

Sweet Bacon Tater Tots

Prep time: 5 minutes | Cook time: 7 minutes | Serves 4

24 frozen tater tots
6 slices cooked bacon

2 tablespoons maple syrup
1 cup shredded Cheddar cheese

1. Preheat the air fryer to 400ºF (204ºC). 2. Put the tater tots in the air fryer basket. Air fry for 10 minutes, shaking the basket halfway through the cooking time. 3. Meanwhile, cut the bacon into 1-inch pieces. 4. Remove the tater tots from the air fryer basket and put into a baking pan. Top with the bacon and drizzle with the maple syrup. Air fry for 5 minutes, or until the tots and bacon are crisp. 5. Top with the cheese and air fry for 2 minutes, or until the cheese is melted. 6. Serve hot.

Black Bean Corn Dip

Prep time: 10 minutes | Cook time: 10 minutes |

Serves 4

½ (15-ounce / 425-g) can black beans, drained and rinsed
½ (15-ounce / 425-g) can corn, drained and rinsed
¼ cup chunky salsa
2 ounces (57 g) reduced-fat cream cheese, softened

¼ cup shredded reduced-fat Cheddar cheese
½ teaspoon ground cumin
½ teaspoon paprika
Salt and freshly ground black pepper, to taste

1. Preheat the air fryer to 325ºF (163ºC). 2. In a medium bowl, mix together the black beans, corn, salsa, cream cheese, Cheddar cheese, cumin, and paprika. Season with salt and pepper and stir until well combined. 3. Spoon the mixture into a baking dish. 4. Place baking dish in the air fryer basket and bake until heated through, about 10 minutes. 5. Serve hot.

Garlic-Roasted Tomatoes and Olives

Prep time: 5 minutes | Cook time: 20 minutes |

Serves 6

2 cups cherry tomatoes
4 garlic cloves, roughly chopped
½ red onion, roughly chopped
1 cup black olives
1 cup green olives

1 tablespoon fresh basil, minced
1 tablespoon fresh oregano, minced
2 tablespoons olive oil
¼ to ½ teaspoon salt

1. Preheat the air fryer to 380°F(193ºC). 2. In a large bowl, combine all of the ingredients and toss together so that the tomatoes and olives are coated well with the olive oil and herbs. 3. Pour the mixture into the air fryer basket, and roast for 10 minutes. Stir the mixture well, then continue roasting for an additional 10 minutes. 4. Remove from the air fryer, transfer to a serving bowl, and enjoy.

Skinny Fries

Prep time: 10 minutes | Cook time: 15 minutes per

batch | Serves 2

2 to 3 russet potatoes, peeled and cut into ¼-inch sticks
2 to 3 teaspoons olive or

vegetable oil
Salt, to taste

1. Cut the potatoes into ¼-inch strips. (A mandolin with a julienne blade is really helpful here.) Rinse the potatoes with cold water several times and let them soak in cold water for at least 10 minutes or as long as overnight. 2. Preheat the air fryer to 380ºF (193ºC). 3. Drain and dry the potato sticks really well, using a clean kitchen towel. Toss the fries with the oil in a bowl and then air fry the fries in two batches at 380ºF (193ºC) for 15 minutes, shaking the basket a couple of times while they cook. 4. Add the first batch of French fries back into the air fryer basket with the finishing batch and let everything warm through for a few minutes. As soon as the fries are done, season them with salt and transfer to a plate or basket. Serve them warm with ketchup or your favorite dip.

Bruschetta with Basil Pesto

Prep time: 10 minutes | Cook time: 5 to 11 minutes |

Serves 4

8 slices French bread, ½ inch thick
2 tablespoons softened butter
1 cup shredded Mozzarella

cheese
½ cup basil pesto
1 cup chopped grape tomatoes
2 green onions, thinly sliced

1. Preheat the air fryer to 350ºF (177ºC). 2. Spread the bread with the butter and place butter-side up in the air fryer basket. Bake for 3 to 5 minutes, or until the bread is light golden brown. 3. Remove the bread from the basket and top each piece with some of the cheese. Return to the basket in 2 batches and bake for 1 to 3 minutes, or until the cheese melts. 4. Meanwhile, combine the pesto, tomatoes, and green onions in a small bowl. 5. When the cheese has melted, remove the bread from the air fryer and place on a serving plate. Top each slice with some of the pesto mixture and serve.

Bacon-Wrapped Shrimp and Jalapeño

Prep time: 20 minutes | Cook time: 26 minutes |

Serves 8

24 large shrimp, peeled and deveined, about ¾ pound (340 g)
5 tablespoons barbecue sauce,

divided
12 strips bacon, cut in half
24 small pickled jalapeño slices

1. Toss together the shrimp and 3 tablespoons of the barbecue sauce. Let stand for 15 minutes. Soak 24 wooden toothpicks in water for 10 minutes. Wrap 1 piece bacon around the shrimp and jalapeño slice, then secure with a toothpick. 2. Preheat the air fryer to 350ºF (177ºC). 3. Working in batches, place half of the shrimp in the air fryer basket, spacing them ½ inch apart. Air fry for 10 minutes. Turn shrimp over with tongs and air fry for 3 minutes more, or until bacon is golden brown and shrimp are cooked through. 4. Brush with the remaining barbecue sauce and serve.

Kale Chips with Sesame

Prep time: 15 minutes | Cook time: 8 minutes | Serves 5

8 cups deribbed kale leaves, torn into 2-inch pieces
1½ tablespoons olive oil
¾ teaspoon chili powder

¼ teaspoon garlic powder
½ teaspoon paprika
2 teaspoons sesame seeds

1. Preheat air fryer to 350ºF (177ºC). 2. In a large bowl, toss the kale with the olive oil, chili powder, garlic powder, paprika, and sesame seeds until well coated. 3. Put the kale in the air fryer basket and air fry for 8 minutes, flipping the kale twice during cooking, or until the kale is crispy. 4. Serve warm.

Kale Chips with Tex-Mex Dip

Prep time: 10 minutes | Cook time: 5 to 6 minutes | Serves 8

1 cup Greek yogurt
1 tablespoon chili powder
⅓ cup low-sodium salsa, well drained

1 bunch curly kale
1 teaspoon olive oil
¼ teaspoon coarse sea salt

1. In a small bowl, combine the yogurt, chili powder, and drained salsa; refrigerate. 2. Rinse the kale thoroughly, and pat dry. Remove the stems and ribs from the kale, using a sharp knife. Cut or tear the leaves into 3-inch pieces. 3. Toss the kale with the olive oil in a large bowl. 4. Air fry the kale in small batches at 390ºF (199ºC) until the leaves are crisp. This should take 5 to 6 minutes. Shake the basket once during cooking time. 5. As you remove the kale chips, sprinkle them with a bit of the sea salt. 6. When all of the kale chips are done, serve with the dip.

Onion Pakoras

Prep time: 30 minutes | Cook time: 10 minutes per batch | Serves 2

2 medium yellow or white onions, sliced (2 cups)
½ cup chopped fresh cilantro
2 tablespoons vegetable oil
1 tablespoon chickpea flour
1 tablespoon rice flour, or 2

tablespoons chickpea flour
1 teaspoon ground turmeric
1 teaspoon cumin seeds
1 teaspoon kosher salt
½ teaspoon cayenne pepper
Vegetable oil spray

1. In a large bowl, combine the onions, cilantro, oil, chickpea flour, rice flour, turmeric, cumin seeds, salt, and cayenne. Stir to combine.

Cover and let stand for 30 minutes or up to overnight. (This allows the onions to release moisture, creating a batter.) Mix well before using. 2. Spray the air fryer basket generously with vegetable oil spray. Drop half of the batter in 6 heaping tablespoons into the basket. Set the air fryer to 350ºF (177ºC) for 8 minutes. Carefully turn the pakoras over and spray with oil spray. Set the air fryer for 2 minutes, or until the batter is cooked through and crisp. 3. Repeat with remaining batter to make 6 more pakoras, checking at 6 minutes for doneness. Serve hot.

Lemon Shrimp with Garlic Olive Oil

Prep time: 5 minutes | Cook time: 6 minutes | Serves 4

1 pound (454 g) medium shrimp, cleaned and deveined
¼ cup plus 2 tablespoons olive oil, divided
Juice of ½ lemon
3 garlic cloves, minced and divided

½ teaspoon salt
¼ teaspoon red pepper flakes
Lemon wedges, for serving (optional)
Marinara sauce, for dipping (optional)

1. Preheat the air fryer to 380ºF(193ºC). 2. In a large bowl, combine the shrimp with 2 tablespoons of the olive oil, as well as the lemon juice, ⅓ of the minced garlic, salt, and red pepper flakes. Toss to coat the shrimp well. 3. In a small ramekin, combine the remaining ¼ cup of olive oil and the remaining minced garlic. 4. Tear off a 12-by-12-inch sheet of aluminum foil. Pour the shrimp into the center of the foil, then fold the sides up and crimp the edges so that it forms an aluminum foil bowl that is open on top. Place this packet into the air fryer basket. 5. Roast the shrimp for 4 minutes, then open the air fryer and place the ramekin with oil and garlic in the basket beside the shrimp packet. Cook for 2 more minutes. 6. Transfer the shrimp on a serving plate or platter with the ramekin of garlic olive oil on the side for dipping. You may also serve with lemon wedges and marinara sauce, if desired.

Spiced Roasted Cashews

Prep time: 5 minutes | Cook time: 10 minutes | Serves 4

2 cups raw cashews
2 tablespoons olive oil
¼ teaspoon salt

¼ teaspoon chili powder
⅛ teaspoon garlic powder
⅛ teaspoon smoked paprika

1. Preheat the air fryer to 360ºF(182ºC). 2. In a large bowl, toss all of the ingredients together. 3. Pour the cashews into the air fryer basket and roast them for 5 minutes. Shake the basket, then cook for 5 minutes more. 4. Serve immediately.

Crispy Mozzarella Sticks

Prep time: 8 minutes | Cook time: 5 minutes | Serves 4

½ cup all-purpose flour

1 egg, beaten

½ cup panko bread crumbs

½ cup grated Parmesan cheese

1 teaspoon Italian seasoning

½ teaspoon garlic salt

6 Mozzarella sticks, halved crosswise

Olive oil spray

1. Put the flour in a small bowl. 2. Put the beaten egg in another small bowl. 3. In a medium bowl, stir together the panko, Parmesan cheese, Italian seasoning, and garlic salt. 4. Roll a Mozzarella-stick half in the flour, dip it into the egg, and then roll it in the panko mixture to coat. Press the coating lightly to make sure the bread crumbs stick to the cheese. Repeat with the remaining 11 Mozzarella sticks. 5. Insert the crisper plate into the basket and the basket into the unit. Preheat the unit by selecting AIR FRY, setting the temperature to 400ºF (204ºC), and setting the time to 3 minutes. Select START/STOP to begin. 6. Once the unit is preheated, spray the crisper plate with olive oil and place a parchment paper liner in the basket. Place the Mozzarella sticks into the basket and lightly spray them with olive oil. 7. Select AIR FRY, set the temperature to 400ºF (204ºC), and set the time to 5 minutes. Select START/STOP to begin. 8. When the cooking is complete, the Mozzarella sticks should be golden and crispy. Let the sticks stand for 1 minute before transferring them to a serving plate. Serve warm.

Asian Rice Logs

Prep time: 30 minutes | Cook time: 5 minutes | Makes 8 rice logs

1½ cups cooked jasmine or sushi rice

¼ teaspoon salt

2 teaspoons five-spice powder

2 teaspoons diced shallots

1 tablespoon tamari sauce

1 egg, beaten

1 teaspoon sesame oil

2 teaspoons water

⅓ cup plain bread crumbs

¾ cup panko bread crumbs

2 tablespoons sesame seeds

Orange Marmalade Dipping Sauce:

½ cup all-natural orange marmalade

1 tablespoon soy sauce

1. Make the rice according to package instructions. While the rice is cooking, make the dipping sauce by combining the marmalade and soy sauce and set aside. 2. Stir together the cooked rice, salt, five-spice powder, shallots, and tamari sauce. 3. Divide rice into 8 equal pieces. With slightly damp hands, mold each piece into a log shape. Chill in freezer for 10 to 15 minutes. 4. Mix the egg, sesame oil, and water together in a shallow bowl. 5. Place the plain bread crumbs on a sheet of wax paper. 6. Mix the panko bread crumbs with the sesame seeds and place on another sheet of wax paper. 7.

Roll the rice logs in plain bread crumbs, then dip in egg wash, and then dip in the panko and sesame seeds. 8. Cook the logs at 390ºF (199ºC) for approximately 5 minutes, until golden brown. 9. Cool slightly before serving with Orange Marmalade Dipping Sauce.

Apple Wedges

Prep time: 10 minutes | Cook time: 8 to 9 minutes | Serves 4

¼ cup panko bread crumbs

¼ cup pecans

1½ teaspoons cinnamon

1½ teaspoons brown sugar

¼ cup cornstarch

1 egg white

2 teaspoons water

1 medium apple

Oil for misting or cooking spray

1. In a food processor, combine panko, pecans, cinnamon, and brown sugar. Process to make small crumbs. 2. Place cornstarch in a plastic bag or bowl with lid. In a shallow dish, beat together the egg white and water until slightly foamy. 3. Preheat the air fryer to 390ºF (199ºC). 4. Cut apple into small wedges. The thickest edge should be no more than ⅜- to ½-inch thick. Cut away the core, but do not peel. 5. Place apple wedges in cornstarch, reseal bag or bowl, and shake to coat. 6. Dip wedges in egg wash, shake off excess, and roll in crumb mixture. Spray with oil. 7. Place apples in air fryer basket in single layer and cook for 5 minutes. Shake basket and break apart any apples that have stuck together. Mist lightly with oil and cook 3 to 4 minutes longer, until crispy.

Roasted Pearl Onion Dip

Prep time: 5 minutes | Cook time: 12 minutes | Serves 4

2 cups peeled pearl onions

3 garlic cloves

3 tablespoons olive oil, divided

½ teaspoon salt

1 cup nonfat plain Greek yogurt

1 tablespoon lemon juice

¼ teaspoon black pepper

⅛ teaspoon red pepper flakes

Pita chips, vegetables, or toasted bread for serving (optional)

1. Preheat the air fryer to 360°F(182ºC). 2. In a large bowl, combine the pearl onions and garlic with 2 tablespoons of the olive oil until the onions are well coated. 3. Pour the garlic-and-onion mixture into the air fryer basket and roast for 12 minutes. 4. Transfer the garlic and onions to a food processor. Pulse the vegetables several times, until the onions are minced but still have some chunks. 5. In a large bowl, combine the garlic and onions and the remaining 1 tablespoon of olive oil, along with the salt, yogurt, lemon juice, black pepper, and red pepper flakes. 6. Cover and chill for 1 hour before serving with pita chips, vegetables, or toasted bread.

Shrimp Toasts with Sesame Seeds

Prep time: 15 minutes | Cook time: 6 to 8 minutes | Serves 4 to 6

½ pound (227 g) raw shrimp, peeled and deveined
1 egg, beaten
2 scallions, chopped, plus more for garnish
2 tablespoons chopped fresh cilantro
2 teaspoons grated fresh ginger

1 to 2 teaspoons sriracha sauce
1 teaspoon soy sauce
½ teaspoon toasted sesame oil
6 slices thinly sliced white sandwich bread
½ cup sesame seeds
Cooking spray
Thai chili sauce, for serving

1. Preheat the air fryer to 400°F (204°C). Spritz the air fryer basket with cooking spray. 2. In a food processor, add the shrimp, egg, scallions, cilantro, ginger, sriracha sauce, soy sauce and sesame oil, and pulse until chopped finely. You'll need to stop the food processor occasionally to scrape down the sides. Transfer the shrimp mixture to a bowl. 3. On a clean work surface, cut the crusts off the sandwich bread. Using a brush, generously brush one side of each slice of bread with shrimp mixture. 4. Place the sesame seeds on a plate. Press bread slices, shrimp-side down, into sesame seeds to coat evenly. Cut each slice diagonally into quarters. 5. Spread the coated slices in a single layer in the air fryer basket. 6. Air fry in batches for 6 to 8 minutes, or until golden and crispy. Flip the bread slices halfway through. Repeat with the remaining bread slices. 7. Transfer to a plate and let cool for 5 minutes. Top with the chopped scallions and serve warm with Thai chili sauce.

Garlic Edamame

Prep time: 5 minutes | Cook time: 10 minutes | Serves 4

Olive oil
1 (16-ounce / 454-g) bag frozen edamame in pods
½ teaspoon salt
½ teaspoon garlic salt

¼ teaspoon freshly ground black pepper
½ teaspoon red pepper flakes (optional)

1. Spray the air fryer basket lightly with olive oil. 2. In a medium bowl, add the frozen edamame and lightly spray with olive oil. Toss to coat. 3. In a small bowl, mix together the salt, garlic salt, black pepper, and red pepper flakes (if using). Add the mixture to the edamame and toss until evenly coated. 4. Place half the edamame in the air fryer basket. Do not overfill the basket. 5. Air fry at 375°F (191°C) for 5 minutes. Shake the basket and cook until the edamame is starting to brown and get crispy, 3 to 5 more minutes. 6. Repeat with the remaining edamame and serve immediately.

Cheesy Steak Fries

Prep time: 5 minutes | Cook time: 20 minutes | Serves 5

1 (28-ounce / 794-g) bag frozen steak fries
Cooking spray
Salt and pepper, to taste
½ cup beef gravy

1 cup shredded Mozzarella cheese
2 scallions, green parts only, chopped

1. Preheat the air fryer to 400°F (204°C). 2. Place the frozen steak fries in the air fryer. Air fry for 10 minutes. Shake the basket and spritz the fries with cooking spray. Sprinkle with salt and pepper. Air fry for an additional 8 minutes. 3. Pour the beef gravy into a medium, microwave-safe bowl. Microwave for 30 seconds, or until the gravy is warm. 4. Sprinkle the fries with the cheese. Air fry for an additional 2 minutes, until the cheese is melted. 5. Transfer the fries to a serving dish. Drizzle the fries with gravy and sprinkle the scallions on top for a green garnish. Serve.

Pepperoni Pizza Dip

Prep time: 10 minutes | Cook time: 10 minutes | Serves 6

6 ounces (170 g) cream cheese, softened
¾ cup shredded Italian cheese blend
¼ cup sour cream
1½ teaspoons dried Italian seasoning
¼ teaspoon garlic salt
¼ teaspoon onion powder

¾ cup pizza sauce
½ cup sliced miniature pepperoni
¼ cup sliced black olives
1 tablespoon thinly sliced green onion
Cut-up raw vegetables, toasted baguette slices, pita chips, or tortilla chips, for serving

1. In a small bowl, combine the cream cheese, ¼ cup of the shredded cheese, the sour cream, Italian seasoning, garlic salt, and onion powder. Stir until smooth and the ingredients are well blended. 2. Spread the mixture in a baking pan. Top with the pizza sauce, spreading to the edges. Sprinkle with the remaining ½ cup shredded cheese. Arrange the pepperoni slices on top of the cheese. Top with the black olives and green onion. 3. Place the pan in the air fryer basket. Set the air fryer to 350°F (177°C) for 10 minutes, or until the pepperoni is beginning to brown on the edges and the cheese is bubbly and lightly browned. 4. Let stand for 5 minutes before serving with vegetables, toasted baguette slices, pita chips, or tortilla chips.

Spicy Tortilla Chips

Prep time: 5 minutes | Cook time: 8 to 12 minutes | Serves 4

½ teaspoon ground cumin
½ teaspoon paprika
½ teaspoon chili powder
½ teaspoon salt

Pinch cayenne pepper
8 (6-inch) corn tortillas, each cut into 6 wedges
Cooking spray

1. Preheat the air fryer to 375ºF (191ºC). Lightly spritz the air fryer basket with cooking spray. 2. Stir together the cumin, paprika, chili powder, salt, and pepper in a small bowl. 3. Working in batches, arrange the tortilla wedges in the air fryer basket in a single layer. Lightly mist them with cooking spray. Sprinkle some seasoning mixture on top of the tortilla wedges. 4. Air fry for 4 to 6 minutes, shaking the basket halfway through, or until the chips are lightly browned and crunchy. 5. Repeat with the remaining tortilla wedges and seasoning mixture. 6. Let the tortilla chips cool for 5 minutes and serve.

Artichoke and Olive Pita Flatbread

Prep time: 5 minutes | Cook time: 10 minutes | Serves 4

2 whole wheat pitas
2 tablespoons olive oil, divided
2 garlic cloves, minced
¼ teaspoon salt
½ cup canned artichoke hearts, sliced

¼ cup Kalamata olives
¼ cup shredded Parmesan
¼ cup crumbled feta
Chopped fresh parsley, for garnish (optional)

1. Preheat the air fryer to 380°F(193ºC). 2. Brush each pita with 1 tablespoon olive oil, then sprinkle the minced garlic and salt over the top. 3. Distribute the artichoke hearts, olives, and cheeses evenly between the two pitas, and place both into the air fryer to bake for 10 minutes. 4. Remove the pitas and cut them into 4 pieces each before serving. Sprinkle parsley over the top, if desired.

Greens Chips with Curried Yogurt Sauce

Prep time: 10 minutes | Cook time: 5 to 6 minutes | Serves 4

1 cup low-fat Greek yogurt
1 tablespoon freshly squeezed lemon juice
1 tablespoon curry powder

½ bunch curly kale, stemmed, ribs removed and discarded, leaves cut into 2- to 3-inch pieces

½ bunch chard, stemmed, ribs removed and discarded, leaves

cut into 2- to 3-inch pieces
1½ teaspoons olive oil

1. In a small bowl, stir together the yogurt, lemon juice, and curry powder. Set aside. 2. In a large bowl, toss the kale and chard with the olive oil, working the oil into the leaves with your hands. This helps break up the fibers in the leaves so the chips are tender. 3. Air fry the greens in batches at 390ºF (199ºC) for 5 to 6 minutes, until crisp, shaking the basket once during cooking. Serve with the yogurt sauce.

Tangy Fried Pickle Spears

Prep time: 5 minutes | Cook time: 15 minutes | Serves 6

2 jars sweet and sour pickle spears, patted dry
2 medium-sized eggs
⅓ cup milk
1 teaspoon garlic powder

1 teaspoon sea salt
½ teaspoon shallot powder
⅓ teaspoon chili powder
⅓ cup all-purpose flour
Cooking spray

1. Preheat the air fryer to 385ºF (196ºC). Spritz the air fryer basket with cooking spray. 2. In a bowl, beat together the eggs with milk. In another bowl, combine garlic powder, sea salt, shallot powder, chili powder and all-purpose flour until well blended. 3. One by one, roll the pickle spears in the powder mixture, then dredge them in the egg mixture. Dip them in the powder mixture a second time for additional coating. 4. Arrange the coated pickles in the prepared basket. Air fry for 15 minutes until golden and crispy, shaking the basket halfway through to ensure even cooking. 5. Transfer to a plate and let cool for 5 minutes before serving.

Poutine with Waffle Fries

Prep time: 10 minutes | Cook time: 15 to 17 minutes | Serves 4

2 cups frozen waffle cut fries
2 teaspoons olive oil
1 red bell pepper, chopped

2 green onions, sliced
1 cup shredded Swiss cheese
½ cup bottled chicken gravy

1. Preheat the air fryer to 380ºF (193ºC). 2. Toss the waffle fries with the olive oil and place in the air fryer basket. Air fry for 10 to 12 minutes, or until the fries are crisp and light golden brown, shaking the basket halfway through the cooking time. 3. Transfer the fries to a baking pan and top with the pepper, green onions, and cheese. Air fry for 3 minutes, or until the vegetables are crisp and tender. 4. Remove the pan from the air fryer and drizzle the gravy over the fries. Air fry for 2 minutes, or until the gravy is hot. 5. Serve immediately.

Spiralized Potato Nest with Tomato Ketchup

Prep time: 10 minutes | Cook time: 15 minutes |

Serves 2

1 large russet potato (about 12 ounces / 340 g)
2 tablespoons vegetable oil
1 tablespoon hot smoked paprika
½ teaspoon garlic powder
Kosher salt and freshly ground black pepper, to taste
½ cup canned crushed tomatoes
2 tablespoons apple cider vinegar
1 tablespoon dark brown sugar
1 tablespoon Worcestershire sauce
1 teaspoon mild hot sauce

1. Using a spiralizer, spiralize the potato, then place in a large colander. (If you don't have a spiralizer, cut the potato into thin ⅛-inch-thick matchsticks.) Rinse the potatoes under cold running water until the water runs clear. Spread the potatoes out on a double-thick layer of paper towels and pat completely dry. 2. In a large bowl, combine the potatoes, oil, paprika, and garlic powder. Season with salt and pepper and toss to combine. Transfer the potatoes to the air fryer and air fry at 400ºF (204ºC) until the potatoes are browned and crisp, 15 minutes, shaking the basket halfway through. 3. Meanwhile, in a small blender, purée the tomatoes, vinegar, brown sugar, Worcestershire, and hot sauce until smooth. Pour into a small saucepan or skillet and simmer over medium heat until reduced by half, 3 to 5 minutes. Pour the homemade ketchup into a bowl and let cool. 4. Remove the spiralized potato nest from the air fryer and serve hot with the ketchup.

Greek Street Tacos

Prep time: 10 minutes | Cook time: 3 minutes |

Makes 8 small tacos

8 small flour tortillas (4-inch diameter)
8 tablespoons hummus
4 tablespoons crumbled feta
cheese
4 tablespoons chopped kalamata or other olives (optional)
Olive oil for misting

1. Place 1 tablespoon of hummus or tapenade in the center of each tortilla. Top with 1 teaspoon of feta crumbles and 1 teaspoon of chopped olives, if using. 2. Using your finger or a small spoon, moisten the edges of the tortilla all around with water. 3. Fold tortilla over to make a half-moon shape. Press center gently. Then press the edges firmly to seal in the filling. 4. Mist both sides with olive oil. 5. Place in air fryer basket very close but try not to overlap. 6. Air fry at 390ºF (199ºC) for 3 minutes, just until lightly browned and crispy.

Italian Rice Balls

Prep time: 20 minutes | Cook time: 10 minutes |

Makes 8 rice balls

1½ cups cooked sticky rice
½ teaspoon Italian seasoning blend
¾ teaspoon salt, divided
8 black olives, pitted
1 ounce (28 g) Mozzarella cheese, cut into tiny pieces
(small enough to stuff into olives)
2 eggs
⅓ cup Italian bread crumbs
¾ cup panko bread crumbs
Cooking spray

1. Preheat air fryer to 390ºF (199ºC). 2. Stuff each black olive with a piece of Mozzarella cheese. Set aside. 3. In a bowl, combine the cooked sticky rice, Italian seasoning blend, and ½ teaspoon of salt and stir to mix well. Form the rice mixture into a log with your hands and divide it into 8 equal portions. Mold each portion around a black olive and roll into a ball. 4. Transfer to the freezer to chill for 10 to 15 minutes until firm. 5. In a shallow dish, place the Italian bread crumbs. In a separate shallow dish, whisk the eggs. In a third shallow dish, combine the panko bread crumbs and remaining salt. 6. One by one, roll the rice balls in the Italian bread crumbs, then dip in the whisked eggs, finally coat them with the panko bread crumbs. 7. Arrange the rice balls in the air fryer basket and spritz both sides with cooking spray. 8. Air fry for 10 minutes until the rice balls are golden brown. Flip the balls halfway through the cooking time. 9. Serve warm.

Fried Artichoke Hearts

Prep time: 10 minutes | Cook time: 12 minutes |

Serves 10

Oil, for spraying
3 (14-ounce / 397-g) cans quartered artichokes, drained and patted dry
½ cup mayonnaise
1 cup panko bread crumbs
⅓ cup grated Parmesan cheese
Salt and freshly ground black pepper, to taste

1. Line the air fryer basket with parchment and spray lightly with oil. 2. Place the artichokes on a plate. Put the mayonnaise and bread crumbs in separate bowls. 3. Working one at a time, dredge each artichoke piece in the mayonnaise, then in the bread crumbs to cover. 4. Place the artichokes in the prepared basket. You may need to work in batches, depending on the size of your air fryer. 5. Air fry at 370ºF (188ºC) for 10 to 12 minutes, or until crispy and golden brown. 6. Sprinkle with the Parmesan cheese and season with salt and black pepper. Serve immediately.

Zucchini Fries with Roasted Garlic Aïoli

Prep time: 20 minutes | Cook time: 12 minutes |
Serves 4

1 tablespoon vegetable oil
½ head green or savoy cabbage, finely shredded
Roasted Garlic Aïoli:
1 teaspoon roasted garlic
½ cup mayonnaise
2 tablespoons olive oil
Juice of ½ lemon
Salt and pepper, to taste

Zucchini Fries:
½ cup flour
2 eggs, beaten
1 cup seasoned bread crumbs
Salt and pepper, to taste
1 large zucchini, cut into ½-inch sticks
Olive oil

1. Make the aïoli: Combine the roasted garlic, mayonnaise, olive oil and lemon juice in a bowl and whisk well. Season the aïoli with salt and pepper to taste. 2. Prepare the zucchini fries. Create a dredging station with three shallow dishes. Place the flour in the first shallow dish and season well with salt and freshly ground black pepper. Put the beaten eggs in the second shallow dish. In the third shallow dish, combine the bread crumbs, salt and pepper. Dredge the zucchini sticks, coating with flour first, then dipping them into the eggs to coat, and finally tossing in bread crumbs. Shake the dish with the bread crumbs and pat the crumbs onto the zucchini sticks gently with your hands so they stick evenly. 3. Place the zucchini fries on a flat surface and let them sit at least 10 minutes before air frying to let them dry out a little. Preheat the air fryer to 400ºF (204ºC). 4. Spray the zucchini sticks with olive oil, and place them into the air fryer basket. You can air fry the zucchini in two layers, placing the second layer in the opposite direction to the first. Air fry for 12 minutes turning and rotating the fries halfway through the cooking time. Spray with additional oil when you turn them over. 5. Serve zucchini fries warm with the roasted garlic aïoli.

Cheesy Hash Brown Bruschetta

Prep time: 5 minutes | Cook time: 6 to 8 minutes |
Serves 4

4 frozen hash brown patties
1 tablespoon olive oil
⅓ cup chopped cherry tomatoes
3 tablespoons diced fresh Mozzarella

2 tablespoons grated Parmesan cheese
1 tablespoon balsamic vinegar
1 tablespoon minced fresh basil

1. Preheat the air fryer to 400ºF (204ºC). 2. Place the hash brown patties in the air fryer in a single layer. Air fry for 6 to 8 minutes, or until the potatoes are crisp, hot, and golden brown. 3. Meanwhile, combine the olive oil, tomatoes, Mozzarella, Parmesan, vinegar, and basil in a small bowl. 4. When the potatoes are done, carefully remove from the basket and arrange on a serving plate. Top with the tomato mixture and serve.

Zucchini Feta Roulades

Prep time: 10 minutes | Cook time: 10 minutes |
Serves 6

½ cup feta
1 garlic clove, minced
2 tablespoons fresh basil, minced
1 tablespoon capers, minced

⅛ teaspoon salt
⅛ teaspoon red pepper flakes
1 tablespoon lemon juice
2 medium zucchini
12 toothpicks

1. Preheat the air fryer to 360ºF (182ºC).(If using a grill attachment, make sure it is inside the air fryer during preheating.) 2. In a small bowl, combine the feta, garlic, basil, capers, salt, red pepper flakes, and lemon juice. 3. Slice the zucchini into ⅛-inch strips lengthwise. (Each zucchini should yield around 6 strips.) 4. Spread 1 tablespoon of the cheese filling onto each slice of zucchini, then roll it up and secure it with a toothpick through the middle. 5. Place the zucchini roulades into the air fryer basket in a single layer, making sure that they don't touch each other. 6. Bake or grill in the air fryer for 10 minutes. 7. Remove the zucchini roulades from the air fryer and gently remove the toothpicks before serving.

Spinach and Crab Meat Cups

Prep time: 10 minutes | Cook time: 10 minutes |
Makes 30 cups

1 (6-ounce / 170-g) can crab meat, drained to yield ⅓ cup meat
¼ cup frozen spinach, thawed, drained, and chopped
1 clove garlic, minced
½ cup grated Parmesan cheese

3 tablespoons plain yogurt
¼ teaspoon lemon juice
½ teaspoon Worcestershire sauce
30 mini frozen phyllo shells, thawed
Cooking spray

1. Preheat the air fryer to 390ºF (199ºC). 2. Remove any bits of shell that might remain in the crab meat. 3. Mix the crab meat, spinach, garlic, and cheese together. 4. Stir in the yogurt, lemon juice, and Worcestershire sauce and mix well. 5. Spoon a teaspoon of filling into each phyllo shell. 6. Spray the air fryer basket with cooking spray and arrange half the shells in the basket. Air fry for 5 minutes. Repeat with the remaining shells. 7. Serve immediately.

Sea Salt Potato Chips

Prep time: 30 minutes | Cook time: 27 minutes | Serves 4

Oil, for spraying
4 medium yellow potatoes
1 tablespoon oil
⅛ to ¼ teaspoon fine sea salt

1. Line the air fryer basket with parchment and spray lightly with oil. 2. Using a mandoline or a very sharp knife, cut the potatoes into very thin slices. 3. Place the slices in a bowl of cold water and let soak for about 20 minutes. 4. Drain the potatoes, transfer them to a plate lined with paper towels, and pat dry. 5. Drizzle the oil over the potatoes, sprinkle with the salt, and toss to combine. Transfer to the prepared basket. 6. Air fry at 200°F (93°C) for 20 minutes. Toss the chips, increase the heat to 400°F (204°C), and cook for another 5 to 7 minutes, until crispy.

Veggie Salmon Nachos

Prep time: 10 minutes | Cook time: 9 to 12 minutes | Serves 6

2 ounces (57 g) baked no-salt corn tortilla chips
1 (5-ounce / 142-g) baked salmon fillet, flaked
½ cup canned low-sodium black beans, rinsed and drained
1 red bell pepper, chopped
½ cup grated carrot
1 jalapeño pepper, minced
⅓ cup shredded low-sodium low-fat Swiss cheese
1 tomato, chopped

1. Preheat the air fryer to 360°F (182°C). 2. In a baking pan, layer the tortilla chips. Top with the salmon, black beans, red bell pepper, carrot, jalapeño, and Swiss cheese. 3. Bake in the air fryer for 9 to 12 minutes, or until the cheese is melted and starts to brown. 4. Top with the tomato and serve.

Cinnamon Apple Chips

Prep time: 5 minutes | Cook time: 7 to 8 hours | Serves 4

4 medium apples, any type, cored and cut into ⅓-inch-thick slices (thin slices yield crunchy
chips)
¼ teaspoon ground cinnamon
¼ teaspoon ground nutmeg

1. Place the apple slices in a large bowl. Sprinkle the cinnamon and nutmeg onto the apple slices and toss to coat. 2. Insert the crisper plate into the basket and the basket into the unit. Preheat the unit by selecting DEHYDRATE, setting the temperature to 135°F (57°C), and setting the time to 3 minutes. Select START/STOP to begin. 3. Once the unit is preheated, place the apple chips into the basket. It is okay to stack them. 4. Select DEHYDRATE, set the temperature to 135°F (57°C), and set the time to 7 or 8 hours. Select START/STOP to begin. 5. When the cooking is complete, cool the apple chips. Serve or store at room temperature in an airtight container for up to 1 week.

Crispy Chili Chickpeas

Prep time: 5 minutes | Cook time: 15 minutes | Serves 4

1 (15-ounce / 425-g) can cooked chickpeas, drained and rinsed
1 tablespoon olive oil
¼ teaspoon salt
⅛ teaspoon chili powder
⅛ teaspoon garlic powder
⅛ teaspoon paprika

1. Preheat the air fryer to 380°F(193°C). 2. In a medium bowl, toss all of the ingredients together until the chickpeas are well coated. 3. Pour the chickpeas into the air fryer and spread them out in a single layer. 4. Roast for 15 minutes, stirring once halfway through the cook time.

Grilled Ham and Cheese on Raisin Bread

Prep time: 5 minutes | Cook time: 10 minutes | Serves 1

2 slices raisin bread
2 tablespoons butter, softened
2 teaspoons honey mustard
3 slices thinly sliced honey ham
(about 3 ounces / 85 g)
4 slices Muenster cheese (about 3 ounces / 85 g)
2 toothpicks

1. Preheat the air fryer to 370°F (188°C). 2. Spread the softened butter on one side of both slices of raisin bread and place the bread, buttered side down on the counter. Spread the honey mustard on the other side of each slice of bread. Layer 2 slices of cheese, the ham and the remaining 2 slices of cheese on one slice of bread and top with the other slice of bread. Remember to leave the buttered side of the bread on the outside. 3. Transfer the sandwich to the air fryer basket and secure the sandwich with toothpicks. 4. Air fry for 5 minutes. Flip the sandwich over, remove the toothpicks and air fry for another 5 minutes. Cut the sandwich in half and enjoy!

Chapter 8 Vegetables and Sides

Chili Fingerling Potatoes

Prep time: 10 minutes | Cook time: 16 minutes |
Serves 4

1 pound (454 g) fingerling potatoes, rinsed and cut into wedges
1 teaspoon olive oil
1 teaspoon salt
1 teaspoon black pepper
1 teaspoon cayenne pepper
1 teaspoon nutritional yeast
½ teaspoon garlic powder

1. Preheat the air fryer to 400ºF (204ºC). 2. Coat the potatoes with the rest of the ingredients. 3. Transfer to the air fryer basket and air fry for 16 minutes, shaking the basket at the halfway point. 4. Serve immediately.

Gorgonzola Mushrooms with Horseradish Mayo

Prep time: 15 minutes | Cook time: 10 minutes |
Serves 5

½ cup bread crumbs
2 cloves garlic, pressed
2 tablespoons chopped fresh coriander
⅓ teaspoon kosher salt
½ teaspoon crushed red pepper flakes
1½ tablespoons olive oil
20 medium mushrooms, stems
removed
½ cup grated Gorgonzola cheese
¼ cup low-fat mayonnaise
1 teaspoon prepared horseradish, well-drained
1 tablespoon finely chopped fresh parsley

1. Preheat the air fryer to 380ºF (193ºC). 2. Combine the bread crumbs together with the garlic, coriander, salt, red pepper, and olive oil. 3. Take equal-sized amounts of the bread crumb mixture and use them to stuff the mushroom caps. Add the grated Gorgonzola on top of each. 4. Put the mushrooms in a baking pan and transfer to the air fryer. 5. Air fry for 10 minutes, ensuring the stuffing is warm throughout. 6. In the meantime, prepare the horseradish mayo. Mix the mayonnaise, horseradish and parsley. 7. When the mushrooms are ready, serve with the mayo.

Cauliflower with Lime Juice

Prep time: 10 minutes | Cook time: 7 minutes |
Serves 4

2 cups chopped cauliflower florets
2 tablespoons coconut oil, melted
2 teaspoons chili powder
½ teaspoon garlic powder
1 medium lime
2 tablespoons chopped cilantro

1. In a large bowl, toss cauliflower with coconut oil. Sprinkle with chili powder and garlic powder. Place seasoned cauliflower into the air fryer basket. 2. Adjust the temperature to 350ºF (177ºC) and set the timer for 7 minutes. 3. Cauliflower will be tender and begin to turn golden at the edges. Place into a serving bowl. 4. Cut the lime into quarters and squeeze juice over cauliflower. Garnish with cilantro.

Cauliflower Rice Balls

Prep time: 10 minutes | Cook time: 8 minutes |
Serves 4

1 (10-ounce / 283-g) steamer bag cauliflower rice, cooked according to package instructions
½ cup shredded Mozzarella cheese
1 large egg
2 ounces (57 g) plain pork rinds, finely crushed
¼ teaspoon salt
½ teaspoon Italian seasoning

1. Place cauliflower into a large bowl and mix with Mozzarella. 2. Whisk egg in a separate medium bowl. Place pork rinds into another large bowl with salt and Italian seasoning. 3. Separate cauliflower mixture into four equal sections and form each into a ball. Carefully dip a ball into whisked egg, then roll in pork rinds. Repeat with remaining balls. 4. Place cauliflower balls into ungreased air fryer basket. Adjust the temperature to 400ºF (204ºC) and air fry for 8 minutes. Rice balls will be golden when done. 5. Use a spatula to carefully move cauliflower balls to a large dish for serving. Serve warm.

Garlic Zucchini and Red Peppers

Prep time: 5 minutes | Cook time: 15 minutes | Serves 6

2 medium zucchini, cubed
1 red bell pepper, diced
2 garlic cloves, sliced
2 tablespoons olive oil
½ teaspoon salt

1. Preheat the air fryer to 380°F(193°C). 2. In a large bowl, mix together the zucchini, bell pepper, and garlic with the olive oil and salt. 3. Pour the mixture into the air fryer basket, and roast for 7 minutes. Shake or stir, then roast for 7 to 8 minutes more.

"Faux-Tato" Hash

Prep time: 10 minutes | Cook time: 12 minutes | Serves 4

1 pound (454 g) radishes, ends removed, quartered
¼ medium yellow onion, peeled and diced
½ medium green bell pepper, seeded and chopped
2 tablespoons salted butter, melted
½ teaspoon garlic powder
¼ teaspoon ground black pepper

1. In a large bowl, combine radishes, onion, and bell pepper. Toss with butter. 2. Sprinkle garlic powder and black pepper over mixture in bowl, then spoon into ungreased air fryer basket. 3. Adjust the temperature to 320ºF (160ºC) and air fry for 12 minutes. Shake basket halfway through cooking. Radishes will be tender when done. Serve warm.

Sesame-Ginger Broccoli

Prep time: 10 minutes | Cook time: 15 minutes | Serves 4

3 tablespoons toasted sesame oil
2 teaspoons sesame seeds
1 tablespoon chili-garlic sauce
2 teaspoons minced fresh ginger
½ teaspoon kosher salt
½ teaspoon black pepper
1 (16-ounce / 454-g) package frozen broccoli florets (do not thaw)

1. In a large bowl, combine the sesame oil, sesame seeds, chili-garlic sauce, ginger, salt, and pepper. Stir until well combined. Add the broccoli and toss until well coated. 2. Arrange the broccoli in the air fryer basket. Set the air fryer to 325°F (163°C) for 15 minutes, or until the broccoli is crisp, tender, and the edges are lightly browned, gently tossing halfway through the cooking time.

Cabbage Wedges with Caraway Butter

Prep time: 30 minutes | Cook time: 35 to 40 minutes | Serves 6

1 tablespoon caraway seeds
½ cup (1 stick) unsalted butter, at room temperature
½ teaspoon grated lemon zest
1 small head green or red
cabbage, cut into 6 wedges
1 tablespoon avocado oil
½ teaspoon sea salt
¼ teaspoon freshly ground black pepper

1. Place the caraway seeds in a small dry skillet over medium-high heat. Toast the seeds for 2 to 3 minutes, then remove them from the heat and let cool. Lightly crush the seeds using a mortar and pestle or with the back of a knife. 2. Place the butter in a small bowl and stir in the crushed caraway seeds and lemon zest. Form the butter into a log and wrap it in parchment paper or plastic wrap. Refrigerate for at least 1 hour or freeze for 20 minutes. 3. Brush or spray the cabbage wedges with the avocado oil, and sprinkle with the salt and pepper. 4. Set the air fryer to 375°F (191°C). Place the cabbage in a single layer in the air fryer basket and roast for 20 minutes. Flip and cook for 15 to 20 minutes more, until the cabbage is tender and lightly charred. Plate the cabbage and dot with caraway butter. Tent with foil for 5 minutes to melt the butter, and serve.

Sesame Carrots and Sugar Snap Peas

Prep time: 10 minutes | Cook time: 16 minutes | Serves 4

1 pound (454 g) carrots, peeled sliced on the bias (½-inch slices)
1 teaspoon olive oil
Salt and freshly ground black pepper, to taste
⅓ cup honey
1 tablespoon sesame oil
1 tablespoon soy sauce
½ teaspoon minced fresh ginger
4 ounces (113 g) sugar snap peas (about 1 cup)
1½ teaspoons sesame seeds

1. Preheat the air fryer to 360°F (182°C). 2. Toss the carrots with the olive oil, season with salt and pepper and air fry for 10 minutes, shaking the basket once or twice during the cooking process. 3. Combine the honey, sesame oil, soy sauce and minced ginger in a large bowl. Add the sugar snap peas and the air-fried carrots to the honey mixture, toss to coat and return everything to the air fryer basket. 4. Turn up the temperature to 400ºF (204ºC) and air fry for an additional 6 minutes, shaking the basket once during the cooking process. 5. Transfer the carrots and sugar snap peas to a serving bowl. Pour the sauce from the bottom of the cooker over the vegetables and sprinkle sesame seeds over top. Serve immediately.

Rosemary New Potatoes

Prep time: 10 minutes | Cook time: 5 to 6 minutes | Serves 4

3 large red potatoes (enough to make 3 cups sliced)
¼ teaspoon ground rosemary
¼ teaspoon ground thyme
⅛ teaspoon salt
⅛ teaspoon ground black pepper
2 teaspoons extra-light olive oil

1. Preheat the air fryer to 330°F (166°C). 2. Place potatoes in large bowl and sprinkle with rosemary, thyme, salt, and pepper. 3. Stir with a spoon to distribute seasonings evenly. 4. Add oil to potatoes and stir again to coat well. 5. Air fry at 330°F (166°C) for 4 minutes. Stir and break apart any that have stuck together. 6. Cook an additional 1 to 2 minutes or until fork-tender.

Citrus-Roasted Broccoli Florets

Prep time: 5 minutes | Cook time: 12 minutes | Serves 6

4 cups broccoli florets (approximately 1 large head)
2 tablespoons olive oil
½ teaspoon salt
½ cup orange juice
1 tablespoon raw honey
Orange wedges, for serving (optional)

1. Preheat the air fryer to 360°F(182°C). 2. In a large bowl, combine the broccoli, olive oil, salt, orange juice, and honey. Toss the broccoli in the liquid until well coated. 3. Pour the broccoli mixture into the air fryer basket and roast for 6 minutes. Stir and roast for 6 minutes more. 4. Serve alone or with orange wedges for additional citrus flavor, if desired.

Parmesan and Herb Sweet Potatoes

Prep time: 10 minutes | Cook time: 18 minutes | Serves 4

2 large sweet potatoes, peeled and cubed
¼ cup olive oil
1 teaspoon dried rosemary
½ teaspoon salt
2 tablespoons shredded Parmesan

1. Preheat the air fryer to 360°F(182°C). 2. In a large bowl, toss the sweet potatoes with the olive oil, rosemary, and salt. 3. Pour the potatoes into the air fryer basket and roast for 10 minutes, then stir the potatoes and sprinkle the Parmesan over the top. Continue roasting for 8 minutes more. 4. Serve hot and enjoy.

Tingly Chili-Roasted Broccoli

Prep time: 5 minutes | Cook time: 10 minutes | Serves 2

12 ounces (340 g) broccoli florets
2 tablespoons Asian hot chili oil
1 teaspoon ground Sichuan peppercorns (or black pepper)
2 garlic cloves, finely chopped
1 (2-inch) piece fresh ginger, peeled and finely chopped
Kosher salt and freshly ground black pepper, to taste

1. In a bowl, toss together the broccoli, chili oil, Sichuan peppercorns, garlic, ginger, and salt and black pepper to taste. 2. Transfer to the air fryer and roast at 375°F (191°C), shaking the basket halfway through, until lightly charred and tender, about 10 minutes. Remove from the air fryer and serve warm.

Zesty Fried Asparagus

Prep time: 3 minutes | Cook time: 10 minutes | Serves 4

Oil, for spraying
10 to 12 spears asparagus, trimmed
2 tablespoons olive oil
1 tablespoon granulated garlic
1 teaspoon chili powder
½ teaspoon ground cumin
¼ teaspoon salt

1. Line the air fryer basket with parchment and spray lightly with oil. 2. If the asparagus are too long to fit easily in the air fryer, cut them in half. 3. Place the asparagus, olive oil, garlic, chili powder, cumin, and salt in a zip-top plastic bag, seal, and toss until evenly coated. 4. Place the asparagus in the prepared basket. 5. Roast at 390°F (199°C) for 5 minutes, flip, and cook for another 5 minutes, or until bright green and firm but tender.

Roasted Potatoes and Asparagus

Prep time: 5 minutes | Cook time: 23 minutes | Serves 4

4 medium potatoes
1 bunch asparagus
⅓ cup cottage cheese
⅓ cup low-fat crème fraiche
1 tablespoon wholegrain mustard
Salt and pepper, to taste
Cooking spray

1. Preheat the air fryer to 390°F (199°C). Spritz the air fryer basket with cooking spray. 2. Place the potatoes in the basket. Air fry the potatoes for 20 minutes. 3. Boil the asparagus in salted water for 3 minutes. 4. Remove the potatoes and mash them with rest of ingredients. Sprinkle with salt and pepper. 5. Serve immediately.

Green Peas with Mint

Prep time: 5 minutes | Cook time: 5 minutes | Serves 4

1 cup shredded lettuce
1 (10-ounce / 283-g) package frozen green peas, thawed

1 tablespoon fresh mint, shredded
1 teaspoon melted butter

1. Lay the shredded lettuce in the air fryer basket. 2. Toss together the peas, mint, and melted butter and spoon over the lettuce. 3. Air fry at 360ºF (182ºC) for 5 minutes, until peas are warm and lettuce wilts.

Crispy Zucchini Sticks

Prep time: 5 minutes | Cook time: 14 minutes | Serves 4

2 small zucchini, cut into 2-inch × ½-inch sticks
3 tablespoons chickpea flour
2 teaspoons arrowroot (or cornstarch)
½ teaspoon garlic granules

¼ teaspoon sea salt
⅛ teaspoon freshly ground black pepper
1 tablespoon water
Cooking spray

1. Preheat the air fryer to 392ºF (200ºC). 2. Combine the zucchini sticks with the chickpea flour, arrowroot, garlic granules, salt, and pepper in a medium bowl and toss to coat. Add the water and stir to mix well. 3. Spritz the air fryer basket with cooking spray and spread out the zucchini sticks in the basket. Mist the zucchini sticks with cooking spray. 4. Air fry for 14 minutes, shaking the basket halfway through, or until the zucchini sticks are crispy and nicely browned. 5. Serve warm.

Marinara Pepperoni Mushroom Pizza

Prep time: 5 minutes | Cook time: 18 minutes | Serves 4

4 large portobello mushrooms, stems removed
4 teaspoons olive oil
1 cup marinara sauce

1 cup shredded Mozzarella cheese
10 slices sugar-free pepperoni

1. Preheat the air fryer to 375ºF (191ºC). 2. Brush each mushroom cap with the olive oil, one teaspoon for each cap. 3. Put on a baking sheet and bake, stem-side down, for 8 minutes. 4. Take out of the air fryer and divide the marinara sauce, Mozzarella cheese and pepperoni evenly among the caps. 5. Air fry for another 10 minutes until browned. 6. Serve hot.

Caesar Whole Cauliflower

Prep time: 20 minutes | Cook time: 30 minutes | Serves 2 to 4

3 tablespoons olive oil
2 tablespoons red wine vinegar
2 tablespoons Worcestershire sauce
2 tablespoons grated Parmesan cheese
1 tablespoon Dijon mustard
4 garlic cloves, minced
4 oil-packed anchovy fillets, drained and finely minced

Kosher salt and freshly ground black pepper, to taste
1 small head cauliflower (about 1 pound / 454 g), green leaves trimmed and stem trimmed flush with the bottom of the head
1 tablespoon roughly chopped fresh flat-leaf parsley (optional)

1. In a liquid measuring cup, whisk together the olive oil, vinegar, Worcestershire, Parmesan, mustard, garlic, anchovies, and salt and pepper to taste. Place the cauliflower head upside down on a cutting board and use a paring knife to make an "x" through the full length of the core. Transfer the cauliflower head to a large bowl and pour half the dressing over it. Turn the cauliflower head to coat it in the dressing, then let it rest, stem-side up, in the dressing for at least 10 minutes and up to 30 minutes to allow the dressing to seep into all its nooks and crannies. 2. Transfer the cauliflower head, stem-side down, to the air fryer and air fry at 340ºF (171ºC) for 25 minutes. Drizzle the remaining dressing over the cauliflower and air fry at 400ºF (204ºC) until the top of the cauliflower is golden brown and the core is tender, about 5 minutes more. 3. Remove the basket from the air fryer and transfer the cauliflower to a large plate. Sprinkle with the parsley, if you like, and serve hot.

Five-Spice Roasted Sweet Potatoes

Prep time: 10 minutes | Cook time: 12 minutes | Serves 4

½ teaspoon ground cinnamon
¼ teaspoon ground cumin
¼ teaspoon paprika
1 teaspoon chile powder
⅛ teaspoon turmeric
½ teaspoon salt (optional)

Freshly ground black pepper, to taste
2 large sweet potatoes, peeled and cut into ¾-inch cubes (about 3 cups)
1 tablespoon olive oil

1. In a large bowl, mix together cinnamon, cumin, paprika, chile powder, turmeric, salt, and pepper to taste. 2. Add potatoes and stir well. 3. Drizzle the seasoned potatoes with the olive oil and stir until evenly coated. 4. Place seasoned potatoes in a baking pan or an ovenproof dish that fits inside your air fryer basket. 5. Cook for 6 minutes at 390ºF (199ºC), stop, and stir well. 6. Cook for an additional 6 minutes.

Kohlrabi Fries

Prep time: 10 minutes | Cook time: 20 to 30 minutes | Serves 4

2 pounds (907 g) kohlrabi, peeled and cut into ¼ to ½-inch fries

2 tablespoons olive oil
Salt and freshly ground black pepper, to taste

1. Preheat the air fryer to 400°F (204°C). 2. In a large bowl, combine the kohlrabi and olive oil. Season to taste with salt and black pepper. Toss gently until thoroughly coated. 3. Working in batches if necessary, spread the kohlrabi in a single layer in the air fryer basket. Pausing halfway through the cooking time to shake the basket, air fry for 20 to 30 minutes until the fries are lightly browned and crunchy.

Tahini-Lemon Kale

Prep time: 5 minutes | Cook time: 15 minutes | Serves 2 to 4

¼ cup tahini
¼ cup fresh lemon juice
2 tablespoons olive oil
1 teaspoon sesame seeds
½ teaspoon garlic powder
¼ teaspoon cayenne pepper

4 cups packed torn kale leaves (stems and ribs removed and leaves torn into palm-size pieces; about 4 ounces / 113 g)
Kosher salt and freshly ground black pepper, to taste

1. In a large bowl, whisk together the tahini, lemon juice, olive oil, sesame seeds, garlic powder, and cayenne until smooth. Add the kale leaves, season with salt and black pepper, and toss in the dressing until completely coated. Transfer the kale leaves to a cake pan. 2. Place the pan in the air fryer and roast at 350°F (177°C), stirring every 5 minutes, until the kale is wilted and the top is lightly browned, about 15 minutes. Remove the pan from the air fryer and serve warm.

Shishito Pepper Roast

Prep time: 4 minutes | Cook time: 9 minutes | Serves 4

Cooking oil spray (sunflower, safflower, or refined coconut)
1 pound (454 g) shishito, Anaheim, or bell peppers, rinsed

1 tablespoon soy sauce
2 teaspoons freshly squeezed lime juice
2 large garlic cloves, pressed

1. Insert the crisper plate into the basket and the basket into the unit. Preheat the unit by selecting AIR ROAST, setting the temperature to 390°F (199°C), and setting the time to 3 minutes. Select START/STOP to begin. 2. Once the unit is preheated, spray the crisper plate and the basket with cooking oil. Place the peppers into the basket and spray them with oil. 3. Select AIR ROAST, set the temperature to 390°F (199°C), and set the time to 9 minutes. Select START/STOP to begin. 4. After 3 minutes, remove the basket and shake the peppers. Spray the peppers with more oil. Reinsert the basket to resume cooking. Repeat this step again after 3 minutes. 5. While the peppers roast, in a medium bowl, whisk the soy sauce, lime juice, and garlic until combined. Set aside. 6. When the cooking is complete, several of the peppers should have lots of nice browned spots on them. If using Anaheim or bell peppers, cut a slit in the side of each pepper and remove the seeds, which can be bitter. 7. Place the roasted peppers in the bowl with the sauce. Toss to coat the peppers evenly and serve.

Indian Eggplant Bharta

Prep time: 15 minutes | Cook time: 20 minutes | Serves 4

1 medium eggplant
2 tablespoons vegetable oil
½ cup finely minced onion
½ cup finely chopped fresh tomato

2 tablespoons fresh lemon juice
2 tablespoons chopped fresh cilantro
½ teaspoon kosher salt
⅛ teaspoon cayenne pepper

1. Rub the eggplant all over with the vegetable oil. Place the eggplant in the air fryer basket. Set the air fryer to 400°F (204°C) for 20 minutes, or until the eggplant skin is blistered and charred. 2. Transfer the eggplant to a resealable plastic bag, seal, and set aside for 15 to 20 minutes (the eggplant will finish cooking in the residual heat trapped in the bag). 3. Transfer the eggplant to a large bowl. Peel off and discard the charred skin. Roughly mash the eggplant flesh. Add the onion, tomato, lemon juice, cilantro, salt, and cayenne. Stir to combine.

Curried Fruit

Prep time: 10 minutes | Cook time: 20 minutes | Serves 6 to 8

1 cup cubed fresh pineapple
1 cup cubed fresh pear (firm, not overly ripe)
8 ounces (227 g) frozen peaches, thawed

1 (15-ounce / 425-g) can dark, sweet, pitted cherries with juice
2 tablespoons brown sugar
1 teaspoon curry powder

1. Combine all ingredients in large bowl. Stir gently to mix in the sugar and curry. 2. Pour into a baking pan and bake at 360°F (182°C) for 10 minutes. 3. Stir fruit and cook 10 more minutes. 4. Serve hot.

Garlic Parmesan-Roasted Cauliflower

Prep time: 5 minutes | Cook time: 15 minutes |

Serves 6

1 medium head cauliflower, leaves and core removed, cut into florets	½ tablespoon salt
	2 cloves garlic, peeled and finely minced
2 tablespoons salted butter, melted	½ cup grated Parmesan cheese, divided

1. Toss cauliflower in a large bowl with butter. Sprinkle with salt, garlic, and ¼ cup Parmesan. 2. Place florets into ungreased air fryer basket. Adjust the temperature to 350ºF (177ºC) and roast for 15 minutes, shaking basket halfway through cooking. Cauliflower will be browned at the edges and tender when done. 3. Transfer florets to a large serving dish and sprinkle with remaining Parmesan. Serve warm.

Garlic Roasted Broccoli

Prep time: 8 minutes | Cook time: 10 to 14 minutes |

Serves 6

1 head broccoli, cut into bite-size florets	Sea salt and freshly ground black pepper, to taste
1 tablespoon avocado oil	1 tablespoon freshly squeezed lemon juice
2 teaspoons minced garlic	
⅛ teaspoon red pepper flakes	½ teaspoon lemon zest

1. In a large bowl, toss together the broccoli, avocado oil, garlic, red pepper flakes, salt, and pepper. 2. Set the air fryer to 375ºF (191ºC). Arrange the broccoli in a single layer in the air fryer basket, working in batches if necessary. Roast for 10 to 14 minutes, until the broccoli is lightly charred. 3. Place the florets in a medium bowl and toss with the lemon juice and lemon zest. Serve.

Creamed Spinach

Prep time: 10 minutes | Cook time: 15 minutes |

Serves 4

Vegetable oil spray	4 ounces (113 g) cream cheese, diced
1 (10-ounce / 283-g) package frozen spinach, thawed and squeezed dry	½ teaspoon ground nutmeg
½ cup chopped onion	1 teaspoon kosher salt
2 cloves garlic, minced	1 teaspoon black pepper
	½ cup grated Parmesan cheese

1. Spray a baking pan with vegetable oil spray. 2. In a medium bowl, combine the spinach, onion, garlic, cream cheese, nutmeg, salt, and pepper. Transfer to the prepared pan. 3. Place the pan in the air fryer basket. Set the air fryer to 350ºF (177ºC) for 10 minutes. Open and stir to thoroughly combine the cream cheese and spinach. 4. Sprinkle the Parmesan cheese on top. Set the air fryer to 400ºF (204ºC) for 5 minutes, or until the cheese has melted and browned.

Mediterranean Zucchini Boats

Prep time: 5 minutes | Cook time: 10 minutes |

Serves 4

1 large zucchini, ends removed, halved lengthwise	¼ cup feta cheese
	1 tablespoon balsamic vinegar
6 grape tomatoes, quartered	1 tablespoon olive oil
¼ teaspoon salt	

1. Use a spoon to scoop out 2 tablespoons from center of each zucchini half, making just enough space to fill with tomatoes and feta. 2. Place tomatoes evenly in centers of zucchini halves and sprinkle with salt. Place into ungreased air fryer basket. Adjust the temperature to 350ºF (177ºC) and roast for 10 minutes. When done, zucchini will be tender. 3. Transfer boats to a serving tray and sprinkle with feta, then drizzle with vinegar and olive oil. Serve warm.

Baked Jalapeño and Cheese Cauliflower Mash

Prep time: 10 minutes | Cook time: 15 minutes |

Serves 6

1 (12-ounce / 340-g) steamer bag cauliflower florets, cooked according to package instructions	softened
	½ cup shredded sharp Cheddar cheese
	¼ cup pickled jalapeños
2 tablespoons salted butter, softened	½ teaspoon salt
2 ounces (57 g) cream cheese,	¼ teaspoon ground black pepper

1. Place cooked cauliflower into a food processor with remaining ingredients. Pulse twenty times until cauliflower is smooth and all ingredients are combined. 2. Spoon mash into an ungreased round nonstick baking dish. Place dish into air fryer basket. Adjust the temperature to 380ºF (193ºC) and bake for 15 minutes. The top will be golden brown when done. Serve warm.

Sesame Taj Tofu

Prep time: 5 minutes | Cook time: 25 minutes |
Serves 4

1 block firm tofu, pressed and
cut into 1-inch thick cubes
2 tablespoons soy sauce
2 teaspoons toasted sesame

seeds
1 teaspoon rice vinegar
1 tablespoon cornstarch

1. Preheat the air fryer to 400ºF (204ºC). 2. Add the tofu, soy sauce, sesame seeds, and rice vinegar in a bowl together and mix well to coat the tofu cubes. Then cover the tofu in cornstarch and put it in the air fryer basket. 3. Air fry for 25 minutes, giving the basket a shake at five-minute intervals to ensure the tofu cooks evenly. 4. Serve immediately.

Lush Vegetable Salad

Prep time: 15 minutes | Cook time: 10 minutes |
Serves 4

6 plum tomatoes, halved
2 large red onions, sliced
4 long red pepper, sliced
2 yellow pepper, sliced
6 cloves garlic, crushed
1 tablespoon extra-virgin olive

oil
1 teaspoon paprika
½ lemon, juiced
Salt and ground black pepper,
to taste
1 tablespoon baby capers

1. Preheat the air fryer to 420ºF (216ºC). 2. Put the tomatoes, onions, peppers, and garlic in a large bowl and cover with the extra-virgin olive oil, paprika, and lemon juice. Sprinkle with salt and pepper as desired. 3. Line the inside of the air fryer basket with aluminum foil. Put the vegetables inside and air fry for 10 minutes, ensuring the edges turn brown. 4. Serve in a salad bowl with the baby capers.

Fig, Chickpea, and Arugula Salad

Prep time: 15 minutes | Cook time: 20 minutes |
Serves 4

8 fresh figs, halved
1½ cups cooked chickpeas
1 teaspoon crushed roasted
cumin seeds
4 tablespoons balsamic vinegar
2 tablespoons extra-virgin olive

oil, plus more for greasing
Salt and ground black pepper,
to taste
3 cups arugula rocket, washed
and dried

1. Preheat the air fryer to 375ºF (191ºC). 2. Cover the air fryer basket with aluminum foil and grease lightly with oil. Put the figs in the air fryer basket and air fry for 10 minutes. 3. In a bowl, combine the chickpeas and cumin seeds. 4. Remove the air fried figs from the air fryer and replace with the chickpeas. Air fry for 10 minutes. Leave to cool. 5. In the meantime, prepare the dressing. Mix the balsamic vinegar, olive oil, salt and pepper. 6. In a salad bowl, combine the arugula rocket with the cooled figs and chickpeas. 7. Toss with the sauce and serve.

Cheesy Loaded Broccoli

Prep time: 10 minutes | Cook time: 10 minutes |
Serves 2

3 cups fresh broccoli florets
1 tablespoon coconut oil
¼ teaspoon salt
½ cup shredded sharp Cheddar
cheese

¼ cup sour cream
4 slices cooked sugar-free
bacon, crumbled
1 medium scallion, trimmed
and sliced on the bias

1. Place broccoli into ungreased air fryer basket, drizzle with coconut oil, and sprinkle with salt. Adjust the temperature to 350ºF (177ºC) and roast for 8 minutes. Shake basket three times during cooking to avoid burned spots. 2. Sprinkle broccoli with Cheddar and cook for 2 additional minutes. When done, cheese will be melted and broccoli will be tender. 3. Serve warm in a large serving dish, topped with sour cream, crumbled bacon, and scallion slices.

Butternut Squash Croquettes

Prep time: 5 minutes | Cook time: 17 minutes |
Serves 4

⅓ butternut squash, peeled and
grated
⅓ cup all-purpose flour
2 eggs, whisked
4 cloves garlic, minced
1½ tablespoons olive oil

1 teaspoon fine sea salt
⅓ teaspoon freshly ground
black pepper, or more to taste
⅓ teaspoon dried sage
A pinch of ground allspice

1. Preheat the air fryer to 345ºF (174ºC). Line the air fryer basket with parchment paper. 2. In a mixing bowl, stir together all the ingredients until well combined. 3. Make the squash croquettes: Use a small cookie scoop to drop tablespoonfuls of the squash mixture onto a lightly floured surface and shape into balls with your hands. Transfer them to the air fryer basket. 4. Air fry for 17 minutes until the squash croquettes are golden brown. 5. Remove from the basket to a plate and serve warm.

Southwestern Roasted Corn

Prep time: 10 minutes | Cook time: 10 minutes | Serves 4

Corn:

1 ½ cups thawed frozen corn kernels

1 cup diced yellow onion

1 cup mixed diced bell peppers

1 jalapeño, diced

1 tablespoon fresh lemon juice

1 teaspoon ground cumin

½ teaspoon ancho chile powder

½ teaspoon kosher salt

For Serving:

¼ cup queso fresco or feta cheese

¼ cup chopped fresh cilantro

1 tablespoon fresh lemon juice

1. For the corn: In a large bowl, stir together the corn, onion, bell peppers, jalapeño, lemon juice, cumin, chile powder, and salt until well incorporated. 2. Pour the spiced vegetables into the air fryer basket. Set the air fryer to 375°F (191°C) for 10 minutes, stirring halfway through the cooking time. 3. Transfer the corn mixture to a serving bowl. Add the cheese, cilantro, and lemon juice and stir well to combine. Serve immediately.

Chapter 9 Vegetarian Mains

Caprese Eggplant Stacks

Prep time: 5 minutes | Cook time: 12 minutes |
Serves 4

1 medium eggplant, cut into
¼-inch slices
2 large tomatoes, cut into
¼-inch slices
4 ounces (113 g) fresh

Mozzarella, cut into ½-ounce /
14-g slices
2 tablespoons olive oil
¼ cup fresh basil, sliced

1. In a baking dish, place four slices of eggplant on the bottom. Place a slice of tomato on top of each eggplant round, then Mozzarella, then eggplant. Repeat as necessary. 2. Drizzle with olive oil. Cover dish with foil and place dish into the air fryer basket. 3. Adjust the temperature to 350ºF (177ºC) and bake for 12 minutes. 4. When done, eggplant will be tender. Garnish with fresh basil to serve.

Garlic White Zucchini Rolls

Prep time: 20 minutes | Cook time: 20 minutes |
Serves 4

2 medium zucchini
2 tablespoons unsalted butter
¼ white onion, peeled and
diced
½ teaspoon finely minced
roasted garlic
¼ cup heavy cream
2 tablespoons vegetable broth
⅛ teaspoon xanthan gum

½ cup full-fat ricotta cheese
¼ teaspoon salt
½ teaspoon garlic powder
¼ teaspoon dried oregano
2 cups spinach, chopped
½ cup sliced baby portobello
mushrooms
¾ cup shredded Mozzarella
cheese, divided

1. Using a mandoline or sharp knife, slice zucchini into long strips lengthwise. Place strips between paper towels to absorb moisture. Set aside. 2. In a medium saucepan over medium heat, melt butter. Add onion and sauté until fragrant. Add garlic and sauté 30 seconds. 3. Pour in heavy cream, broth, and xanthan gum. Turn off heat and whisk mixture until it begins to thicken, about 3 minutes. 4. In a medium bowl, add ricotta, salt, garlic powder, and oregano and mix well. Fold in spinach, mushrooms, and ½ cup Mozzarella. 5. Pour half of the sauce into a round baking pan. To assemble the rolls, place two strips of zucchini on a work surface. Spoon 2 tablespoons of ricotta mixture onto the slices and roll up. Place seam side down on top of sauce. Repeat with remaining ingredients. 6. Pour remaining sauce over the rolls and sprinkle with remaining Mozzarella. Cover with foil and place into the air fryer basket. 7. Adjust the temperature to 350ºF (177ºC) and bake for 20 minutes. 8. In the last 5 minutes, remove the foil to brown the cheese. Serve immediately.

Cauliflower, Chickpea, and Avocado Mash

Prep time: 10 minutes | Cook time: 25 minutes |
Serves 4

1 medium head cauliflower, cut
into florets
1 can chickpeas, drained and
rinsed
1 tablespoon extra-virgin olive
oil

2 tablespoons lemon juice
Salt and ground black pepper,
to taste
4 flatbreads, toasted
2 ripe avocados, mashed

1. Preheat the air fryer to 425ºF (218ºC). 2. In a bowl, mix the chickpeas, cauliflower, lemon juice and olive oil. Sprinkle salt and pepper as desired. 3. Put inside the air fryer basket and air fry for 25 minutes. 4. Spread on top of the flatbread along with the mashed avocado. Sprinkle with more pepper and salt and serve.

Eggplant and Zucchini Bites

Prep time: 30 minutes | Cook time: 30 minutes |
Serves 8

2 teaspoons fresh mint leaves,
chopped
1½ teaspoons red pepper chili
flakes
2 tablespoons melted butter

1 pound (454 g) eggplant,
peeled and cubed
1 pound (454 g) zucchini,
peeled and cubed
3 tablespoons olive oil

1. Toss all the above ingredients in a large-sized mixing dish. 2. Roast the eggplant and zucchini bites for 30 minutes at 325ºF (163ºC) in your air fryer, turning once or twice. 3. Serve with a homemade dipping sauce.

Basmati Risotto

Prep time: 10 minutes | Cook time: 30 minutes |
Serves 2

1 onion, diced	1 clove garlic, minced
1 small carrot, diced	¾ cup long-grain basmati rice
2 cups vegetable broth, boiling	1 tablespoon olive oil
½ cup grated Cheddar cheese	1 tablespoon unsalted butter

1. Preheat the air fryer to 390ºF (199ºC). 2. Grease a baking tin with oil and stir in the butter, garlic, carrot, and onion. 3. Put the tin in the air fryer and bake for 4 minutes. 4. Pour in the rice and bake for a further 4 minutes, stirring three times throughout the baking time. 5. Turn the temperature down to 320ºF (160ºC). 6. Add the vegetable broth and give the dish a gentle stir. Bake for 22 minutes, leaving the air fryer uncovered. 7. Pour in the cheese, stir once more and serve.

Roasted Vegetables with Rice

Prep time: 5 minutes | Cook time: 12 minutes |
Serves 4

2 teaspoons melted butter	1 red onion, chopped
1 cup chopped mushrooms	1 garlic clove, minced
1 cup cooked rice	Salt and black pepper, to taste
1 cup peas	2 hard-boiled eggs, grated
1 carrot, chopped	1 tablespoon soy sauce

1. Preheat the air fryer to 380ºF (193ºC). Coat a baking dish with melted butter. 2. Stir together the mushrooms, cooked rice, peas, carrot, onion, garlic, salt, and pepper in a large bowl until well mixed. 3. Pour the mixture into the prepared baking dish and transfer to the air fryer basket. 4. Roast in the preheated air fryer for 12 minutes until the vegetables are tender. 5. Divide the mixture among four plates. Serve warm with a sprinkle of grated eggs and a drizzle of soy sauce.

Broccoli Crust Pizza

Prep time: 15 minutes | Cook time: 12 minutes |
Serves 4

3 cups riced broccoli, steamed and drained well	3 tablespoons low-carb Alfredo sauce
1 large egg	½ cup shredded Mozzarella cheese
½ cup grated vegetarian Parmesan cheese	

1. In a large bowl, mix broccoli, egg, and Parmesan. 2. Cut a piece of parchment to fit your air fryer basket. Press out the pizza mixture to fit on the parchment, working in two batches if necessary. Place into the air fryer basket. 3. Adjust the temperature to 370ºF (188ºC) and air fry for 5 minutes. 4. The crust should be firm enough to flip. If not, add 2 additional minutes. Flip crust. 5. Top with Alfredo sauce and Mozzarella. Return to the air fryer basket and cook an additional 7 minutes or until cheese is golden and bubbling. Serve warm.

Rosemary Beets with Balsamic Glaze

Prep time: 5 minutes | Cook time: 10 minutes |
Serves 2

Beet:	Salt and black pepper, to taste
2 beets, cubed	Balsamic Glaze:
2 tablespoons olive oil	⅓ cup balsamic vinegar
2 springs rosemary, chopped	1 tablespoon honey

1. Preheat the air fryer to 400ºF (204ºC). 2. Combine the beets, olive oil, rosemary, salt, and pepper in a mixing bowl and toss until the beets are completely coated. 3. Place the beets in the air fryer basket and air fry for 10 minutes until the beets are crisp and browned at the edges. Shake the basket halfway through the cooking time. 4. Meanwhile, make the balsamic glaze: Place the balsamic vinegar and honey in a small saucepan and bring to a boil over medium heat. When the sauce starts to boil, reduce the heat to medium-low heat and simmer until the liquid is reduced by half. 5. When ready, remove the beets from the basket to a platter. Pour the balsamic glaze over the top and serve immediately.

Broccoli with Garlic Sauce

Prep time: 19 minutes | Cook time: 15 minutes |
Serves 4

2 tablespoons olive oil	crushed
Kosher salt and freshly ground black pepper, to taste	3 garlic cloves, minced
1 pound (454 g) broccoli florets	⅓ teaspoon dried marjoram, crushed
Dipping Sauce:	¼ cup sour cream
2 teaspoons dried rosemary,	⅓ cup mayonnaise

1. Lightly grease your broccoli with a thin layer of olive oil. Season with salt and ground black pepper. 2. Arrange the seasoned broccoli in the air fryer basket. Bake at 395ºF (202ºC) for 15 minutes, shaking once or twice. In the meantime, prepare the dipping sauce by mixing all the sauce ingredients. Serve warm broccoli with the dipping sauce and enjoy!

Roasted Spaghetti Squash

Prep time: 10 minutes | Cook time: 45 minutes |
Serves 6

1 (4-pound / 1.8-kg) spaghetti
squash, halved and seeded
2 tablespoons coconut oil
4 tablespoons salted butter,

melted
1 teaspoon garlic powder
2 teaspoons dried parsley

1. Brush shell of spaghetti squash with coconut oil. Brush inside with butter. Sprinkle inside with garlic powder and parsley. 2. Place squash skin side down into ungreased air fryer basket, working in batches if needed. Adjust the temperature to 350ºF (177ºC) and set the timer for 30 minutes. When the timer beeps, flip squash and cook an additional 15 minutes until fork-tender. 3. Use a fork to remove spaghetti strands from shell and serve warm.

Air Fryer Winter Vegetables

Prep time: 5 minutes | Cook time: 16 minutes |
Serves 2

1 parsnip, sliced
1 cup sliced butternut squash
1 small red onion, cut into
wedges
½ chopped celery stalk

1 tablespoon chopped fresh
thyme
2 teaspoons olive oil
Salt and black pepper, to taste

1. Preheat the air fryer to 380ºF (193ºC). 2. Toss all the ingredients in a large bowl until the vegetables are well coated. 3. Transfer the vegetables to the air fryer basket and air fry for 16 minutes, shaking the basket halfway through, or until the vegetables are golden brown and tender. 4. Remove from the basket and serve warm.

Fried Root Vegetable Medley with Thyme

Prep time: 10 minutes | Cook time: 22 minutes |
Serves 4

2 carrots, sliced
2 potatoes, cut into chunks
1 rutabaga, cut into chunks
1 turnip, cut into chunks
1 beet, cut into chunks
8 shallots, halved

2 tablespoons olive oil
Salt and black pepper, to taste
2 tablespoons tomato pesto
2 tablespoons water
2 tablespoons chopped fresh
thyme

1. Preheat the air fryer to 400ºF (204ºC). 2. Toss the carrots, potatoes, rutabaga, turnip, beet, shallots, olive oil, salt, and pepper in a large mixing bowl until the root vegetables are evenly coated. 3. Place the root vegetables in the air fryer basket and air fry for 12 minutes. Shake the basket and air fry for another 10 minutes until they are cooked to your preferred doneness. 4. Meanwhile, in a small bowl, whisk together the tomato pesto and water until smooth. 5. When ready, remove the root vegetables from the basket to a platter. Drizzle with the tomato pesto mixture and sprinkle with the thyme. Serve immediately.

Russet Potato Gratin

Prep time: 10 minutes | Cook time: 35 minutes |
Serves 6

½ cup milk
7 medium russet potatoes,
peeled
Salt, to taste
1 teaspoon black pepper

½ cup heavy whipping cream
½ cup grated semi-mature
cheese
½ teaspoon nutmeg

1. Preheat the air fryer to 390ºF (199ºC). 2. Cut the potatoes into wafer-thin slices. 3. In a bowl, combine the milk and cream and sprinkle with salt, pepper, and nutmeg. 4. Use the milk mixture to coat the slices of potatoes. Put in a baking dish. Top the potatoes with the rest of the milk mixture. 5. Put the baking dish into the air fryer basket and bake for 25 minutes. 6. Pour the cheese over the potatoes. 7. Bake for an additional 10 minutes, ensuring the top is nicely browned before serving.

Herbed Broccoli with Cheese

Prep time: 5 minutes | Cook time: 18 minutes |
Serves 4

1 large-sized head broccoli,
stemmed and cut into small
florets
2½ tablespoons canola oil
2 teaspoons dried basil

2 teaspoons dried rosemary
Salt and ground black pepper,
to taste
⅓ cup grated yellow cheese

1. Bring a pot of lightly salted water to a boil. Add the broccoli florets to the boiling water and let boil for about 3 minutes. 2. Drain the broccoli florets well and transfer to a large bowl. Add the canola oil, basil, rosemary, salt, and black pepper to the bowl and toss until the broccoli is fully coated. 3. Preheat the air fryer to 390ºF (199ºC). 4. Place the broccoli in the air fryer basket and air fry for about 15 minutes, shaking the basket halfway through, or until the broccoli is crisp. 5. Serve the broccoli warm with grated cheese sprinkled on top.

Pesto Vegetable Skewers

Prep time: 30 minutes | Cook time: 8 minutes |
Makes 8 skewers

1 medium zucchini, trimmed and cut into ½-inch slices	squares
½ medium yellow onion, peeled and cut into 1-inch squares	16 whole cremini mushrooms
	⅓ cup basil pesto
1 medium red bell pepper, seeded and cut into 1-inch	½ teaspoon salt
	¼ teaspoon ground black pepper

1. Divide zucchini slices, onion, and bell pepper into eight even portions. Place on 6-inch skewers for a total of eight kebabs. Add 2 mushrooms to each skewer and brush kebabs generously with pesto. 2. Sprinkle each kebab with salt and black pepper on all sides, then place into ungreased air fryer basket. Adjust the temperature to 375°F (191°C) and air fry for 8 minutes, turning kebabs halfway through cooking. Vegetables will be browned at the edges and tender-crisp when done. Serve warm.

Zucchini-Ricotta Tart

Prep time: 15 minutes | Cook time: 60 minutes |
Serves 6

½ cup grated Parmesan cheese, divided	1 zucchini, thinly sliced (about 2 cups)
1½ cups almond flour	1 cup ricotta cheese
1 tablespoon coconut flour	3 eggs
½ teaspoon garlic powder	2 tablespoons heavy cream
¾ teaspoon salt, divided	2 cloves garlic, minced
¼ cup unsalted butter, melted	½ teaspoon dried tarragon

1. Preheat the air fryer to 330°F (166°C). Coat a round pan with olive oil and set aside. 2. In a large bowl, whisk ¼ cup of the Parmesan with the almond flour, coconut flour, garlic powder, and ¼ teaspoon of the salt. Stir in the melted butter until the dough resembles coarse crumbs. Press the dough firmly into the bottom and up the sides of the prepared pan. Air fry for 12 to 15 minutes until the crust begins to brown. Let cool to room temperature. 3. Meanwhile, place the zucchini in a colander and sprinkle with the remaining ½ teaspoon salt. Toss gently to distribute the salt and let sit for 30 minutes. Use paper towels to pat the zucchini dry. 4. In a large bowl, whisk together the ricotta, eggs, heavy cream, garlic, and tarragon. Gently stir in the zucchini slices. Pour the cheese mixture into the cooled crust and sprinkle with the remaining ¼

cup Parmesan. 5. Increase the air fryer to 350°F (177°C). Place the pan in the air fryer basket and air fry for 45 to 50 minutes, or until set and a tester inserted into the center of the tart comes out clean. Serve warm or at room temperature.

Spinach Cheese Casserole

Prep time: 15 minutes | Cook time: 15 minutes |
Serves 4

1 tablespoon salted butter, melted	¼ cup chopped pickled jalapeños
¼ cup diced yellow onion	2 cups fresh spinach, chopped
8 ounces (227 g) full-fat cream cheese, softened	2 cups cauliflower florets, chopped
⅓ cup full-fat mayonnaise	1 cup artichoke hearts, chopped
⅓ cup full-fat sour cream	

1. In a large bowl, mix butter, onion, cream cheese, mayonnaise, and sour cream. Fold in jalapeños, spinach, cauliflower, and artichokes. 2. Pour the mixture into a round baking dish. Cover with foil and place into the air fryer basket. 3. Adjust the temperature to 370°F (188°C) and set the timer for 15 minutes. In the last 2 minutes of cooking, remove the foil to brown the top. Serve warm.

White Cheddar and Mushroom Soufflés

Prep time: 15 minutes | Cook time: 12 minutes |
Serves 4

3 large eggs, whites and yolks separated	¼ teaspoon cream of tartar
	¼ teaspoon salt
½ cup sharp white Cheddar cheese	¼ teaspoon ground black pepper
3 ounces (85 g) cream cheese, softened	½ cup cremini mushrooms, sliced

1. In a large bowl, whip egg whites until stiff peaks form, about 2 minutes. In a separate large bowl, beat Cheddar, egg yolks, cream cheese, cream of tartar, salt, and pepper together until combined. 2. Fold egg whites into cheese mixture, being careful not to stir. Fold in mushrooms, then pour mixture evenly into four ungreased ramekins. Place ramekins into air fryer basket. Adjust the temperature to 350°F (177°C) and bake for 12 minutes. Eggs will be browned on the top and firm in the center when done. Serve warm.

Crispy Tofu

Prep time: 30 minutes | Cook time: 15 to 20 minutes | Serves 4

1 (16-ounce / 454-g) block extra-firm tofu
2 tablespoons coconut aminos
1 tablespoon toasted sesame oil
1 tablespoon olive oil

1 tablespoon chili-garlic sauce
1½ teaspoons black sesame seeds
1 scallion, thinly sliced

1. Press the tofu for at least 15 minutes by wrapping it in paper towels and setting a heavy pan on top so that the moisture drains. 2. Slice the tofu into bite-size cubes and transfer to a bowl. Drizzle with the coconut aminos, sesame oil, olive oil, and chili-garlic sauce. Cover and refrigerate for 1 hour or up to overnight. 3. Preheat the air fryer to 400ºF (204ºC). 4. Arrange the tofu in a single layer in the air fryer basket. Pausing to shake the pan halfway through the cooking time, air fry for 15 to 20 minutes until crisp. Serve with any juices that accumulate in the bottom of the air fryer, sprinkled with the sesame seeds and sliced scallion.

Cayenne Tahini Kale

Prep time: 5 minutes | Cook time: 15 minutes | Serves 2 to 4

Dressing:
¼ cup tahini
¼ cup fresh lemon juice
2 tablespoons olive oil
1 teaspoon sesame seeds
½ teaspoon garlic powder

¼ teaspoon cayenne pepper
Kale:
4 cups packed torn kale leaves (stems and ribs removed and leaves torn into palm-size pieces)
Kosher salt and freshly ground black pepper, to taste

1. Preheat the air fryer to 350ºF (177ºC). 2. Make the dressing: Whisk together the tahini, lemon juice, olive oil, sesame seeds, garlic powder, and cayenne pepper in a large bowl until well mixed. 3. Add the kale and massage the dressing thoroughly all over the leaves. Sprinkle the salt and pepper to season. 4. Place the kale in the air fryer basket in a single layer and air fry for about 15 minutes, or until the leaves are slightly wilted and crispy. 5. Remove from the basket and serve on a plate.

Chapter 10 Desserts

Coconut-Custard Pie

Prep time: 10 minutes | Cook time: 20 to 23 minutes | Serves 4

1 cup milk

¼ cup plus 2 tablespoons sugar

¼ cup biscuit baking mix

1 teaspoon vanilla

2 eggs

2 tablespoons melted butter

Cooking spray

½ cup shredded, sweetened coconut

1. Place all ingredients except coconut in a medium bowl. 2. Using a hand mixer, beat on high speed for 3 minutes. 3. Let sit for 5 minutes. 4. Preheat the air fryer to 330°F (166°C). 5. Spray a baking pan with cooking spray and place pan in air fryer basket. 6. Pour filling into pan and sprinkle coconut over top. 7. Cook pie at 330°F (166°C) for 20 to 23 minutes or until center sets.

Tortilla Fried Pies

Prep time: 10 minutes | Cook time: 5 minutes per batch | Makes 12 pies

12 small flour tortillas (4-inch diameter)

½ cup fig preserves

¼ cup sliced almonds

2 tablespoons shredded, unsweetened coconut

Oil for misting or cooking spray

1. Wrap refrigerated tortillas in damp paper towels and heat in microwave 30 seconds to warm. 2. Working with one tortilla at a time, place 2 teaspoons fig preserves, 1 teaspoon sliced almonds, and ½ teaspoon coconut in the center of each. 3. Moisten outer edges of tortilla all around. 4. Fold one side of tortilla over filling to make a half-moon shape and press down lightly on center. Using the tines of a fork, press down firmly on edges of tortilla to seal in filling. 5. Mist both sides with oil or cooking spray. 6. Place hand pies in air fryer basket close but not overlapping. It's fine to lean some against the sides and corners of the basket. You may need to cook in 2 batches. 7. Air fry at 390°F (199°C) for 5 minutes or until lightly browned. Serve hot. 8. Refrigerate any leftover pies in a closed container. To serve later, toss them back in the air fryer basket and cook for 2 or 3 minutes to reheat.

Baked Brazilian Pineapple

Prep time: 10 minutes | Cook time: 10 minutes | Serves 4

½ cup brown sugar

2 teaspoons ground cinnamon

1 small pineapple, peeled,

cored, and cut into spears

3 tablespoons unsalted butter, melted

1. In a small bowl, mix the brown sugar and cinnamon until thoroughly combined. 2. Brush the pineapple spears with the melted butter. Sprinkle the cinnamon-sugar over the spears, pressing lightly to ensure it adheres well. 3. Place the spears in the air fryer basket in a single layer. (Depending on the size of your air fryer, you may have to do this in batches.) Set the air fryer to 400°F (204°C) for 10 minutes for the first batch (6 to 8 minutes for the next batch, as the fryer will be preheated). Halfway through the cooking time, brush the spears with butter. 4. The pineapple spears are done when they are heated through and the sugar is bubbling. Serve hot.

Butter and Chocolate Chip Cookies

Prep time: 20 minutes | Cook time: 11 minutes | Serves 8

1 stick butter, at room temperature

1¼ cups Swerve

¼ cup chunky peanut butter

1 teaspoon vanilla paste

1 fine almond flour

⅔ cup coconut flour

⅓ cup cocoa powder, unsweetened

1½ teaspoons baking powder

¼ teaspoon ground cinnamon

¼ teaspoon ginger

½ cup chocolate chips, unsweetened

1. In a mixing dish, beat the butter and Swerve until creamy and uniform. Stir in the peanut butter and vanilla. 2. In another mixing dish, thoroughly combine the flour, cocoa powder, baking powder, cinnamon, and ginger. 3. Add the flour mixture to the peanut butter mixture; mix to combine well. Afterwards, fold in the chocolate chips. Drop by large spoonfuls onto a parchment-lined air fryer basket. Bake at 365°F (185°C) for 11 minutes or until golden brown on the top. Bon appétit!

Bourbon Bread Pudding

Prep time: 10 minutes | Cook time: 20 minutes | Serves 4

3 slices whole grain bread, cubed

1 large egg

1 cup whole milk

2 tablespoons bourbon

½ teaspoons vanilla extract

¼ cup maple syrup, divided

½ teaspoons ground cinnamon

2 teaspoons sparkling sugar

1. Preheat the air fryer to 270ºF (132ºC). 2. Spray a baking pan with nonstick cooking spray, then place the bread cubes in the pan. 3. In a medium bowl, whisk together the egg, milk, bourbon, vanilla extract, 3 tablespoons of maple syrup, and cinnamon. Pour the egg mixture over the bread and press down with a spatula to coat all the bread, then sprinkle the sparkling sugar on top and bake for 20 minutes. 4. Remove the pudding from the air fryer and allow to cool in the pan on a wire rack for 10 minutes. Drizzle the remaining 1 tablespoon of maple syrup on top. Slice and serve warm.

Lemon Bars

Prep time: 15 minutes | Cook time: 25 minutes | Serves 6

¾ cup whole-wheat pastry flour

2 tablespoons confectioners' sugar

¼ cup butter, melted

½ cup granulated sugar

1 tablespoon packed grated lemon zest

¼ cup freshly squeezed lemon

juice

⅛ teaspoon sea salt

¼ cup unsweetened plain applesauce

2 teaspoons cornstarch

¾ teaspoon baking powder

Cooking oil spray (sunflower, safflower, or refined coconut)

1. In a small bowl, stir together the flour, confectioners' sugar, and melted butter just until well combined. Place in the refrigerator. 2. In a medium bowl, stir together the granulated sugar, lemon zest and juice, salt, applesauce, cornstarch, and baking powder. 3. Insert the crisper plate into the basket and the basket into the unit. Preheat the unit by selecting BAKE, setting the temperature to 350ºF (177ºC), and setting the time to 3 minutes. Select START/STOP to begin. 4. Spray a 6-by-2-inch round pan lightly with cooking oil. Remove the crust mixture from the refrigerator and gently press it into the bottom of the prepared pan in an even layer. 5. Once the unit is preheated, place the pan into the basket. 6. Select BAKE, set the temperature to 350ºF (177ºC), and set the time to 25 minutes. Select START/STOP to begin. 7. After 5 minutes, check the crust. It should be slightly firm to the touch. Remove the pan and spread the lemon filling over the crust. Reinsert the pan into the basket and resume baking for 18 to 20 minutes, or until the top is nicely browned. 8. When baking is complete, let cool for 30 minutes. Refrigerate to cool completely. Cut into pieces and serve.

Hazelnut Butter Cookies

Prep time: 30 minutes | Cook time: 20 minutes | Serves 10

4 tablespoons liquid monk fruit

½ cup hazelnuts, ground

1 stick butter, room temperature

2 cups almond flour

1 cup coconut flour

2 ounces (57 g) granulated Swerve

2 teaspoons ground cinnamon

1. Firstly, cream liquid monk fruit with butter until the mixture becomes fluffy. Sift in both types of flour. 2. Now, stir in the hazelnuts. Now, knead the mixture to form a dough; place in the refrigerator for about 35 minutes. 3. To finish, shape the prepared dough into the bite-sized balls; arrange them on a baking dish; flatten the balls using the back of a spoon. 4. Mix granulated Swerve with ground cinnamon. Press your cookies in the cinnamon mixture until they are completely covered. 5. Bake the cookies for 20 minutes at 310ºF (154ºC). 6. Leave them to cool for about 10 minutes before transferring them to a wire rack. Bon appétit!

Lemon Raspberry Muffins

Prep time: 5 minutes | Cook time: 15 minutes | Serves 6

2 cups almond flour

¾ cup Swerve

1¼ teaspoons baking powder

⅓ teaspoon ground allspice

⅓ teaspoon ground anise star

½ teaspoon grated lemon zest

¼ teaspoon salt

2 eggs

1 cup sour cream

½ cup coconut oil

½ cup raspberries

1. Preheat the air fryer to 345ºF (174ºC). Line a muffin pan with 6 paper liners. 2. In a mixing bowl, mix the almond flour, Swerve, baking powder, allspice, anise, lemon zest, and salt. 3. In another mixing bowl, beat the eggs, sour cream, and coconut oil until well mixed. Add the egg mixture to the flour mixture and stir to combine. Mix in the raspberries. 4. Scrape the batter into the prepared muffin cups, filling each about three-quarters full. 5. Bake for 15 minutes, or until the tops are golden and a toothpick inserted in the middle comes out clean. 6. Allow the muffins to cool for 10 minutes in the muffin pan before removing and serving.

Chocolate Lava Cakes

Prep time: 5 minutes | Cook time: 15 minutes |
Serves 2

2 large eggs, whisked

¼ cup blanched finely ground almond flour

½ teaspoon vanilla extract

2 ounces (57 g) low-carb chocolate chips, melted

1. In a medium bowl, mix eggs with flour and vanilla. Fold in chocolate until fully combined. 2. Pour batter into two ramekins greased with cooking spray. Place ramekins into air fryer basket. Adjust the temperature to 320°F (160°C) and bake for 15 minutes. Cakes will be set at the edges and firm in the center when done. Let cool 5 minutes before serving.

Oatmeal Raisin Bars

Prep time: 15 minutes | Cook time: 15 minutes |
Serves 8

⅓ cup all-purpose flour

¼ teaspoon kosher salt

¼ teaspoon baking powder

¼ teaspoon ground cinnamon

¼ cup light brown sugar, lightly packed

¼ cup granulated sugar

½ cup canola oil

1 large egg

1 teaspoon vanilla extract

1⅓ cups quick-cooking oats

⅓ cup raisins

1. Preheat the air fryer to 360°F (182°C). 2. In a large bowl, combine the all-purpose flour, kosher salt, baking powder, ground cinnamon, light brown sugar, granulated sugar, canola oil, egg, vanilla extract, quick-cooking oats, and raisins. 3. Spray a baking pan with nonstick cooking spray, then pour the oat mixture into the pan and press down to evenly distribute. Place the pan in the air fryer and bake for 15 minutes or until golden brown. 4. Remove from the air fryer and allow to cool in the pan on a wire rack for 20 minutes before slicing and serving.

Almond Shortbread

Prep time: 10 minutes | Cook time: 12 minutes |
Serves 8

½ cup (1 stick) unsalted butter

½ cup sugar

1 teaspoon pure almond extract

1 cup all-purpose flour

1. In bowl of a stand mixer fitted with the paddle attachment, beat the butter and sugar on medium speed until light and fluffy, 3 to 4 minutes. Add the almond extract and beat until combined, about 30 seconds. Turn the mixer to low. Add the flour a little at a time and beat for about 2 minutes more until well-incorporated. 2. Pat the dough into an even layer in a baking pan. Place the pan in the air fryer basket. Set the air fryer to 375°F (191°C) for 12 minutes. 3. Carefully remove the pan from air fryer basket. While the shortbread is still warm and soft, cut it into 8 wedges. 4. Let cool in the pan on a wire rack for 5 minutes. Remove the wedges from the pan and let cool completely on the rack before serving.

Vanilla Pound Cake

Prep time: 10 minutes | Cook time: 25 minutes |
Serves 6

1 cup blanched finely ground almond flour

¼ cup salted butter, melted

½ cup granular erythritol

1 teaspoon vanilla extract

1 teaspoon baking powder

½ cup full-fat sour cream

1 ounce (28 g) full-fat cream cheese, softened

2 large eggs

1. In a large bowl, mix almond flour, butter, and erythritol. 2. Add in vanilla, baking powder, sour cream, and cream cheese and mix until well combined. Add eggs and mix. 3. Pour batter into a round baking pan. Place pan into the air fryer basket. 4. Adjust the temperature to 300°F (149°C) and bake for 25 minutes. 5. When the cake is done, a toothpick inserted in center will come out clean. The center should not feel wet. Allow it to cool completely, or the cake will crumble when moved.

Breaded Bananas with Chocolate Topping

Prep time: 10 minutes | Cook time: 10 minutes |
Serves 6

¼ cup cornstarch

¼ cup plain bread crumbs

1 large egg, beaten

3 bananas, halved crosswise

Cooking spray

Chocolate sauce, for serving

1. Preheat the air fryer to 350°F (177°C) 2. Place the cornstarch, bread crumbs, and egg in three separate bowls. 3. Roll the bananas in the cornstarch, then in the beaten egg, and finally in the bread crumbs to coat well. 4. Spritz the air fryer basket with the cooking spray. 5. Arrange the banana halves in the basket and mist them with the cooking spray. Air fry for 5 minutes. Flip the bananas and continue to air fry for another 2 minutes. 6. Remove the bananas from the basket to a serving plate. Serve with the chocolate sauce drizzled over the top.

Strawberry Shortcake

Prep time: 10 minutes | Cook time: 25 minutes |
Serves 6

2 tablespoons coconut oil

1 cup blanched finely ground almond flour

2 large eggs, whisked

½ cup granular erythritol

1 teaspoon baking powder

1 teaspoon vanilla extract

2 cups sugar-free whipped cream

6 medium fresh strawberries, hulled and sliced

1. In a large bowl, combine coconut oil, flour, eggs, erythritol, baking powder, and vanilla. Pour batter into an ungreased round nonstick baking dish. 2. Place dish into air fryer basket. Adjust the temperature to 300ºF (149ºC) and bake for 25 minutes. When done, shortcake should be golden and a toothpick inserted in the middle will come out clean. 3. Remove dish from fryer and let cool 1 hour. 4. Once cooled, top cake with whipped cream and strawberries to serve.

Molten Chocolate Almond Cakes

Prep time: 5 minutes | Cook time: 13 minutes |
Serves 3

Butter and flour for the ramekins

4 ounces (113 g) bittersweet chocolate, chopped

½ cup (1 stick) unsalted butter

2 eggs

2 egg yolks

¼ cup sugar

½ teaspoon pure vanilla extract,

or almond extract

1 tablespoon all-purpose flour

3 tablespoons ground almonds

8 to 12 semisweet chocolate discs (or 4 chunks of chocolate)

Cocoa powder or powdered sugar, for dusting

Toasted almonds, coarsely chopped

1. Butter and flour three (6-ounce / 170-g) ramekins. (Butter the ramekins and then coat the butter with flour by shaking it around in the ramekin and dumping out any excess.) 2. Melt the chocolate and butter together, either in the microwave or in a double boiler. In a separate bowl, beat the eggs, egg yolks and sugar together until light and smooth. Add the vanilla extract. Whisk the chocolate mixture into the egg mixture. Stir in the flour and ground almonds. 3. Preheat the air fryer to 330ºF (166ºC). 4. Transfer the batter carefully to the buttered ramekins, filling halfway. Place two or three chocolate discs in the center of the batter and then fill the ramekins to ½-inch below the top with the remaining batter. Place the ramekins into the air fryer basket and air fry at 330ºF (166ºC) for 13 minutes. The sides of the cake should be set, but the centers should be slightly soft. Remove the ramekins from the air fryer and let the cakes sit for 5 minutes. (If you'd like the cake a little less

molten, air fry for 14 minutes and let the cakes sit for 4 minutes.) 5. Run a butter knife around the edge of the ramekins and invert the cakes onto a plate. Lift the ramekin off the plate slowly and carefully so that the cake doesn't break. Dust with cocoa powder or powdered sugar and serve with a scoop of ice cream and some coarsely chopped toasted almonds.

Pecan and Cherry Stuffed Apples

Prep time: 10 minutes | Cook time: 20 minutes |
Serves 4

4 apples (about 1¼ pounds / 567 g)

¼ cup chopped pecans

⅓ cup dried tart cherries

1 tablespoon melted butter

3 tablespoons brown sugar

¼ teaspoon allspice

Pinch salt

Ice cream, for serving

1. Cut off top ½ inch from each apple; reserve tops. With a melon baller, core through stem ends without breaking through the bottom. (Do not trim bases.) 2. Preheat the air fryer to 350ºF (177ºC). Combine pecans, cherries, butter, brown sugar, allspice, and a pinch of salt. Stuff mixture into the hollow centers of the apples. Cover with apple tops. Put in the air fryer basket, using tongs. Air fry for 20 to 25 minutes, or just until tender. 3. Serve warm with ice cream.

Crumbly Coconut-Pecan Cookies

Prep time: 10 minutes | Cook time: 25 minutes |
Serves 10

1½ cups coconut flour

1½ cups extra-fine almond flour

½ teaspoon baking powder

⅓ teaspoon baking soda

3 eggs plus an egg yolk, beaten

¾ cup coconut oil, at room temperature

1 cup unsalted pecan nuts, roughly chopped

¾ cup monk fruit

¼ teaspoon freshly grated nutmeg

⅓ teaspoon ground cloves

½ teaspoon pure vanilla extract

½ teaspoon pure coconut extract

⅛ teaspoon fine sea salt

1. Preheat the air fryer to 370ºF (188ºC). Line the air fryer basket with parchment paper. 2. Mix the coconut flour, almond flour, baking powder, and baking soda in a large mixing bowl. 3. In another mixing bowl, stir together the eggs and coconut oil. Add the wet mixture to the dry mixture. 4. Mix in the remaining ingredients and stir until a soft dough forms. 5. Drop about 2 tablespoons of dough on the parchment paper for each cookie and flatten each biscuit until it's 1 inch thick. 6. Bake for about 25 minutes until the cookies are golden and firm to the touch. Remove from the basket to a plate. Let the cookies cool to room temperature and serve.

Simple Pineapple Sticks

Prep time: 5 minutes | Cook time: 10 minutes |
Serves 4

½ fresh pineapple, cut into sticks
¼ cup desiccated coconut

1. Preheat the air fryer to 400ºF (204ºC). 2. Coat the pineapple sticks in the desiccated coconut and put each one in the air fryer basket. 3. Air fry for 10 minutes. 4. Serve immediately

Grilled Pineapple Dessert

Prep time: 5 minutes | Cook time: 12 minutes |
Serves 4

Oil for misting or cooking spray
4 ½-inch-thick slices fresh pineapple, core removed
1 tablespoon honey
¼ teaspoon brandy

2 tablespoons slivered almonds, toasted
Vanilla frozen yogurt or coconut sorbet

1. Spray both sides of pineapple slices with oil or cooking spray. Place into air fryer basket. 2. Air fry at 390ºF (199ºC) for 6 minutes. Turn slices over and cook for an additional 6 minutes. 3. Mix together the honey and brandy. 4. Remove cooked pineapple slices from air fryer, sprinkle with toasted almonds, and drizzle with honey mixture. 5. Serve with a scoop of frozen yogurt or sorbet on the side.

Berry Crumble

Prep time: 10 minutes | Cook time: 15 minutes |
Serves 4

For the Filling:
2 cups mixed berries
2 tablespoons sugar
1 tablespoon cornstarch
1 tablespoon fresh lemon juice
For the Topping:
¼ cup all-purpose flour

¼ cup rolled oats
1 tablespoon sugar
2 tablespoons cold unsalted butter, cut into small cubes
Whipped cream or ice cream (optional)

1. Preheat the air fryer to 400ºF (204ºC). 2. For the filling: In a round baking pan, gently mix the berries, sugar, cornstarch, and lemon juice until thoroughly combined. 3. For the topping: In a small bowl, combine the flour, oats, and sugar. Stir the butter into the flour mixture until the mixture has the consistency of bread crumbs. 4. Sprinkle the topping over the berries. 5. Put the pan

in the air fryer basket and air fry for 15 minutes. Let cool for 5 minutes on a wire rack. 6. Serve topped with whipped cream or ice cream, if desired.

Spiced Apple Cake

Prep time: 15 minutes | Cook time: 30 minutes |
Serves 6

Vegetable oil
2 cups diced peeled Gala apples (about 2 apples)
1 tablespoon fresh lemon juice
¼ cup (½ stick) unsalted butter, softened
⅓ cup granulated sugar
2 large eggs
1 ¼ cups unbleached all-purpose flour

1 ½ teaspoons baking powder
1 tablespoon apple pie spice
½ teaspoon ground ginger
¼ teaspoon ground cardamom
¼ teaspoon ground nutmeg
½ teaspoon kosher salt
¼ cup whole milk
Confectioners' sugar, for dusting

1. Grease a 3-cup Bundt pan with oil; set aside. 2. In a medium bowl, toss the apples with the lemon juice until well coated; set aside. 3. In a large bowl, combine the butter and sugar. Beat with an electric hand mixer on medium speed until the sugar has dissolved. Add the eggs and beat until fluffy. Add the flour, baking powder, apple pie spice, ginger, cardamom, nutmeg, salt, and milk. Mix until the batter is thick but pourable. 4. Pour the batter into the prepared pan. Top batter evenly with the apple mixture. Place the pan in the air fryer basket. Set the air fryer to 350ºF (177ºC) for 30 minutes, or until a toothpick inserted in the center of the cake comes out clean. Close the air fryer and let the cake rest for 10 minutes. Turn the cake out onto a wire rack and cool completely. 5. Right before serving, dust the cake with confectioners' sugar.

Olive Oil Cake

Prep time: 10 minutes | Cook time: 30 minutes |
Serves 8

2 cups blanched finely ground almond flour
5 large eggs, whisked
¾ cup extra-virgin olive oil

⅓ cup granular erythritol
1 teaspoon vanilla extract
1 teaspoon baking powder

1. In a large bowl, mix all ingredients. Pour batter into an ungreased round nonstick baking dish. 2. Place dish into air fryer basket. Adjust the temperature to 300ºF (149ºC) and bake for 30 minutes. The cake will be golden on top and firm in the center when done. 3. Let cake cool in dish 30 minutes before slicing and serving.

Shortcut Spiced Apple Butter

Prep time: 5 minutes | Cook time: 1 hour | Makes 1¼ cups

Cooking spray	3 tablespoons fresh lemon juice
2 cups store-bought	½ teaspoon kosher salt
unsweetened applesauce	¼ teaspoon ground cinnamon
⅔ cup packed light brown sugar	⅛ teaspoon ground allspice

1. Spray a cake pan with cooking spray. Whisk together all the ingredients in a bowl until smooth, then pour into the greased pan. Set the pan in the air fryer and bake at 340°F (171°C) until the apple mixture is caramelized, reduced to a thick purée, and fragrant, about 1 hour. 2. Remove the pan from the air fryer, stir to combine the caramelized bits at the edge with the rest, then let cool completely to thicken. Scrape the apple butter into a jar and store in the refrigerator for up to 2 weeks.

Cinnamon Cupcakes with Cream Cheese Frosting

Prep time: 10 minutes | Cook time: 20 to 25 minutes | Serves 6

½ cup plus 2 tablespoons almond flour	½ teaspoon vanilla extract
2 tablespoons low-carb vanilla protein powder	2 tablespoons heavy cream
⅛ teaspoon salt	Cream Cheese Frosting:
1 teaspoon baking powder	4 ounces (113 g) cream cheese, softened
¼ teaspoon ground cinnamon	2 tablespoons unsalted butter, softened
¼ cup unsalted butter	½ teaspoon vanilla extract
¼ cup Swerve	2 tablespoons powdered Swerve
2 eggs	1 to 2 tablespoons heavy cream

1. Preheat the air fryer to 320°F (160°C). Lightly coat 6 silicone muffin cups with oil and set aside. 2. In a medium bowl, combine the almond flour, protein powder, salt, baking powder, and cinnamon; set aside. 3. In a stand mixer fitted with a paddle attachment, beat the butter and Swerve until creamy. Add the eggs, vanilla, and heavy cream, and beat again until thoroughly combined. Add half the flour mixture at a time to the butter mixture, mixing after each addition, until you have a smooth, creamy batter. 4. Divide the batter evenly among the muffin cups, filling each one about three-fourths full. Arrange the muffin cups in the air fryer and air fry for 20 to 25 minutes, or until a toothpick inserted into the center of a cupcake comes out clean. Transfer the cupcakes to a rack and let cool completely. 5. To make the cream cheese frosting:

In a stand mixer fitted with a paddle attachment, beat the cream cheese, butter, and vanilla until fluffy. Add the Swerve and mix again until thoroughly combined. With the mixer running, add the heavy cream a tablespoon at a time until the frosting is smooth and creamy. Frost the cupcakes as desired.

Apple Fries

Prep time: 10 minutes | Cook time: 7 minutes | Serves 8

Oil, for spraying	1 teaspoon ground cinnamon
1 cup all-purpose flour	3 large Gala apples, peeled,
3 large eggs, beaten	cored, and cut into wedges
1 cup graham cracker crumbs	1 cup caramel sauce, warmed
¼ cup sugar	

1. Preheat the air fryer to 380°F (193°C). Line the air fryer basket with parchment and spray lightly with oil. 2. Place the flour and beaten eggs in separate bowls and set aside. In another bowl, mix together the graham cracker crumbs, sugar, and cinnamon. 3. Working one at a time, coat the apple wedges in the flour, dip in the egg, and dredge in the graham cracker mix until evenly coated. 4. Place the apples in the prepared basket, taking care not to overlap, and spray lightly with oil. You may need to work in batches, depending on the size of your air fryer. 5. Cook for 5 minutes, flip, spray with oil, and cook for another 2 minutes, or until crunchy and golden brown. 6. Drizzle the caramel sauce over the top and serve.

Crispy Pineapple Rings

Prep time: 5 minutes | Cook time: 6 to 8 minutes | Serves 6

1 cup rice milk	½ teaspoon baking powder
⅔ cup flour	½ teaspoon vanilla essence
½ cup water	½ teaspoon ground cinnamon
¼ cup unsweetened flaked coconut	¼ teaspoon ground anise star
4 tablespoons sugar	Pinch of kosher salt
½ teaspoon baking soda	1 medium pineapple, peeled and sliced

1. Preheat the air fryer to 380°F (193°C). 2. In a large bowl, stir together all the ingredients except the pineapple. 3. Dip each pineapple slice into the batter until evenly coated. 4. Arrange the pineapple slices in the basket and air fry for 6 to 8 minutes until golden brown. 5. Remove from the basket to a plate and cool for 5 minutes before serving.arm.

Eggless Farina Cake

Prep time: 30 minutes | Cook time: 25 minutes | Serves 6

Vegetable oil

2 cups hot water

1 cup chopped dried fruit, such as apricots, golden raisins, figs, and/or dates

1 cup farina (or very fine semolina)

1 cup milk

1 cup sugar

¼ cup ghee, butter, or coconut oil, melted

2 tablespoons plain Greek yogurt or sour cream

1 teaspoon ground cardamom

1 teaspoon baking powder

½ teaspoon baking soda

Whipped cream, for serving

1. Grease a baking pan with vegetable oil. 2. In a small bowl, combine the hot water and dried fruit; set aside for 20 minutes to plump the fruit. 3. Meanwhile, in a large bowl, whisk together the farina, milk, sugar, ghee, yogurt, and cardamom. Let stand for 20 minutes to allow the farina to soften and absorb some of the liquid. 4. Drain the dried fruit and gently stir it into the batter. Add the baking powder and baking soda and stir until thoroughly combined. 5. Pour the batter into the prepared pan. Set the pan in the air fryer basket. Set the air fryer to 325ºF (163ºC) for 25 minutes, or until a toothpick inserted into the center of the cake comes out clean. 6. Let the cake cool in the pan on a wire rack for 10 minutes. Remove the cake from the pan and let cool on the rack for 20 minutes before slicing. 7. Slice and serve topped with whipped cream.

Appendix 1: Air Fryer Cooking Chart

Air Fryer Cooking Chart

Beef

Item	Temp (°F)	Time (mins)	Item	Temp (°F)	Time (mins)
Beef Eye Round Roast (4 lbs.)	400 °F	45 to 55	Meatballs (1-inch)	370 °F	7
Burger Patty (4 oz.)	370 °F	16 to 20	Meatballs (3-inch)	380 °F	10
Filet Mignon (8 oz.)	400 °F	18	Ribeye, bone-in (1-inch, 8 oz)	400 °F	10 to 15
Flank Steak (1.5 lbs.)	400 °F	12	Sirloin steaks (1-inch, 12 oz)	400 °F	9 to 14
Flank Steak (2 lbs.)	400 °F	20 to 28			

Chicken

Item	Temp (°F)	Time (mins)	Item	Temp (°F)	Time (mins)
Breasts, bone in (1 ¼ lb.)	370 °F	25	Legs, bone-in (1 ¾ lb.)	380 °F	30
Breasts, boneless (4 oz)	380 °F	12	Thighs, boneless (1 ½ lb.)	380 °F	18 to 20
Drumsticks (2 ½ lb.)	370 °F	20	Wings (2 lb.)	400 °F	12
Game Hen (halved 2 lb.)	390 °F	20	Whole Chicken	360 °F	75
Thighs, bone-in (2 lb.)	380 °F	22	Tenders	360 °F	8 to 10

Pork & Lamb

Item	Temp (°F)	Time (mins)	Item	Temp (°F)	Time (mins)
Bacon (regular)	400 °F	5 to 7	Pork Tenderloin	370 °F	15
Bacon (thick cut)	400 °F	6 to 10	Sausages	380 °F	15
Pork Loin (2 lb.)	360 °F	55	Lamb Loin Chops (1-inch thick)	400 °F	8 to 12
Pork Chops, bone in (1-inch, 6.5 oz)	400 °F	12	Rack of Lamb (1.5 – 2 lb.)	380 °F	22

Fish & Seafood

Item	Temp (°F)	Time (mins)	Item	Temp (°F)	Time (mins)
Calamari (8 oz)	400 °F	4	Tuna Steak	400 °F	7 to 10
Fish Fillet (1-inch, 8 oz)	400 °F	10	Scallops	400 °F	5 to 7
Salmon, fillet (6 oz)	380 °F	12	Shrimp	400 °F	5
Swordfish steak	400 °F	10			

Air Fryer Cooking Chart

Vegetables					
INGREDIENT	**AMOUNT**	**PREPARATION**	**OIL**	**TEMP**	**COOK TIME**
Asparagus	2 bunches	Cut in half, trim stems	2 Tbsp	420°F	12-15 mins
Beets	1½ lbs	Peel, cut in ½-inch cubes	1Tbsp	390°F	28-30 mins
Bell peppers (for roasting)	4 peppers	Cut in quarters, remove seeds	1Tbsp	400°F	15-20 mins
Broccoli	1 large head	Cut in 1-2-inch florets	1Tbsp	400°F	15-20 mins
Brussels sprouts	1lb	Cut in half, remove stems	1Tbsp	425°F	15-20 mins
Carrots	1lb	Peel, cut in ¼-inch rounds	1 Tbsp	425°F	10-15 mins
Cauliflower	1 head	Cut in 1-2-inch florets	2 Tbsp	400°F	20-22 mins
Corn on the cob	7 ears	Whole ears, remove husks	1 Tbps	400°F	14-17 mins
Green beans	1 bag (12 oz)	Trim	1 Tbps	420°F	18-20 mins
Kale (for chips)	4 oz	Tear into pieces,remove stems	None	325°F	5-8 mins
Mushrooms	16 oz	Rinse, slice thinly	1 Tbps	390°F	25-30 mins
Potatoes, russet	1½ lbs	Cut in 1-inch wedges	1 Tbps	390°F	25-30 mins
Potatoes, russet	1lb	Hand-cut fries, soak 30 mins in cold water, then pat dry	½ -3 Tbps	400°F	25-28 mins
Potatoes, sweet	1lb	Hand-cut fries, soak 30 mins in cold water, then pat dry	1 Tbps	400°F	25-28 mins
Zucchini	1lb	Cut in eighths lengthwise, then cut in half	1 Tbps	400°F	15-20 mins

Made in the USA
Las Vegas, NV
12 November 2023

80729547R00057